Jeanne Guyon's Mystical Interpretation of Divinization, Volume 2

Jeanne Guyon's Mystical Interpretation of Divinization, Volume 2

Her Biblical Commentary on St. Matthew's Gospel

By JEANNE DE LA MOTHE GUYON

Introduction and translation from the original French by
NANCY CAROL JAMES

Foreword by THOMAS PATRICK KUFFEL

PICKWICK *Publications* · Eugene, Oregon

JEANNE GUYON'S MYSTICAL INTERPRETATION OF DIVINIZATION, VOLUME 2
Her Biblical Commentary on St. Matthew's Gospel

Copyright © 2026 Nancy Carol James. All rights reserved. Except for brief quotations in critical publications or reviews, no part of this book may be reproduced in any manner without prior written permission from the publisher. Write: Permissions, Wipf and Stock Publishers, 199 W. 8th Ave., Suite 3, Eugene, OR 97401.

Pickwick Publications
An Imprint of Wipf and Stock Publishers
199 W. 8th Ave., Suite 3
Eugene, OR 97401

www.wipfandstock.com

PAPERBACK ISBN: 979-8-3852-4518-5
HARDCOVER ISBN: 979-8-3852-4519-2
EBOOK ISBN: 979-8-3852-4520-8

Cataloguing-in-Publication data:

Names: Guyon, Jeanne de la Mothe [author]. | James, Nancy Carol [editor and translator]. | Kuffel, Thomas Patrick [foreword writer].

Title: Jeanne Guyon's mystical interpretation of divinization, volume 2 : her biblical commentary on St. Matthew's Gospel / by Jeanne de la Mothe Guyon ; translated by Nancy Carol James.

Description: Eugene, OR: Pickwick Publications, 2026 | Includes bibliographical references and index.

Identifiers: ISBN 979-8-3852-4518-5 (paperback) | ISBN 979-8-3852-4519-2 (hardcover) | ISBN 979-8-3852-4520-8 (ebook)

Subjects: LCSH: Guyon, Jeanne Marie Bouvier de La Motte, 1648–1717. | Bible. Matthew—Commentaries—Early works to 1800. | Spiritual life—Catholic Church. | Quietism.

Classification: BS2575 G89 2026 (paperback) | BS2575 (ebook)

VERSION NUMBER 03/18/26

Unless otherwise noted, Scripture quotations are from the ESV® Bible (The Holy Bible, English Standard Version®), © 2001 by Crossway, a publishing ministry of Good News Publishers. Used by permission. All rights reserved.

Scriptures marked Douay-Rheims are from the Douay-Rheims 1899 American edition in the public domain.

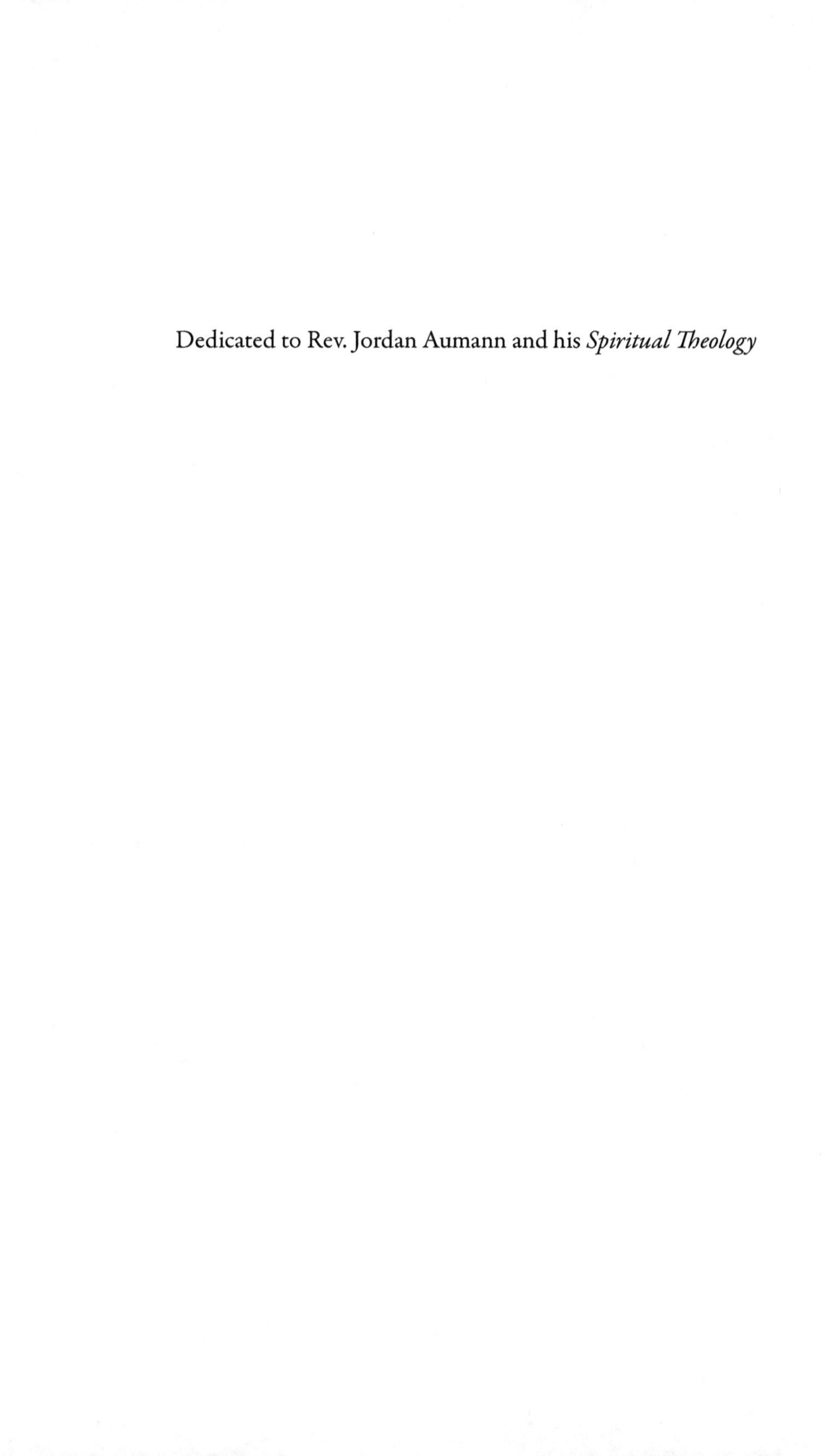

Dedicated to Rev. Jordan Aumann and his *Spiritual Theology*

Contents

Foreword

by Thomas Patrick Kuffel

Madame Guyon received great acclaim as a theologian and mystic, while still accomplishing her powerful role in King Louis XIV's court at Versailles. A prolific writer, Guyon wrote extensively on applied mystical theology and wrote a commentary on every book in the Bible to show the understanding of interior life. In her commentary on Matthew, she described the soul's transformation and divinization under the healing and power of the Holy Spirit, understood as mysticism. Jordan Aumann writes, "Mysticism is an awareness of the divine activity on the soul."[1] Truly, Guyon experienced this divine activity and expressed her mysticism of pure love faithfully and spiritually.

In mysticism, the Holy Spirit works in our lives, bringing through divine enlightenment a superior and deeper knowledge of God but "also an experiential, intuitive knowledge of the divine."[2] Guyon described the normal development of a Christian seeking and asking God to reveal himself through grace, the very gift of his life-giving love, to transform us, divinizing our whole self with Christian perfection. Mysticism, then, is the refulgent splendor of God filling our souls with his wisdom.

Guyon attributed to St. Paul this divine understanding, calling him the mystic master. He understands the roots of mysticism as the mystery that reveals God's heart and mind. He writes to those who are "servants of Christ and stewards of the mysteries. That they may be found trustworthy" (1 Cor 4:1–2). In Colossians, he writes: "I became a minister according to the divine office, which was given to me for you, to make the word of God fully known, the mystery hidden for ages and generations but

1. Aumann, *Spiritual Theology*, 123.

2. Aumann, *Spiritual Theology*, 6.

now made manifest to his saints" (Col 1:25–26). Hidden and secret, the mystery is intricately connected to the unveiling of God's presence working in our lives as well as the unveiling of apocalypse: Jesus the Bridegroom coming to redeem his bride (Rev 19:11–16). It is not something we develop but something we experience and then discern to receive the divine roots of this encounter.

Mystics and mysticism penetrate the wisdom of God, delving deeply into the divine mysteries. Guyon sought pure love. In other words, she wanted to live and love God's will alone.

St. Paul also sought this mystical divinization and union. "I have been crucified with Christ; it is no longer I who live, but Christ who lives in me; and the life I now live in the flesh I live by faith in the Son of God, who loved me and gave himself for me" (Gal 2:20). Mystics partake in God's pure love purely, for they seek wisdom and wisdom purified the heart. Purified, the real indwelling of God's pure love abides in the heart.

In her commentary on Matthew, Guyon also interprets other mystical saints such as St. Angela of Foligno, St. Catherine of Genoa, and St. Macarius the Great as wanting to live and move in God alone. Dwelling in this mystical journey, believers will also encounter evil, and Guyon emphasizes in this commentary that all of these saints knew evil as they sought pure love.

Why do believers seek the mystical pure love? As Nancy James writes, "The deathless fire of pure love calls us to lofty goals that lead us to fulfillment."[3] This encapsulates Guyon's heart for God. She sought perfect union with God and wanted to teach this communion to others. To do this she wrote many books, articles, poems, and letters expressing her views and ways. Her book *Short Method of Prayer* became a popular bestseller. In this book, Guyon describes prayer as "the affection of the heart and love."[4] She describes this: "Nothing is so easily gained as the possession and enjoyment of God. God is more in ourselves than we are in ourselves. God desires to give the divine heart more than we wish to possess it. You can live in God as easily and continuously as you live in the air you breathe."[5]

Mysticism then is the ineffable encounter with Divine Love in which a soul is transformed and transfigured into the image and likeness of Jesus Christ. Influenced by mysticism, spiritual theology then is the

3. James, *Pure Love*, vii.

4. James, *Complete Madame Guyon*, 45.

5. James, *Complete Madame Guyon*, 46.

summit of all theology as it seeks to understand and apply faith, hope, and charity, so the soul dwells in perfect surrender to the Holy Spirit. This definition unites the truths contained and revealed within Scriptures, including moral theology; the virtues; perfection of applied theology to the human behavior seeking perfection; and eschatology of understanding the purpose and ultimate reason of living a life in Christ while praying for eternal life. In reality, spiritual theology is the ineffable and inexhaustible desire to be united to Divine Love.

As the Christian experiences and encounters Divine Love, this harmonizes the purpose and plan God has with the heart of each believer. This person asks, seeks, and knocks on the door to Divine Love. Surrender allows Divine Love to penetrate the heart so that any person may behold and encounter Jesus as the Way, the Truth, and Life of their soul. Each has his own path, but human openness and willingness allow the Holy Spirit to guide, correct, and eventually lead to union with Divine Love.

In conforming our will to God's will, does the human will lose its power to discern, reason, and choose? As Pope Benedict XVI writes, "God's will is no longer for me an alien will . . . but now my own will."[6] No longer alien, the Divine Heart unites with the human heart. Pope Benedict continues, "Our will and God's will increasingly coincide," because we want the same thing and reject the same thing. I am not diminished by another's will, especially God's will for me; rather I am enhanced. I want what you want, and you want what I want. We all want what is good, true, and beautiful. This is the divine longing in the soul to find fulfillment in Divine Love. To rest in Divine Love completes us.

In conforming our wills to God's, we want God, and God wants us. This does not mean I lose my identity and ability to choose. Rather, it is reciprocal, each keeping their own identity and individuality, but God and the soul are lost in the beauty of true love for each other, becoming a conforming and transforming union.

St. Thomas Aquinas also expounds on the power of pure love. He explains in the following:

> Christ could will what God did not; but in His will as reason He always wished the same as God, which appears from what He says (Matt. 26:39): *Not what I will but what Thou wilt.* It is not fate

6. Benedict XVI, *Deus Caritas Est* 17.

> by which we live but by faith: an entrustment of our will into the divine will.[7]

Mysticism participates in the divine life. We share, partake, and adhere to the goodness, truth, and beauty of Divine Love. Partaking in God's life is so foreign to the "modernity's mechanistic autonomy (techne), hedonistic utilitarianism, and radical pragmatism" of the Enlightenment.[8] In contrast to this individual autonomy divorced from God's presence in our world, St. Peter counters.

> His divine power has granted to us all things that pertain to life and godliness, through the knowledge of him who called us to his own glory and excellence, [4] by which he has granted to us his precious and very great promises, so that through them you may become partakers of the divine nature, having escaped from the corruption that is in the world because of sinful desire. (2 Pet 1:3–4)

Made partakers in God's nature, a total transformation takes place. No longer do rationalism, pragmatism, and materialism satisfy; rather we long for an interior personal transformation that purifies the heart. This transformation, which takes place through grace, as a caterpillar becomes a butterfly, develops an intimate relationship with Divine Love through the Son and Spirit. Relishing the Divine Presence, we receive with gratitude the in-flowing of the Holy Spirit. Or as St. Teresa of Avila writes: "The important thing is not to think much, but to love much; do, then, whatever most arouses you to love."[9]

GUYON'S FOURFOLD METHOD OF INTERPRETING SCRIPTURE

To understand Guyon's commentary on Matthew's Gospel, we need to know that Guyon interpreted Scripture using the theological method of Thomas Aquinas, who identified this four-pronged theological method. The catechism of the Catholic Church describes these forms of scriptural interpretation in this short description.

7. Aquinas, *Summa Theologica* III, q. 18, a. 5.
8. Millare, *Living Sacrifice*, 20.
9. Teresa of Avila, *Interior Castle*, 84.

> The Letter speaks of deeds; Allegory to faith; The Moral how to act; Anagogy our destiny.[10]

First, in the literal form of interpretation, we read the literal and historical reality. A variety of literary styles from poetry, history, narratives, philosophy, prophecy, and even mythology, along with vastly diverse cultures, customs, and beliefs, give Scripture an array of literal images, stories, and personages. This form of interpretation reads the word in context with the whole of Scripture so that what is understood accords with reason. It accords with truth, and the truths contained in Scripture accord with charity, that God's loving presence revealed is the overriding principle in scriptural interpretation. God's loving presence unveils a deeper or typological interpretation and includes the narrative of Christ, which St. Thomas describes as "the things of the Old Law signify[ing] the things of the New Law."[11]

The typological sense or mystical sense is different. It sees deeper realities within the literal sense—how the words or events unveil Jesus, his moral teachings, and the promise of eternal life with him. Reading Scripture literally founds the mystical sense, but if reading according to one's own century's mindset, typological nuances and subtleties are missed.

First, the mystical sense explores the three transcendentals of truth, goodness, and beauty. To miss these or misinterpret these creates a vacuum, missing pieces in the icon.

Second, the allegorical form of interpretation reveals the first transcendental truth, that Jesus Christ is God and man. The incarnation of Jesus Christ reveals this truth.

Third, the moral or tropological form of interpretation reveals the second transcendental, goodness. Christ as goodness himself commands we keep the law through his grace, which makes us good. St. Thomas says, "So far as the things done in Christ, or so far as the things which signify Christ, are types of what we ought to do, there is the moral sense."[12]

Fourth, the anagogical interpretation reveals the third transcendental, beauty. Christ as the fulfillment and purpose of divine revelation gives the vision of the pure beauty of heaven. In the last transcendental, our Bridegroom Christ calls and then divinizes every person who responds

10. Catholic Church, *Catechism of the Catholic Church*, 33.

11. Aquinas, *Summa Theologica* I, q. 1, a. 10.

12. Aquinas, *Summa Theologica* I, q. 1, a. 10.

faithfully to his invitation. St. Thomas writes that this invitation means "they signify what relates to eternal glory."[13]

This method of scriptural interpretation can be seen in Matt 26:6–7, when a woman whom Guyon identifies as Mary Magdalene approaches Jesus with an alabaster flask of expensive ointment to pour on his head. In her commentary on Matthew, Guyon describes this pure love of the heart in a most touching scene. Mary Magdalene enters and smashes the alabaster jar filled with aromatic nard. How can she do this act of love? Guyon describes Magdalene's interior life.

> Magdalene, already purified by her perfect conversion that the almighty gaze of the Savior had operated and carried into her soul, became like an alabaster by its candor and purity, the precious perfume of the interior and divine anointing because Mary was not only converted from sin to grace, but from exterior to interior.

Once the soul is made like valuable alabaster, Guyon continues, "Everything comes from the Word, everything must flow back into the Word: if humans retain this for themselves, they steal it." For Guyon the soul itself must become annihilated, as she explains, like the smashing of the alabaster jar so that Jesus may expand her with his power to "communicate to her in an immense way."

In this passage, we see the four types of scriptural interpretation. In the literal understanding, Mary Magdalene is a historical person who is known to love Jesus. She carries an alabaster jar, a precious, translucent mineral that is soft and known to let light through. Alabaster was frequently used to hold expensive ointment, as well as used in church altars and other holy objects.

In the allegorical understanding, as she anoints Jesus she reveals her understanding of Jesus as the Son of God. Guyon writes, "Spreading her fragrant liquid on the head of our Lord, she declares by this action, that she recognizes that because everything comes from the Word, everything must flow back into the Word." Jesus annihilates our soul, calling us to smash the exterior observations—seeing Jesus as a mere man—and embrace him as the Son of God who chooses to give his life for us because like the alabaster jar, we, though sinners like Magdalene, are of great value, translucent with light, receiving the divine anointing.

In the tropological understanding, Mary Magdalene shows in her actions that the human has a moral obligation to return to the Word what

13. Aquinas, *Summa Theologica* I, q. 1, a. 10.

Jesus Christ has given humanity. Guyon writes, "Everything must flow back into the Word: if humans retain this for themselves, they steal it."

In the anagogical understanding, Mary Magdalene understands that she prepares Jesus Christ for his death, prophesied about for centuries. Guyon interprets the analogy between the alabaster jar and Magdalene's soul. As the jar is broken to allow the outflowing of the ointment, the human soul must be broken open and annihilated to allow the soul to melt with love and flow into Jesus Christ, who enlarges their capacity. Guyon writes that Jesus understands this as the restoration of the great glory that he can receive by applying themselves to him in love and concerned only with loving him. This divinization brings life into our human lives, preparing us for both our natural and mystical death and resurrection.

Further along in her commentary on Matthew, Guyon describes in detail immolation and annihilation. In Jesus's prayer, he prays for grace to be annihilated. "My Father, if it be possible let this cup pass from me, nevertheless, not as I will, but as you will" (Matt 26:39). Guyon understands that in the suffering of Jesus, Jesus's pure love for the Father embraces his sacrifice. In her commentary, she calls his confrontation with suffering a free act of self-immolation as she describes his agony.

> Thus, the sadness of Jesus in the garden was the most interior sadness and pain. This intimate sacrifice caused him an incomprehensible torment, capable of reducing him to dust, if he had not borrowed the forces of divine power to prolong his martyrdom, so that he would only end on the cross. It was even to make his passion more painful that he weakened himself in the garden, suspending the vigorous and sensitive assistance of his supreme part, so that the inferior was abandoned to a crueler torment. The suffering of the cross was extreme, but it was still accompanied by more force than appeared in this agony of the garden. On the cross Jesus shows no weakness, he speaks with great firmness and utters powerful cries, showing unparalleled constancy. But here he complains to his disciples of his sadness, and he begs them to remain with him, and to watch, as if he needed their consolation, or that their vigilance was necessary for his preservation. And although the Savior wanted to experience these weaknesses to console us among those that happen to us in such a strange sacrifice, he also did it again to make known to his disciples, the few people who wanted to keep his company in such a terrible state as if he wanted to say to them, "Since I will hardly find anyone who wants to enter with me into this sacrifice, you at least, who are those of

> my apostles whom I have chosen to participate, remain with me in this extreme immolation, and do not refuse to bear this state one day. Watch with me and remain abandoned for all the rest. In entering into this agony, stay passive to the sacrifice that will take place in you. Keep me company and relieve my pain by whichever part you want to take." O how few are capable of this sacrifice!

Continuing her theology of sacrifice, Guyon states that accepting God's will in real sacrifices must be chosen freely in imitation to Christ. She explains:

> By the foundation of abandonment that she bears, she cannot refuse anything that is proposed to her as the will of God, whereas in times of the real sacrifice, she is bound and carried away by the torrent of providence, so that she must follow him.

That she must follow him does not mean she has no choice. Rather she made her choice to follow God's will, as Mary Magdalene did. We too may follow what Magdalene did by complete abandonment into the divine will of God, despite the suffering or sacrifice it entails.

Pure love acts, engaging and moving the soul to touch those who are weary, broken, or confused. Such merciful deeds bring pure love into life's reality. Instead of distancing herself, the soul experiences pure love in real time as she prays. Mysticism, then, is not solely ethereal but also concrete. It is not enough to say I have faith and love; I also need deeds that prove that faith and love. Why? Jesus requires it, declaring, "As you did it to one of the least of these my brethren, you did it to me" (Matt 25:40). Guyon had faith, understanding why she did what she believed. Her faith was more than a concept, but was in a person, Jesus.

In her commentary on John's Gospel, Guyon desires union with Jesus through the bread of life, stating, "How it is necessary to believe this great mystery revealed." What is the great mystery?

> Jesus Christ is the bread that communicates life. How does he communicate this? By eating. He speaks of a thing that is eaten by the mouth of the body, as manna was. The sacrifices of Jesus Christ were real sacrifices. When Jesus Christ wills to accomplish these sacrifices and gives reality to these things, did he do it in figures of speech, images, or in faith? He did it in reality and truth. If Jesus Christ is a real sacrifice, I say that he is really given to eat, as the Israelites really ate manna that is not just a figure.[14]

14. Guyon, *Jeanne Guyon's Mystical Perfection*, 98.

Guyon's commentary on the bread of life reveals the power of pure love, who gives life to the soul by sacrificing his own life on the cross. She writes,

> He wants to be eaten so they do not die. O wonderful advantage of the holy communion! What good you produce and what a difference you make for those who commune frequently with those who commune rarely.[15]

In her commentaries, Guyon expresses not only her delight in receiving the bread of life but also her desire to join with pure love through reconciliation. As Jesus breathed upon the apostles and gave them the Holy Spirit, he gave them power to forgive sins (John 20:21–23). In her commentary, Guyon states, "He gives them the Holy Spirit and the apostolic mission with the power to deliver from sins. This passage supports the priest hearing confessions."[16] Guyon understands pure love has the power to forgive, but he empowers his apostles to forgive also. Pure love puts Jesus first so our relationship with him does not waver due to feelings and emotions or, worse, persecution and betrayal but enjoys communion with him out of love: a choice to remain with him. We choose to live in harmony with Jesus despite any struggle or suffering.

In her commentary on Matthew, Guyon also distinguishes between the sensible and spiritual world and unveils the prophetic meaning of the Law and the Prophets. Jesus states, "I say to you, till heaven and earth pass away, not an iota, not a dot will pass from the law until all is accomplished" (Matt 5:18). Responding to this passage, Guyon declares,

> This prophecy includes the soul being purified of the terrestrial to become celestial and divine. This happens only as the law is accomplished in the soul according to the degree of which she is capable. She completes and fulfills the law according to her ability and following the designs of God for her.

She develops her thought even more profoundly in life within the interior of the human being.

> If we could discover by the light that God gives us how the whole law is fulfilled in interior souls and how Jesus Christ is expressed there with all his states! We saw with admiration, *I say to you, until heaven and earth pass away, not an iota, not a dot, will pass from the*

15. Guyon, *Jeanne Guyon's Mystical Perfection*, 99.
16. Guyon, *Jeanne Guyon's Mystical Perfection*, 263.

> *law until all is accomplished* in these souls by union and conformity with Jesus Christ since they bear the states of Jesus Christ and Jesus Christ in his states.

Conformity to Christ is perfection of love. It has, as Guyon states, "substance and integrity." St. Paul speaks of the pure love as the eternal weight of glory (2 Cor 4:17), which empowers us to live by faith, not by sight. In other words, we live in the presence of pure love, not the feelings and emotions that arise from our love for Jesus.

As Guyon continues her explanation of pure love and its meaning, she surmises the following.

> The lack of perfection in the observation of the law according to whether it is greater or less great makes the soul more or less great in the celestial Kingdom. For the measure of the interior state will be the measure of glory. Ah! For those who live from the exterior are blind!

Many resist entering into the interior states of Jesus Christ. We fear and fail to understand the marvelous relationship that our hearts will have with his. The profundity of her thought reveals the division between living exteriorly, that is, according to worldly desires and subjective pleasures with feelings and emotions versus living interiorly, that is, in the heart, mind, and soul by faith, hope, and charity. Guyon's thought complements St. Paul's understanding of love: "God our Savior, desires all men to be saved and to come to the knowledge of the truth" (1 Tim 2:3–4). Pure love expresses divine truth, and this Divine Love wants to purify our hearts so that our human will conforms to his divine will. Or as Jesus states: "Not my will, but yours, be done" (Luke 22:42). Conforming to God's will, fulfilling the Great Commandment of loving God and neighbor, pure love perfects our love from all that is exterior. No better insight exists that explains pure love as Guyon's commentary on Jesus's ultimate commandment: "Be perfect as your heavenly Father is perfect" (Matt 5:48). She states:

> We find perfection in God alone, and this may not be found outside of God. In this perfection we are transported into our eternal origin and pass into union with divinity with all of God's goodness and advantages. So that not being able to distinguish itself in anything, nor anything that belongs to it, it only feels through its center *that God may be all in all.*

In spiritual theology, with our ineffable and inexhaustible desire to be united to Divine Love, the soul encounters Divine Love's power to transform and transfigure it into the image and likeness of Jesus Christ. Inspired by this intimacy, the soul obeys out of love, not force. Passivity and annihilation open the doors to a transcendent communion with pure love in an intimate and spousal relationship with God. "Our Bridegroom Christ calls and then divinizes every person who responds faithfully to his invitation, revealing to them the beautiful, mystical marriage of the wedding feast of the Lamb's Supper, the Kingdom of Heaven."[17] All of Scripture prophesies Jesus's coming, and Jesus speaks to us directly, for he is the fulfillment of all Scripture.

The whole of Scripture then is a prophetic unveiling of the mysteries of God's interaction with us, so we come to know and then love him as a bride knowing the Bridegroom, Jesus Christ.

THOMAS PATRICK KUFFEL

17. Kuffel and James, The Ascent to God, 22.

Preface

At the University of Virginia, gifted author and professor Dr. Carlos Eire directed my PhD dissertation, called "The Apophatic Mysticism of Madame Guyon." I appreciate very much everything he did to make this scholarship on Madame Jeanne Guyon possible. I traveled to Europe and researched at the Bodleian Library at the University at Oxford and the Vatican Archives in Rome as well as many other research centers and libraries. In the bibliography, there is a podcast Dr. Eire did on Madame Guyon that is extraordinary. I am eternally grateful for Dr. Eire's scholarship and knowledge, as well as spiritual understandings.

I have already translated and published Guyon's Commentaries on Galatians, Ephesians, Colossians, Revelation, Luke, and John. Madame Guyon wrote at length in her commentary on St. Matthew, and so at its earliest publication this was divided into two volumes. *Jeanne Guyon's Mystical Interpretation of Divinization: Her Biblical Commentary on St. Matthew's Gospel*, volume 1, includes Matthew chapters 1–17. Her *Biblical Commentary on St. Matthew's Gospel*, volume 2, includes Matthew chapters 16–28. I have also finished translating her commentary on Mark, and that will quickly be published also. So soon all of Guyon's commentaries on the Gospels will be available to be read by an English-speaking audience.

Madame Guyon wrote this in 1682–83 and used the form of early punctuation in practice at that time. In this translation, I have conformed her commentary to the practices of her original document. In place of quotation marks, she used italics. When she also wanted to emphasize a phrase, she put it in italics. After years of translating her work, I have come to appreciate this form of early punctuation as direct and immediate communication to the reader, which she finds particularly important. I hope you enjoy the creative power of her thinking.

Madame Guyon expresses her most mature wisdom in her commentaries on the Gospels. Her commentary on Matthew incorporates much of her most valuable theology. Every hour I have spent translating has been richly rewarded by increased understanding of how we live a spiritual life.

I present this to you, the reader of Jeanne Guyon, in prayerful expectation that you, too, will find a peaceful expression of life lived in the expectation of entering divinization.

NANCY CAROL JAMES
July 14, 2025

Acknowledgements

Many people have contributed to this volume. I am grateful for the support of Dr. Carlos Eire of Yale University during my University of Virginia dissertation work on Jeanne Guyon. I thank the Rev. Thomas Kuffel for his understanding of Jeanne Guyon's theology of divinization. I thank Roberta Morell, gifted therapist and friend, for her dialogues and writing on spirituality and theology.

I thank the Diocese of Alaska for their many events and their warm welcome of Jeanne Guyon's Christian witness. In particular, I thank Father Scott Fisher for his passion for God, which brings joy to our faith. I thank St. Matthew's Episcopal Church, Fairbanks, Alaska, for the talks I have given on Jeanne Guyon at this parish. I thank St. John's Episcopal Church, Lafayette Sq., Washington, DC, for their support for my publications of Madame Guyon's works.

Many thanks go to those who share my passion for the work of Jeanne Guyon. Maria has read, explored, and researched Jeanne Guyon along with me. I am grateful that we share this love.

Above all, I think my readers, who share a love for Jeanne Guyon and her ideas about interior faith. Guyon's books have been kept alive by those who continue to seek a profound interior life where Jesus Christ lives and moves and has his being. I pray that Guyon's Christian interior faith lives for centuries yet to come.

Introduction

By Nancy Carol James

A brilliant Scripture scholar, Madame Guyon writes prolifically about the Christian interior life, where Jesus Christ dwells in our mind, body, and soul. In her *Autobiography*, she describes frequently writing all night with ideas flowing directly into her heart and mind. She called these bursts of inspiration "spiritual torrents." Intimately knowing Scriptures and theology from all eras, including St. Thomas Aquinas and St. Augustine of Hippo, she wrote a commentary on every book of the Bible. Known for her mystical comparisons and connections drawn from among all of the books of the Bible, Guyon used Thomas Aquinas's four types of scriptural interpretation. Called the *quadriga*, this fourfold interpretation breathes life and power into Scripture's written word. Guyon's understanding of the literal meaning, as well as her rich thought on scriptural allegories, moral injunctions, and the future events, including the second coming, makes her commentary on Matthew unique. Guyon describes the believer's experiences of pain, crosses, suffering, and evil the believer may experience before the reception of the vast and encompassing vision of the interior Kingdom of heaven.

Madame Guyon prays in her commentary on Matthew, imploring God's blessing on her writing. She writes, "Give, O Uncreated Wisdom, your blessing to this work only undertaken to give more light to the Christian interior, showing it in many ways under the clear clouds of your Scriptures!" Guyon's touchstone insight was her belief in the power of our complete surrender and abandonment to Jesus Christ, which releases interior understandings of God. She testifies that this power assured the survival of her own horrific persecutions, humiliations, and even incarcerations. In her commentary on Matthew, Guyon emphasizes the interior torment and suffering believers may go through and shares how to understand the tremendous pain some will know because of their faith. Guyon's lasting ability to reach out beyond her own self to touch the hearts, minds, and souls of people for over three hundred years confirms the belief that God gave Guyon her powerful words and ministry to help others. In divinization, God blesses the faithful who stay with him through trials and suffering to find the eternal presence of Jesus Christ.

Written in 1682–83, Guyon's commentary on Matthew eloquently describes the hidden and mystical interpretation of the gospel message for the interior life in divinization. She completely expresses her mystical thoughts using allegorical, moral, and anagogical interpretations of divinization, which opens our very soul to the interior Kingdom of heaven, where dwells the living Lord, who desires intimacy and love within us. When we live and seek him with heart, mind, and soul, Jesus Christ answers us and dwells within us. He moves our sluggish souls to follow him, and then our souls become a living force or power within ourselves and the world. In divinization, our souls go on a long journey with Jesus Christ into the Kingdom of heaven, while still living on the earth.

Guyon describes the wonder of this journey in this commentary. She forthrightly addresses her own seventeenth-century French historical situation and states that the Roman Catholic Church pursued many persecutions of those following this interior journey. She writes that in her era, priest confessors and spiritual directors at times refused absolution and the Eucharist to those who practiced this contemplation. King Louis XIV even arrested those advocating these ideas, yet Guyon continued writing about this interior kingdom, helping others to find the fulfilling Kingdom of heaven within our very being. As we know, King Louis XIV turned his immense power against Guyon for doing this, and she spent nearly eight years incarcerated. When she was finally exonerated and released from the Bastille, the king told Guyon not to advocate for the interior life, but she ignored the danger and actually confronted the legal authorities by telling them they were in error and should stop misrepresenting the Christian gospel. Guyon continued her powerful testimony to Jesus Christ living within her soul.

In Guyon's commentary on Matthew, Guyon expresses her most powerful and detailed exposition of the interior life living in the mystical power of divinization. She lifts the veil from symbolic language to show the hidden operations of God within the soul. She describes her interpretation of Scriptures in the following quote.

> All that God operates secretly in souls is written about in the divine books and is included with all its principles and examples. When God is pleased to lift the veil that covers the symbolic figures, we cannot admire them enough. God draws aside the veil only as one advances through the experience of these spiritual states which are depicted in this table of truth. Already there are a thousand places that convince us of the reality of these states that even those with a mediocre understanding can witness in the word of God. The particular goal of this work to prove the interior life as solid truth is advanced in this place. The adversaries of the interior life *are in error* because they do not *know* and consult *the Scriptures*.

In this interior life, Guyon describes the soul's journey as one in which the delicacy and beauty of the spiritual vision delights us with purity and light, inviting us into the interior Kingdom. Our souls become a living altar where Jesus Christ pours his holy and life-giving Spirit within our soul and celebrates the Eucharist upon our soul. Faith outlines our destiny on our soul, and pure love fills this outline with the nuance of living in God's glory for eternity.

As Thomas Kuffel says in his introduction, in our time many have lost both the vision and experience of our interior faith. Reading Guyon on mysticism keeps our hope for the reality of the Kingdom of heaven alive. If we dwell only in our sensuality, she writes, we have a brute for a master, and we become increasingly isolated and lonely. Living in our senses denies the reality of the living soul and leaves us isolated from the ability to know and love the Holy Spirit. For discernment of this, Guyon refers us to St. Catherine of Genoa in *The Spiritual Dialogue*, who describes living only in the body: "I became enmeshed in sin, I became arid and heavy, a thing of the earth."[1]

To live in the Spirit, interior people follow a spiritual principle found in the foundation of our soul. Guyon states that in this principle we are to be equally content in whichever state God places and holds us. In both times of plenty and need, the believer cares only for God, finding and possessing him in all things, allowing our self to be emptied and filled through God's will and in God's time.

Guyon interprets the complexity of Scriptures using all of Thomas Aquinas's four methods: the literal, allegorical, moral or tropological, and anagogical. She writes, "It is nevertheless certain that Jesus Christ did not say a word that did not have several meanings." Throughout her

1. Catherine of Genoa, *Spiritual Dialogue*, 106.

commentary on Matthew, she involves all four of these methods to release the mystical meaning of these Scriptures.

The basis of this meaning lies in Jesus Christ's desire to communicate his word to everybody. His word is life, and Jesus Christ's great joy lies in eternal and spiritual generation, which means giving birth to our living soul and purifying this soul from the corruption of Adam. Jesus Christ then nourishes our soul. He gives us what is needed for the sanctification and divinization of our souls. Guyon writes that he pours out profound gifts and "gives the greatest of graces deserved for souls with whom he will unite in marriage: the purification of his spouses, the trials showing their fidelity, the consummation of their love, and their eternal marriage with the King of glory."

An example of this is found the narrative of the rich young man, invited to sell his possessions and follow Jesus Christ. For Guyon, the symbolism here is that the rich young man literally needed to separate from his wealth, but in the allegorical meaning, God needed to purify his soul and give needed trials and joys to develop his love of God. The paradox of the interior life is the more we dispossess the exterior, the more fruitful and rich our interior life becomes. To sell the soul's possessions is to take off the superficial concerns of the exterior life and clothe our interior life with the truth and beauty of the Spirit. This is Guyon's moral or tropological interpretation of this passage. Few enter this narrow path to perfection, because we fear losing external possessions.

> Many make good progress wrapped in rich spiritual goods and practices. But almost all lack courage, turn back, and fail, when invited into a great discipline. This offer will clothe them with truth, yet their self-love and nature will not support this. Ah! We do not understand the purity of our vocation and do not penetrate to our interior desire. External loss is a shadow of our interior transformation.

The Spirit calls us to participate in God's perfection and the Kingdom of heaven. Yet we want to retain what we already have and add more to this. Guyon writes about this interior transformation.

> God gives us the Kingdom in the interior if we allow the annihilation and get through this narrow door opening to the greatest riches. As soon as a soul is released from self, she is clothed in Jesus Christ. Under these precious vestments, she enters easily into God, having nothing in her that resists. Like fondue, her soul,

melted and dissolved, flows without difficulty into God, like pure and clear water passes into the smallest place.

GUYON'S DESCRIPTION OF THE SOUL'S TRANSFORMATION DESCRIBED IN MATTHEW

Throughout volume 2 of the Gospel of Matthew commentary, Guyon traces the journey to divinization that the soul may go on. She calls the soul sluggish at times until the interior vision of the Kingdom of heaven becomes alive in the soul. The transformation goes through certain stages, although every soul experiences these in a unique way and order. Divinization, the infusion of God's grace and perfection, creates the interior Kingdom of heaven within the soul. She writes, "The observation of the commandments assures salvation but does not bring perfection which involves the disappropriation of spiritual and temporal wealth. We understand the cleansing of the soul in *sell your possessions.* Our Lord proposes our imitation of his life." In our love, we enter a new and intense relationship with God that will require suffering and trials. The rewards will be intense as the believer moves into the presence of holiness. Guyon continues, "Few enter, though our Master of perfection calls us to this." Here are the stages that Guyon describes for those who follow Jesus Christ in this story.

STAGE ONE: DRIVING OUT THE MONEY CHANGERS (MATT 21:12–13)

Guyon uses the quadriga interpretations to reveal the mystical meaning of Jesus driving out the money changers from the temple.

First, in the literal translation, Jesus Christ entered the temple to drive out all that were selling and buying in the temple area. "He said to them, 'It is written, "My house shall be called a house of prayer"; but you are making it a den of robbers'" (Matt 21:13).

Guyon honors the literal meaning while she interprets this also as an allegory of what Christ does within the human soul. In our soul, we may invite the spirit of the world, amusements and interest in others, self-interest, and ambition to rule our soul, thus making the soul cluttered with propriety full of ungodly interests. When Jesus Christ enters the soul, he drives away what Guyon calls this "nonsense." When we hold on to our right to cling to these worldly occupations and commerce, our soul becomes a "den of thieves."

> Once Jesus Christ *enters into* a soul as the *temple of God*, he drives out the *money changers* and banishes all commerce with creatures. . . . We must be *a house of prayer* with a free and continual prayer, as the spirit of God suggests and operates in the hearts of those who are subject to him.

Guyon considers allowing this cleansing of our soul justice that we owe to God. We are to "know him as the only occupation of our heart and the sovereign preference of all our views. All other things must be chased from the soul and the soul must remain empty, so that God remains there alone."

STAGE TWO: THE HEAVENLY FEAST (MATT 22:1–6)

In this narrative, Jesus tells the story of the king who gave a wedding feast for his son and sends his servants to call those to the feast. Sadly, those invited did not come to the feast for reasons of commerce and business which has filled their soul. Scripture reads, "But they paid no attention and went off, one to his farm, another to his business, [6] while the rest seized his servants, treated them shamefully, and killed them" (Matt 22:5–6).

When the soul has been cleansed from the money changers, now the soul filled with the Spirit of God may know the joys of a feast. Guyon interprets this as all are invited to the feast in our interior life where they enjoy the Kingdom of heaven. God sends his servants who are the ministers of the word to announce with joy that everybody is invited. God continually offers an interior feast to us. Yet if the human soul is still filled with money changing, the human acts contemptuously to this invitation.

When those first invited to come to the feast say no, God sends out his servants to the main roads, inviting everybody to come to the feast. The apostles and God's most faithful servants announce this, saying to those to whom they give the invitation, "You are invited to the continual feast with unfailing joy! You will be kissed with the kiss of reconciliation and find your treasure is your heart."

Yet most turn down this pressing invitation because they are attached only to the earth and not to the soul. They destroy the soul's foundation, where the table for the feast is set. They reject those who seek God in the interior who have discovered human treasure is not in the external life. Our heart filled with God is the feast and the treasure.

What is the goal of the transforming soul? In Matt 25 we receive an invitation to the wedding feast, "yet we are so insensitive to our happiness that we refuse." In this anagogical interpretation, our destiny is to share in God's feast in the heavenly banquet. In the power of divinization, we may indeed experience some of this in this lifetime. Yet many souls resist this call from God to join in the feast with joy. "Instead of returning to the divine table, they move away from their foundation where the table is set to participate in the commerce of creatures." This is the anagogical sense of Scripture about the heavenly realities received in contemplation.

STAGE THREE: THE TEN VIRGINS (MATT 25:1–13)

The soul now filled with joy and understanding seeks to unite with God in a pure and perfect alliance. She has offered herself to Jesus Christ and awaits the fulfillment of the coming, that we all may be one.

Jesus tells this story of the ten virgins to emphasize the need for our interior, anointed prayer as we seek a more perfect union with God. The literal meaning of this narrative states, there are ten virgins, all with the same external and respectable life. All prepare their lamps, which is the sign of preparation through exterior life. All wait for the Bridegroom, yet only five have brought oil for their lamps. All ten virgins fall asleep, yet the five without oil sleep in ignorance of when the Bridegroom will come. The five with the oil rest in the power of the grace of continual prayer. The Bridegroom comes at midnight, which is an allegorical comparison with the incarnation at Jesus's birth at Bethlehem in the middle of night. The foolish virgins without the anointing of light in the lamps cannot see the Bridegroom to unite with him and sadly find the door shut that keeps them outside. Those with oil see the Bridegroom and enter the wedding feast and are received in God with Jesus Christ.

> Our Savior wants us to see in this comparison that the exterior is nothing without the interior. The interior is the oil that must give life from within to all the actions that appear outside. Now this interior is Jesus himself as the oil of life, as the bride declares when she says to him, *Your name is like an oil poured out* (Song 1:2).

Guyon states that the souls of the wise virgins receive the Bridegroom only when the soul rests in the oil of prayer and silence to listen for the coming of the Word of God. She writes, "Souls therefore who are ready, being lifted out of themselves, are taken and received: they *enter the wedding feast with the Bridegroom* and are seated in God with Jesus Christ, who hides them and encloses them with him in the bosom of the Father."

The anagogical narrative about the ten virgins who wait for the wedding describe the glories of eternity spent with the Bridegroom. She describes the interior experience of the soul who prepares to unite with God.

> When the Bridegroom is to come, as long as we watch, he makes himself heard. A cry made in the depths of the soul announces the coming of the Bridegroom. . . . It is then that there is a great silence in the interior sky, and at the same time we hear a voice crying out. O cry! O silence! O silence that cries out! O cry which is made without noise! And what does this cry say? He says the Bridegroom is coming. O happy news! But what else does he add? That you have to get up and go to meet him. You have to come out of yourself which is the last step in order to be admitted to the wedding. The soul is no sooner out of itself than the Bridegroom appears.

The soul then meets and unites with Jesus Christ, who carries the soul into the bosom of the Father. The soul has been purified of being a money changer, has accepted the invitation to the feast, and has entered the marriage with the Bridegroom. Yet suffering and trials await the faithful soul, even as suffering and trials clung to Jesus Christ during his earthly ministry.

Guyon states that the interior Christian lives in similar states to that of Jesus Christ. We are to know his states of being, of baptism, joy, wisdom, and union with God the Father. The interior Christian also will know the suffering and crosses that Jesus Christ knew. She writes that these crosses are to be expected, and the believer should show gratitude for them, as they prepare the soul for complete union and participation with God the Father in resurrected divinization.

> External crosses almost always accompany interior crosses. We must expect persecutions and venomous hatred because of the name of Jesus Christ. People who do only evil stir up the bloodiest

> persecutions against us. Why? For the name of Jesus Christ, the cause for whom we work, to make him known and loved. Many are horrified to see his loving name like an aromatic oil spread everywhere. These faithful hearts of whom we speak find themselves in love with his love.

The crosses approach as a test of the faithfulness of the soul yearning to stay in union with Jesus Christ.

STAGE FOUR: THE AGONY IN THE GARDEN OF GETHSEMANE (MATT 26:26–36)

In this unique section of the commentary on Matthew, Guyon describes in great detail when the interior Christian may experience times of isolation, desolation, deprivation, spiritual abuse, all of which may be accompanied by physical torture and death. Indeed, her life contained many forms of this violence and abuse, and she writes about this with understanding. One of the greatest contributions of her commentary on Matthew are these understandings that can help those who are suffering great persecution or have suffered this persecution. She encourages us to remember that the Kingdom of heaven is within us, and Jesus Christ continues to be present in our world. We think of Christians throughout the world who suffer for the name of Jesus Christ, as Guyon herself suffered. Jesus Christ offers his body and blood to all who suffer; Guyon's understanding here of the horrors of persecution offers hope to all who go through similar experiences. Guyon describes the stages and levels of Jesus Christ, who suffers unbearable agony in the garden.

In the literal understanding of the garden of Gethsemane, Jesus takes with him Peter and the two sons of Zebedee and asks them to remain with him and watch. He asks them to witness his sorrow as he cries out to the Father and asks if the cup of suffering can pass from him. Jesus understands the evils that will happen to him, without hope of consolation or support. Without divine help, this voluntary acceptance of suffering is impossible, for nature will not accept a death that can be avoided.

Jesus also knows he will fully bear shame and martyrdom while being clothed with the appearance of criminality and sin. No life will be given to his soul. This will be the ultimate interior sadness, pain, and torment. Yet his chosen disciples sleep and do not give him the consolation of watching and prayer. Jesus Christ's interior pain in the garden of Gethsemane is greater than the physical pain he will suffer in the crucifixion.

In the allegorical interpretation, Guyon says that the interior person will also receive an impression on the soul from the hand of God that shows them the pains, circumstances, and consequences of their sacrifice and abandonment to God. Our human nature has a repugnance to this sacrifice. However, when the human and divine will unite, the soul will also bear the agony of Jesus Christ in the garden of Gethsemane. When God wills to conform the soul to Jesus Christ, suffering will occur. The soul might bear the rigors of divine justice, which is not a punishment for sin but a strong, saving reality. Finally, the soul receives a most sublime participation to carry this very same state as Jesus Christ. Guyon writes, of the agony of the interior person,

> Jesus Christ saw himself charged with all sins, placing him in this agony. The same happens in proportion to a soul whom God causes to pass into this state. The sin with which she sees herself covered and clothed, after having seen herself all brilliant in virtues and rich in good works, horrifies her intolerably. She sees herself clothed in sin without any trace of the divinity that once shone within her.

Guyon reveals her profound understanding of the depth of human suffering that will happen to the interior person.

> To say what this last state is and the extent of its sufferings cannot be said. All other sorrows are only shadows compared to these, but God carries everything; the more the soul has become divine, the more Jesus is in the soul with the fullness of his states.

Judas received thirty pieces of silver to betray Jesus, which is called *blood money*. Judas despairs and gives the money back, but the chief priests refuse help to Judas and declare that the blood money cannot be put in the treasury. Instead, they use this money to buy a burial ground for foreigners, called a potter's field. Guyon reacts to the harsh treatment Judas receives from the high priests.

> But who will not be surprised at the hardness of these priests, who seeing this repentance of Judas, and the declaration he made to them of having handed over an innocent man to them, far from correcting themselves, become even harsher? Whether you have delivered up a just man or an innocent one, they tell him, that is none of our business. What then is your business, O blind men!

> If the obvious danger of committing such injustice does not affect you, if a just man has been handed over to you, will you be able to condemn him justly? Or did he become a criminal just because he was handed over to you? The hardness of heart in people whose lives are not visibly disordered is worse than that of the greatest sinners, because when covered with self-esteem and supported by obstinacy, it is no longer curable.

After exposing the sins of those who refused assistance to Judas's attempt to repent, Guyon interprets Judas's blood money and the purchase of the potter's field as an allegory, saying that Jesus Christ wants his crucifixion to serve the benefit of all human beings. Guyon says the blood money purified the burial ground for foreigners in the same way that Jesus's blood purifies our soul. Jesus takes our lives like a broken pot and restores us to wholeness. The blood money purchasing this burial ground is like blood pouring into the burial ground. This allegory shows the expansion of this redemptive power of Jesus's blood also poured out upon foreigners and non-Christians for their salvation. The symbol of the field of blood where foreigners were buried means that all humanity had Jesus Christ's blood poured out for them also. In the anagogic interpretation, we look at the death of Judas, while meditating the meaning of destiny and death in light of this purifying blood, which brings us salvation and hopes for the Kingdom of heaven.

STAGE FIVE: JESUS CHRIST'S CRUCIFIXION ON GOLGOTHA (MATT 27:32–56)

In the literal understanding of this Scripture, Jesus Christ suffers death on the cross. His only support in his life had been divinity, and now at his death, he will be deprived of divinity. Without his Father, he could not survive, for the flow of divinity within him was deprived. He suffered this agony and mortal abandonment felt like an immense solitude. Jesus Christ cries out about this in this immense pain: "My God, My God, why have you forsaken me?" Feeling abandoned by God, Jesus Christ's cry consummates his sacrifice.

In the allegorical understanding, Guyon says that some souls will also experience this strange suffering of betrayal and crucifixion. She says that interior people can hide and bear some suffering quietly, yet this is nothing close to this ultimate pain of crucifixion. She says that when we cry out in our crucifying pain, we know that "the more extreme it is, the nearer it approaches to the end." The soul has come out of herself by this terrible abandonment that consummates her sacrifice.

Guyon continues her allegorical interpretation, saying that the *tearing of the curtain* of the temple into two parts when Jesus dies is to show Jesus Christ's division of the soul from his body. In allegorical interpretation, this tearing of the curtain into two also shows the mystical death of his most chosen souls, who must die as Jesus Christ did on Calvary. Even while alive, through abandonment, the soul comes out of herself with a cry. Now the soul will live only in God. The curtain of the temple being torn in two reveals the mystical interpretation in which the superior part of the soul entirely divides from the inferior part. In an allegorical interpretation, that the stones were split shows that the soul has lost its first form and is now freed from propriety and hell. Like a stone being made into glass, the soul, penetrated by light, will know the happiness of its resurrection.

STAGE SIX: THE RESURRECTION (MATT 28:1–8)

In the literal and historical interpretation, at his resurrection, Jesus Christ rose victorious from the tomb. The resurrection takes place at the end of the Sabbath night in the deepest darkness.

In the allegorical interpretation, Jesus Christ also rises victorious in all souls who are happy to have a share in his death. God does not bring a soul into death with a plan to leave her there but with the intention of new life. In the resurrection, the soul experiences an absorption into God that is delicate and profound. She experiences an enlargement of the soul with the angel of the Lord like a powerful and sudden grace announcing the coming of Jesus Christ, who deserved this grace for her. The soul enters into a reciprocal love between God and herself. Nothing will be able to remove her from the love of Jesus Christ.

The soul now united to the truth of God through faith hopes uniquely in God with all her strength, has joy in her well-being, rests in the will of God, remains abandoned to all God's commands, and subjected to God's Kingdom. In our pure love and simplicity, we have now offered our empty soul to Christ who fills us with praises. Guyon writes, "The soul rests in no other power than the will of God and follows only the way of providence, which accomplishes from moment to moment the revelation of eternity in time." God infuses his perfection within us, and all our being experiences the sweetness of his love. Guyon exclaims, "O day of glory and triumph for my God, for whom I am passionate!"

CONCLUSION

Guyon describes this spiritual journey called divinization by interpreting the hidden, symbolical meaning of the many narratives in Matthew. To do this, she uses Thomas Aquinas's fourfold method of scriptural interpretation, the quadriga, and uses the details from Matthew to reveal the mystical meaning. For the believer, the providence of God will guide the soul even in this world, living in the believer's heart. Jesus Christ invites, and in faith we respond for salvation and living in the Kingdom of heaven within our purified soul. This divinization is our greatest spiritual gift offered to us through the sacrifice of Jesus Christ upon the cross.

NANCY CAROL JAMES
July 14, 2025

Commentary on St. Matthew, Volume 2

By the Author Jeanne de la Mothe Guyon

Translated by Nancy Carol James

> At that time the disciples came to Jesus, saying, "Who is the greatest in the kingdom of heaven?" [2] And calling to him a child, he put him in the midst of them [3] and said, "Truly, I say to you, unless you turn and become like children, you will never enter the kingdom of heaven." (Matt 18:1–3)

The whole economy of perfection is contained in these words of Jesus Christ. First, we must convert and return within. This necessary conversion involves turning from sin to grace and also from exterior life to interior life. We enter into the interior Kingdom through littleness in order to become a child. Children abandon themselves to the conduct of their parents without care or concern. If we do not enter into this spiritual childhood, we will not arrive at God in this life or even in the next. We pass through a purifying fire, all the more terrible if we resist this grace of littleness.

> Whoever humbles himself like this child is the greatest in the kingdom of heaven. (Matt 18:4)

We advance to the degree of our humility. The more a soul is small, simple, docile, and submitted to the way of God, the more advanced the soul is in God and seeking union with God. Smallness connected with love makes true *humility* and works an interior annihilation not known in external life. Interior people are humble people. Everyone wants to be something, and yet one must be nothing.

> Whoever receives one such child in my name receives me, [6] but whoever causes one of these little ones who believe in me to sin, it would be better for him to have a great millstone fastened around his neck and to be drowned in the depth of the sea. (Matt 18:5–6)

Those who will receive favorably these despised, little, and poor interiors for the love of Jesus will receive him himself. But on the contrary, those who load them with slander, calumnies, and persecutions and prevent them by their rigorous pursuits from giving themselves to the interior life and entering into littleness: ah, how rigorously they will be punished! They have liberty for a time to outrage these innocent persons who do not resist them and do not even complain. Yet a day will come when God himself will take their defense in hand, reserving to himself to equally punish the outrages and reward the benefits that the humble interior persons will have received.

> Woe to the world for temptations to sin! For it is necessary that temptations come, but woe to the one by whom the temptation comes! [8] And if your hand or your foot causes you to sin, cut it off and throw it away. It is better for you to enter life crippled or lame than with two hands or two feet to be thrown into the eternal fire. [9] And if your eye causes you to sin, tear it out and throw it away. It is better for you to enter life with one eye than with two eyes to be thrown into the hell of fire. (Matt 18:7–9)

The Master does not want people who are small and interior to be scandalized, which means the scandal given openly to lead others into sin. He repeats in their favor what he has already said about scandal in general. I stop at that which is committed with regard to the interior, which is my principal aim in all that I write, to write about the interior.

Scandal is that which causes some fall or some spiritual loss. The Savior speaks of this and not of the false scandal of certain persons who are scandalized by good. They wish to prevent others from praying and devoting themselves to the interior because they say they are scandalized by it. People were indeed scandalized in this way by the actions and doctrine of Jesus Christ; and did Jesus for that reason cease to act and teach all the same? But those who truly scandalize souls are those who turn them away from the interior way. O people of good will! Even if these persons scandalizing you seemed as necessary as your hands and feet, and as dear as eyes, even if this confessor or this other person of authority appeared to you the greatest support in the world, leave them. It is better for you to enter into God who is true life then not to enter or be delayed by these specious supports.

Interior persons with a gift and vocation from God also experience another pernicious scandal when others prevent the good they do. They stop them in two ways. First, they take away from them the power necessary for their actions. Second, they slander them, in order to make them odious and ridiculous. It is necessary that this scandal happen so that their souls may be purified, tried, and strengthened by the crosses and confusions that they are made to suffer. But *woe to those by whom this scandal comes!*

However, the children of grace who were beginning to drink the spiritual milk or the great ones who already eat the more solid bread of the interior must not fear or be discouraged when their mothers and fathers in our Lord are taken away from them. Let them remain attached only to Jesus Christ with an entire submission to the Spirit of his grace. They will see that nothing will be lacking for them. For one can indeed tear away the channel, but one cannot take away the source. One can indeed remove the person representing the word of Spirit and life to them, but it is impossible that one prevents their only guide and their true Moses from speaking to them immediately to the heart and from leading them to the *springs of living water* (Rev 7:17). Let them sing then to console themselves what David wrote singularly for them: *For my father and my mother have forsaken me, but the Lord will take me in* (Ps 27:10), for it is certain *God never abandons those who seek only him* (Ps 9:10).

> Take care that you do not despise one of these little ones; for, I tell you, in heaven their angels continually see the face of my Father in heaven. (Matt 18:10)

Jesus Christ commands us with strength *not to despise one of these little*, annihilated *ones*. Nevertheless, they are humiliated and taunted by the whole world. Yet these people so despised enjoy ineffable happiness and live like *angels* on earth. In faith they have a continuous view and a very real enjoyment of God. This true beatitude of life makes them profoundly penetrate what will be the happiness of the other world. In a word, they enjoy God without seeing him, in a union so intimate and permanent that, with the reserve of the beatific vision, there is no enjoyment more truthful or more continual than that which they experience. Also, these interior people care little about everything that is said against them. Far from impeding the joy of the sovereign good within them, it increases their joy. In the midst of these contradictions, concentrated in their interior sanctuary, they testify that God has *delivered* them from their sins and proprieties, and they are with him. They remain content when everyone's hands are aiming against them.

> For the Son of man is come to save that which was lost. [12] What do you think? If a shepherd has a hundred sheep, and one of them has gone astray, does he not leave the ninety-nine on the mountains and go in search of the one that went astray? [13] And if he finds it, truly I tell you, he rejoices over it more than over the ninety–nine that never went astray. (Matt 18:11–13)

The Son of Man *is come to save* souls who are *lost* and bring back those who are gone *astray*. O all of you by a false humility do not want to go to Jesus Christ, saying that you want to wait until you do not sin anymore. Know that you are foolish! This is the gross error that prevents sinners from being converted and the imperfection that stops your entry into the way of perfection. Who can save you, O sinner, and save you from your sins, if you do not give yourself to your Savior? And if you do not go to meet him before he comes to you first, if you run away from him when he is looking for you, and if you are waiting to leave your sins before you approach Jesus, when will you approach him? A patient who would like to wait until he is cured to speak to the doctor, would not he be mad? Ah! If sinners come with trust and pain to throw themselves at the feet of Jesus, they will quickly be converted! The Gospels are full of examples of sudden conversions that Jesus does when the biggest sinners come to him. This is a reason to be astonished that Christians neglect this practice and that their leaders do not inspire them to do this. They talk to them about so many things before telling them to speak to Jesus Christ. We give them many methods and our own inventions before sending them to the Savior and giving them the freedom to spread their hearts before him that it is not surprising we have so much pain and see so little fruit.

It is the same with confessors who are in this error and divert people of good will away from prayer because they still sin. We get carried away with a bitter and violent zeal to prevent many souls from praying because they are still imperfect. The most excellent way to stop sinning and become perfect is to pray. The perfect do not need to do so much, being always united to God. Or rather, they do not need to be exhorted, being there on their own and never ceasing to pray. But sinners and weak beginners must urgently enter into the interior temple to offer the sacrifice every day. Tell a poor man that because he is poor, he should not ask for alms; is that not ridiculous? If all the world prayed, there would be no sinners or imperfect wars. These devotees who are not praying are as imperfect after twenty years as when they began to convert.

As soon as Jesus *finds his sheep* for whom he has searched, he *rejoices*. The Son of Man has descended from heaven to *search* for sinners, and yet we want to prevent them from going to him. O sinners, whoever you are! Leave the circumstances of your sin, and with a sincere heart full of trust, throw yourself into the arms of Jesus Christ. Show him your cheeks; ask him to bandage and heal them. This charitable Samaritan will not fail to do so. Enter your heart, hate your sins, and ask God sincerely for your conversion. He will not fail to grant it to you.

> So it is not the will of your Father in heaven that one of these little ones should be lost."(Matt 18:14)

He *will not lose any of the little ones* because they have enough docility to go to Jesus Christ and enough submission to remain with him. But these superb lovers of themselves who are content with a certain temperament that they affect to keep in all things are full of horrible vanity. They do not appear as bad as others because they are strong and firm in their practices. They believe themselves to be without fault. Lacking charity, they rebuke sinners. They are, I say, in a more obvious danger of ruin because of their great blindness. A sinner appears disordered, and this cannot be ignored. He suffers from sins on his way to conversion. But those who consider themselves superb do not see their faults and take them as virtues. This is why God allows the falls of the flesh, to permit them to see the sins of the spirit to which they are blind.

> If another member of the church sins against you, go and point out the fault when the two of you are alone. If the member listens to you, you have regained that one. [16] But if you are not listened to, take one or two others along with you, so that every word may be confirmed by the evidence of two or three witnesses. [17] If the member refuses to listen to them, tell it to the church; and if the offender refuses to listen even to the church, let such a one be to you as a Gentile and a tax collector. (Matt 18:15–17)

The sin that Jesus talks about here is a real evil that our brother does against us or in our presence. This law does not include imaginary pleasures and light faults that shock our delicate temperament because we may interpret events badly out of a bad mood. Our Lord says, *If your brother sins* or sins *against you* in a true offense, he offends or scandalizes you. This supposes a true and recognized sin. However, the charity that we owe to our brother obliges us to warn him gently and give him a wise correction.

This principle of our Savior is not observed widely. Why is this? Instead of reproaching our brother with love, we applaud him in secret and in public we blame and decry him. You have to tell the brother what bad you notice about him and not tell anyone else. After this secret correction, if the sin continues, we must take some charitable people with us to convince our brother of the sin in order to win him back. And if this does nothing, people of authority and pastors must warn the person. Then if the brother warned with love does not convert, we must avoid his company so we do not indulge his sins and ourselves experience a fall. But alas! We do the opposite of that. We see scandalous people, and we do not correct them. We see pious people, and we mistrust them mercilessly.

> Truly I tell you, whatever you bind on earth will be bound in heaven, and whatever you loose on earth will be loosed in heaven. (Matt 18:18)

This passage, along with the one above, strongly proves the necessity of confession, as well as the power the church has received to cut off and excommunicate. As to confession, clearly no one can bind or unbind what the confessor does not know, and so this must be known so the confessor can do the right thing in just discernment. If Jesus Christ had reserved the power of confession for himself, he would also have reserved the power of absolution and condemnation for himself. To absolve sins, one must know the knowledge of the cause. The Holy Spirit said through James, *Therefore confess your sins to one another* (Jas 5:16). What would be the use of confessing them to one who did not have the power to absolve them? And what good would it be to have the power to absolve if we do not confess them? One of these passages mutually explains and supports the other. We confess our sins so that the ministry of the church may judge them and put them away or retain them. For our salvation, we confess to those established by God to absolve us. There we see the power of God given to his church and priest to absolve our sins. We need to declare our sins out loud in the sacrament of confession, which is the gentlest way of doing this and the most appropriate way for judgment to be exercised.

In this way, the corrupted members of the church may be separated out so they do not corrupt others. They may receive communion when they leave their rebellion, because they are in a state of healing.

Something similar happens in the interior that is admired by those who receive this. God gives a singular power to those he calls to the apostolate in favor of souls. Yet they must declare to the priest what is happening in their heart and faithfully communicate all things to the priest. Certainly priests have an admirable gift of restoring peace to them in their troubles and relieving as much as possible their sorrows, because the priest has the power to command or declare interior movements in their heart. The priest also may deliver them from painful states when he deems it useful to their souls. The priest has received *the keys of heaven* for the benefit of those he serves. The apostolic state gives this authority before performing these acts according to the order of God.

> Again, truly I tell you, if two of you agree on earth about anything you ask, it will be done for you by my Father in heaven. 20 For where two or three are gathered in my name, I am there among them. (Matt 18:19–20)

Jesus Christ speaks here of true interior union of the church, which unites her members in an admirable harmony. The reason that Christians have so little union is that they are Christians only in the exterior and do not have the Spirit. With only exterior union, they are under the mantle of union through criminal ties or unfortunate oppositions.

But interior persons *wherever they meet* are united in such a strong and intimate relationship that the unions of nature and the closest relationships do not equal this. This pure, simple, and clean union is not made by humans. We are as united to them when far away as when near. The interiors experience this union because they are animated by the same Spirit and holiness in their heart and soul of the church. This means that from the first time they surrender, they find themselves seized with warmth and a confidence as free and complete as if they had seen and frequented with each other for a hundred years. This pleasantly surprises them. They have the advantage that when they confer together on their experiences in imitation of the apostles, they all happen to have only one language and country, without doubt because they have the same Master. St. Paul describes this in the following.

> I went up in response to a revelation. Then I laid before them (though only in a private meeting with the acknowledged leaders) the gospel that I proclaim among the Gentiles, in order to make sure that I was not running, or had not run, in vain. (Gal 2:2)

Walking in the same way and truth, they tend to have the same life. God gives these consolations to his poor and little servants to give them refreshment on their painful and long journey, to give them a glimpse of some ray of light through the testimony of others, as they walk through all the darkness with which the mystical way is covered. This causes the same joys that the apostles and their disciples knew: *For I am longing to see you so that I may share with you some spiritual gift to strengthen you—or rather so that we may be mutually encouraged by each other's faith, both yours and mine* (Rom 1:11–12). No one understands this better than interior people.

But in the middle of this, God unites particular people who are in the same degree of prayer. Their union is so pure it is inconceivable. They talk to each other more from the heart than the mouth. The remoteness of place does not prevent this interior conversation. God *unites* ordinarily *two or three people* in this way in a grand union, that they are lost in God together and can no longer be distinguished. God does this for his glory and that they work together for the salvation of souls. These united hearts *ask*, and it will be *granted.* With their conformity to one another, they have the very same feelings. When one has the thought to ask for something, the other has the thought to do it. Jesus *is* always *in the midst of them* because they are always united in him. Jesus is all the more in them, the more they are in him and united in him.

O unions! They differ from human unions and dangerous attachments! They are united to God, the more they are united to one another. One may even experience something surprising, that during the interior vicissitudes of death and life, pain and rest, when we know great danger, God uses these experiences as a purification for the bond.

> Then Peter came to Jesus and asked, "Lord, how many times shall I forgive my brother or sister who sins against me? Up to seven times?" 22 Jesus answered, "I tell you, not seven times, but seventy-seven times." (Matt 18:21–22)

Peter speaks not only for himself and in particular situations but also in the name of the entire church. The divine Master instructs him for himself and the church. As for the particular details, we must not put limits on the forgiveness of injuries because God does not limit his forgiveness of our sins. And for the priests who participate in Peter's power for the remission of sins, they must have a great compassion for sinners and not reject them. If the sins are more weakness than malice, what the sinner does not get at one time, they will get in another. Rigor does not create healing and conversion. Instead, gentleness, charity, and patience have this effect. If we carry sinners into their interior, they understand this easily. If we teach them *I cried to the Lord with my voice: with my voice I made supplication to the Lord* (Ps 141:2) they will not have the problem of frequent relapses and will soon be converted. Sweetness attracts trust, and rigor rebukes it. As soon as trust starts to come, we can easily enter in the heart to win the soul and carry him to God.

> For this reason the kingdom of heaven may be compared to a king who wished to settle accounts with his slaves. [24] When he began the reckoning, one who owed him ten thousand talents was brought to him; [25] and, as he could not pay, his lord ordered him to be sold, together with his wife and children and all his possessions, and payment to be made. [26] So the slave fell on his knees before him, saying, "Have patience with me, and I will pay you everything." [27] And out of pity for him, the lord of that slave released him and forgave him the debt. (Matt 18:23–27)

Each of us individually is this *servant who owes* infinitely to God. We are all his debtors, both for the communal debts for all human beings and for the particular obligations that we owe God and for the debts we have contracted by our personal faults. Therefore God, like the *master* in this Gospel, asks us what we owe him, not to force us to pay but in order to commit ourselves by asking for forgiveness. God takes pleasure in granting it to us, giving us what we owe him with all the more kindness as we are less able to satisfy a debt so strong.

> But that same slave, as he went out, came upon one of his fellow slaves who owed him a hundred denarii; and seizing him by the throat, he said, "Pay what you owe." [29] Then his fellow slave fell down and pleaded with him, "Have patience with me, and I will pay you." [30] But he refused; then he went and threw him into prison until he would pay the debt. (Matt 18:28–30)

This is the way we deal with our neighbor. In his great mercy, God gives us everything that we owe him, yet we demand our debts from others with extreme rigor. Mercy will be paid with mercy. But those who need but do not want mercy make themselves unworthy of is. The same truth is expressed here. *Blessed are the merciful, for they shall receive mercy* (Matt 5:7). We also declare, *He who has not shown mercy will be judged without mercy* (Jas 2:13). This is confirmed by the following passage.

> When the other servants saw what had happened, they were outraged and went and told their master everything that had

> happened. [32] Then the master called the servant in. "You wicked servant," he said, "I canceled all that debt of yours because you begged me to. [33] Shouldn't you have had mercy on your fellow servant just as I had on you?" [34] In anger his master handed him over to the jailers to be tortured, until he should pay back all he owed. [35] This is how my heavenly Father will treat each of you unless you forgive your brother or sister from your heart. (Matt 19:31–35)

This is clearly explained so that there is nothing more to add. We owe to God goods, honor, and life. We also must give to our neighbor all that we *owe* him in regard to these things and *forgive* him also for the usurpation of property, outrages against honor, and the assault on our person and life. We must reserve nothing from forgiveness to our neighbor, as God has reserved nothing from forgiving us.

> Some Pharisees came to him, and to test him they asked, "Is it lawful for a man to divorce his wife for any cause?" [4] He answered, "Have you not read that the one who made them at the beginning 'made them male and female,' [5] and said, 'For this reason a man shall leave his father and mother and be joined to his wife, and the two shall become one flesh'? [6] So they are no longer two, but one flesh. Therefore what God has joined together, let no one separate." (Matt 19:3–6)

The marriage of Adam with Eve was the figure of the marriage of Jesus Christ with the church and also with each pure soul.

The church was taken from the side of Jesus when Jesus's side was opened in his sleep on the cross, as Eve was taken from the side of Adam. This bride the church was created to be united with her husband but an impeccable husband with whom she could not sin and under whose protection she could not sin either. She was made of the same flesh, Jesus being in her by an indissoluble bond. Therefore, she is one and all pure, as it is written of her in the Song of Songs that she is *altogether beautiful and without sin* (Song 4:7). Her beauty is always preserved. As the Bridegroom cannot be separated from his wife, the church can no longer can be separated from her husband Jesus. As long as she remains united to her husband, she remains in his integrity. She can be separated from her husband only because of adultery. But who could convince her to commit adultery, since her infallible husband has promised that *the gates of hell will not prevail against it* (Matt 16:18). Jesus is bound to her in an eternal marriage, and she will never be separated from him for a single moment.

Therefore, the church is united to Jesus but in an indissoluble marriage union. By his Eucharist, he remains with her throughout the centuries in order to fulfill all the laws of marriage.

The church is the *sealed fountain* and the very strong and *closed garden* that does not fear the attacks made against it because her invincible husband is himself her stamp. He himself is *as a seal on her heart and on the arms of his spouse.* This happens on her heart so that she never has any other sentiments or other movements affecting her faith and dogmas, which are signified by the heart, than those he would communicate by his Spirit. She might also be regulated by him in ordinances in exterior actions, which is well designated by the arms. Hence, she does not do anything to her children not in accordance with her husband's wishes, nor does she offer to them any object of faith that is not in his Spirit.

The marriage of Adam is also the figure of the spiritual marriage that the Word makes with the pure soul to give her his Spirit. He leaves paradise, so to speak, to give himself to her with such affection as if she were his only lover. She must therefore leave everything to attach herself to him alone. She must *leave her father and her mother.* This father is Adam's unlawfulness. The mother is propriety. The lover will not be united to her divine lover unless she leaves all of this. This is done so the husband *joins with his wife*, and this is their union. *The two are made one flesh.* Here is union. Here is the loss of distinction and the divine transformation clearly expressed under the shadow of bodily unions. Human beings must not, nor can ever, *separate what God has joined together* in this way.

> And I say to you, whoever divorces his wife, except for unchastity, and marries another commits adultery and he who marries a divorced woman commits adultery. (Matt 19:9)

Jesus Christ never *abandons* a soul with whom he is united in a spiritual marriage. This union subsists in a durable manner so long as the soul does not withdraw from it to prostitute itself to the creature, which would be a crime all the greater being so tightly held by her husband, having enjoyed his embraces, she could tear herself away from it only with incredible violence. The soul who is united can still be separated, but the one who is transformed and changed into the one who possesses her, how could she be separated from him? A soul who is in God by transformation and withdraws from God for a moment would be under demonic influence, as it has been explained many times.

> His disciples said to him, "If such is the case of a man with his wife, it is better not to marry." [11] But he said to them, "Not everyone can accept this teaching, but only those to whom it is given. [12] For there are eunuchs who have been so from birth, and there are eunuchs who have been made eunuchs by others, and there are eunuchs who have made themselves eunuchs for the sake of the kingdom of heaven. Let anyone accept this who can." (Matt 19:10–12)

Not all are able to keep celibacy, but those who can are happy. The grace of continence can come only from God, and it is in vain that we claim celibacy if God does not give this. Even Jesus Christ does not judge that all are able to accept what he teaches. He contents himself with proposing this state and approving it, without, however, making it a precept, so that some do not grieve that they cannot lead a perfect life. Some would through a precipitous fervor enter into a state to which they are not called and cannot persevere. There are people who bring purity from their birth and in whom this inclination seems quite natural, so that they have no difficulty in remaining virgins. There are *eunuchs who have been so from birth*, and there are *eunuchs who have been made eunuchs by others* by an excess of violence, making those who do this criminal before God. Some fathers and mothers in order to enrich the elders of the houses force their daughters to become nuns and their sons to enter the state of priesthood. Ah! What account will they render to God! This is the cause of all the disorder that happens in communities and among priests, namely, that we engage them by human views and temporal interests in states for which they have no vocation. The gift of chastity not being given to them from on high, they frequently commit enormous crimes. Others, finally, have neither the facility to keep chastity like the first nor the constraint of the last. But for the love of God and to possess the interior with more tranquility, they became eunuchs, that is to say, they separate themselves from the commerce of creatures to sacrifice themselves entirely to God. These are the ones who deserve the most. The former usually have the ostentation and the vain indulgence of virginity yet hardly have the merit of it. Those who have never been tempted by this are usually proprietary. When God wants to draw them out of their propriety and wrest from them the pride that blinds them, God allows the loss of a good by which they blind themselves. God makes them open their eyes and lets it cost them the virginity of the flesh to acquire the virginity of the spirit. Some have the need for continence, but they do not have a full will to do this. They still have merit if they make good and voluntary use of their sacrifice that in the beginning had been violent. The latter have all the advantages of purity and not the faults, particularly if they are advanced in the interior.

> Then little children were being brought to him in order that he might lay his hands on them and pray. The disciples spoke sternly to those who brought them; [14] but Jesus said, "Let the little children come to me, and do not stop them; for it is to such as these that the kingdom of heaven belongs." [15] And he laid his hands on them and went on his way. (Matt 19:13–15)

Who could know what graces are communicated by the *laying on of* these divine *hands*! Happy the *children* who have the blessing of being confirmed by the sovereign Priest! It is believable that they were all confirmed in grace by Jesus, who declared himself so strongly in their favor. He made many saints, successors of his disciples, pillars of his church, and illustrious martyrs. Jesus did not lay his hands on them without communicating the fullness of his Spirit over all innocent children in whom he found no resistance to the torrent of his graces. O children! You have been marked by eternity by the Father in his Word to have a considerable rank among the predestined. You have been recognized by the same incarnate Word. His providence, which always serves for predestination, brings you to him so that he may touch you and sanctify you. He fills you with his love, destining you to be noble victims shortly before he goes away to die for you! Who would not envy you this happiness, O promise of the conquests of Jesus! Touched by him from childhood, you do not offend him or stop loving him all the rest of your days. *It is good for a person to have borne the yoke of the Lord from his youth* (Lam 3:27). But how advantageous to have been entrusted with this by the Lord's own hands since infancy, as it happened to those blessed innocents! Who will tell us how effective this divine touch was? The mere memory of this grace fills the soul with anointing when it looks at it with the eye of lively faith. O saints of your childhood! My heart feels a singular devotion for you. Obtain for us from Jesus a similar imposition of his hands as that with which you were gratified so that he communicates to us spiritual childhood, true treasure of all holiness, with purity of love. Make this through your intercessions so powerful that it spreads throughout the church.

Many imitate the apostles in their contempt of wanting to prevent simple and childish souls from approaching Jesus Christ and abandoning themselves to his conduct. Although the apostles' intention is good, they are genuinely mistaken. Also, our Lord himself takes the defense of these innocent people, inviting them to come to him, forbidding the spiritual directors to prevent them. Jesus declares that the interior Kingdom is for them, that is to say, they are purer than any other. Most doctors say that prayer is not for simple, poor, or secular people. However, Jesus has merited prayer for them and for simple people to whom he preaches. And what gospel? The gospel of the Kingdom, which Jesus deserved for all, yet to the simple people he preached the most, as they followed him the most and listened to him most out of docility. He himself said that the gospel is proclaimed to the poor (Matt 11:5). And which gospel? Prayer is mainly the gospel of the Kingdom since it is through this that God reigns in souls, and they make themselves worthy to reign with him. Prayer is therefore for the poor. One must be poor to pray well because prayer works more with our perfect denial of all things to arrive at the poverty of spirit to which our Lord promises the Kingdom of heaven.

> And behold, a man came up to him, saying, "Teacher, what good deed must I do to have eternal life?" 17 And he said to him, "Why do you ask me about what is good? There is only one who is good. If you would enter life, keep the commandments." (Matt 19:16–17)

Jesus Christ, who as God is the essential goodness, does not want to be called good. He says this to teach us the truth of God alone, just as he alone is God. Any statement without God contains only malice and corruption. As soon as he takes something of God, claiming it for his own, he defiles it by stealing it. O God, all good and only good! You alone must be in the soul so that we participate without injustice in your goodness. Without this, the malignity of human nature would corrupt the goodness that you would like to put there! We need annihilation. These truths can be penetrated only by the favor of the interior ray, which makes us cast every crown at the foot of the throne of God and eternally confess that God is the only good, only holy, only just, only being, and only all.

To enter into the true life of Jesus Christ by whom all that is alive lives, one must keep the commandments. The soul united with the will of God already dwells in the divine. She accomplishes all the commandments naturally through the will of God, who leads her there gently and infallibly according to God's providence. St. Paul says, *The law is not laid down for the just but for the lawless and disobedient* (1 Tim 1:9). The just living in the justice of God stand united to God, fulfilling the whole law admirably.

> He said to him, "Which ones?" And Jesus said, "You shall not murder; You shall not commit adultery; You shall not steal; You shall not bear false witness; [19] Honor your father and mother; also, You shall love your neighbor as yourself." [20] The young man said to him, "I have kept all these; what do I still lack?" [21] Jesus said to him, "If you wish to be perfect, go, sell your possessions, and give the money to the poor, and you will have treasure in heaven; then come, follow me." [22] When the young man heard this word, he went away grieving, for he had many possessions. (Matt 19:18–22)

The observation of the commandments assures salvation but does not bring perfection, which involves the disappropriation of spiritual and temporal wealth. We understand the cleansing of the soul in *sell your possessions*. Our Lord proposes our imitation of his life.

This man of good will refuses the loss of external goods, making him lose eternal perfection. We too want to conserve what we have while gaining new wealth. St. Paul states, *We groan under our burden, because we wish not to be unclothed but to be further clothed* (2 Cor 5:4). Many make good progress wrapped in rich spiritual goods and practices. But almost all lack courage, turn back, and fail when invited into a great discipline. This offer will clothe them with truth, yet their self-love and nature will not support this. Few enter, though our Master of perfection calls us to this. Ah! We do not understand the purity of our vocation and do not penetrate to our interior desire. External loss is a shadow of our interior transformation.

> Then Jesus said to his disciples, "Truly I tell you, it will be hard for a rich person to enter the kingdom of heaven. [24] Again I tell you, it is easier for a camel to go through the eye of a needle than for someone who is rich to enter the kingdom of God." (Matt 19:23–24)

Our Lord assures us that *truly, it will be hard for a rich person*, those proprietary in spiritual and holy things, *to enter the kingdom of heaven*. Jesus uses an impossible thing to show this: *a camel going through the eye of a needle*. God gives us the Kingdom in the interior if we allow the annihilation and get through this narrow door opening to the greatest riches. As soon as a soul is released from self, she is clothed in Jesus Christ. Under these precious vestments, she enters easily into God, having nothing in her that resists. Like fondue, her soul, melted and dissolved, flows without difficulty into God, like pure and clear water passes into the smallest place.

> When the disciples heard this, they were greatly astounded and said, "Then who can be saved?" [26] But Jesus looked at them and said, "For mortals it is impossible, but for God all things are possible." (Matt 19:25–26)

The astonished disciples, still weak before the death of Jesus Christ, understand all things from the perspective of weak humanity. But their Master in his response *looked at them*, communicating the knowledge that only God treats the soul's interior. *For mortals it is impossible* to strip away all propriety, because the divine light shows even the smallest atoms of imperfection. Therefore, we must let God infallibly prepare us if we faithfully abandon ourselves. After the faithful active life, we must surrender to the passive way to arrive at Christian perfection.

> Then Peter said in reply, "Look, we have left everything and followed you. What then will we have?" [28] Jesus said to them, "Truly I tell you, at the renewal of all things, when the Son of Man is seated on the throne of his glory, you who have followed me will also sit on twelve thrones, judging the twelve tribes of Israel." (Matt 19:27–28)

Peter's question to Jesus instructs both the apostles and us. O Love! To leave everything to follow you is the best of all crowns. Isn't following you a generous reward in itself given for our love of Jesus Christ? Ah! If I had something left to lose, I would willingly lose it for the sole good of following you, even to Calvary! This grace of graces in having things stripped away brings God the greatest glory as our perfect sacrifice. We have both the reward of happiness and of following you. When you give glory in this life, you give a divine taste to interior people so they discern whether other people have the presence of God or not.

> And everyone who has left houses or brothers or sisters or father or mother or children or fields, for my name's sake, will receive a hundredfold, and will inherit eternal life. (Matt 19:29)

Oh, the advantage of having everything stripped away without exception! To *leave* one's self and everything held dear is rewarded in this life with repose, peace, and inconceivable liberty, true paradise indeed! Through this loss, some souls enter into possession of the Word, which is *eternal life*. Jesus Christ alone communicates this life to those who follow him as the way and who listen to the truth.

> But many who are first will be last, and the last will be first. (Matt 19:30)

In the interior sense, people remain innocent by giving themselves to God and remaining in this state. If they attach themselves to their own sense of justice and their manner of life, they stop their advancement. If they recognize they are poor sinners at the height of disorder, they throw themselves into the hands of God and let him guide them. They then advance and arrive quickly.

Sinners experience horror at themselves. They are like poor, plundered people seeing their house burned down. They must leave their own country to go find a happier one. Whereas others, seeing their own house well adorned, are pleased with themselves and do not pass into God.

The great sinners who convert to Jesus Christ became more sanctified than just people remaining at home. Jesus Christ's single word, glance, and touch of his robe would have advanced them more than twenty years of their own activities.

The great secret is to go first and straight and always to Jesus Christ. Do not stop before we go to Jesus.

> For the kingdom of heaven is like a master of a house who went out early in the morning to hire laborers for his vineyard. [2] After agreeing with the laborers for a denarius a day, he sent them into his vineyard. [3] And going out about the third hour he saw others standing idle in the marketplace, [4] and to them he said, "You go into the vineyard too, and whatever is right I will give you." [5] So they went. Going out again about the sixth hour and the ninth hour, he did the same. [6] And about the eleventh hour he went out and found others standing. And he said to them, "Why do you stand here idle all day?" [7] They said to him, "Because no one has hired us." He said to them, "You go into the vineyard too." (Matt 20:1–7)

Clearly we see here that all people have vocations, not only for heaven but also for the interior life. If we work in the vineyard of the Lord by prompt repentance, Christ rewards us with the possession of the interior Kingdom. Christian brothers and sisters, whoever you are, just or sinners, young or old, poor or rich, wealthy or weak, do not hesitate to commit yourselves to so good a Master. *Do whatever he tells you* (John

2:5). Jesus changes our lukewarm water into a strong and pure wine of ardent charity.

In our vineyard, with the very pure wine of perfect charity, Jesus Christ unites us to him like a single grape to a cluster. We will no longer be divided. Jesus Christ says, *That they may all be one, just as you, Father, are in me, and I in you* (John 17:21). Our total sacrifice becomes like crushed grapes, making an exquisite wine that the church his bride presents to our divine Master. Truly worthy to be drunk and favored by him, we become formed into his unity. O admirable union of spirits! The true Spirit of the church is this beautiful vine, which bears grapes who differ but compose only one wine. The members' Spirit of pure charity makes a pure and united wine. We are conceived and received in the unity of God alone, the true Spirit of the interior and the true Spirit of the church.

> And when evening came, the owner of the vineyard said to his foreman, "Call the laborers and pay them their wages, beginning with the last, up to the first." 9 And when those hired about the eleventh hour came, each of them received a denarius. 10 Now when those hired first came, they thought they would receive more, but each of them also received a denarius. 11 And on receiving it they grumbled at the master of the house, 12 saying, "These last worked only one hour, and you have made them equal to us who have borne the burden of the day and the scorching heat." (Matt 20:8–12)

The just Judge gives the same reward to many, although their works are quite different because he measures them by the price of love and perseverance in letting oneself be led to God. The last to come to the vineyard were the first to be rewarded because they expected nothing from their merit but from the pure account of the master. The others, on the contrary, puffed up with the work they had done, wanted more than they had been promised. They did not regard the payment as a gratification but as something that was due to them. Those who claim nothing from God are those who will receive more. *Love does not insist on its own way* (1 Cor 13:5), yet contains the fullness of all goods.

Pure love does not insist on payment but believes it deserves nothing and so claims no reward. The best reward is the work, finding delight in doing good to others and that all serve the Father of the family. Following the example of St. Paul, the faithful are ready to be anathema for his brothers, far from being jealous of their happiness (Rom 9:3). Ah! The reward is an effect of the goodness of God crowning our merits and his gifts. It must be noted that these workers whom the master took for his vineyard did nothing else than to stand *exposed in the marketplace* to be taken. Let us expose ourselves in this way before God, and he will not fail to take us. If we cease to serve sin and have no other master, God will infallibly take us into his service.

> But he replied to one of them, "Friend, I am doing you no wrong. Did you not agree with me for a denarius? [14] Take what belongs to you and go. I choose to give to this last worker as I give to you. [15] Am I not allowed to do what I choose with what belongs to me? Or do you begrudge my generosity?" [16] So the last will be first, and the first last. (Matt 20:13–16)

The goodness of God leads him to do us good. We must not envy the graces of others but be content with those that he grants us. There are people so weak that they covet all the good that God does to others. If they understood well that the best of goods is to serve God alone, preferring the honor of serving him to any reward, they would be far removed from these self-interested sentiments.

A soul who serves God without any return or even suffers punishment while serving him, yet still serves him with all faithfulness the more rigorous its punishments, rests in the purity of the most perfect love. When God wishes to advance a soul greatly, he treats it with this force for a long time. He apparently rejects all the services she renders him and always seems to be angry with her, notwithstanding all that she does to please him. He has only the rod and the punishment in hand. The more her affection to serve him increases, the more he redoubles his blows. Even with these afflictions, she passionately wants to do the will of her God. He rejects her on one side and he draws her on the other but in such a hidden way that this lover, so troubled, knows nothing about it, except that she wants to love and cannot. She would like to accomplish exactly all the wills of God, and she believes she is doing quite the opposite. This torments her, for it seems that God becomes all the more irritated with her, the more she tries to appease him. But these are only means to test and purify the fidelity of his spouse, to lead her only disinterestedly, so that she thinks only of serving, without inquiring whether her service is seen or accepted and without pretending to ever be rewarded for it.

Thus, *the last become the first*; when this soul who believes herself to be the last of all finds herself in a short time and without thinking about it arriving at her consummation, while the one for whom everything seems to succeed and who believes she has amassed treasures remains very far from the purity of her love.

> And as Jesus was going up to Jerusalem, he took the twelve disciples aside, and on the way he said to them, [18] "See, we are going up to Jerusalem. And the Son of Man will be delivered over to the chief priests and scribes, and they will condemn him to death [19] and deliver him over to the Gentiles to be mocked and flogged and crucified, and he will be raised on the third day." (Matt 20:17–19)

Jesus Christ speaks to those who are truly his at length about his cross in order to dispose them thereby to suffer. Especially when he destines them for extraordinary pains, he gives them many presentiments of them, at the same time kindling in their hearts an ardent love of the cross. But why must the principal doctors and people of authority make the Son of God suffer in all places? They are the ones who oppose his Kingdom and who without knowing him persecute him to death. They also condemn his conduct in souls. He is then *delivered* by his own children into the hands of those who do not know him, while they tolerate the visible disorder of sinners without opposing their crimes. Instead, the Pharisees unite with sinners to fight against the reign of Jesus in souls. But Jesus Christ will soon escape from their hands, and he will stand glorious from his sepulcher. He will dominate with the iron rod those who have not wanted to let themselves be led to him by the path of love and obedience.

> Then the mother of the sons of Zebedee came to him with her sons, and kneeling before him, she asked a favor of him. [21] And he said to her, "What do you want?" She said to him, "Declare that these two sons of mine will sit, one at your right hand and one at your left, in your kingdom." [22] But Jesus answered, "You do not know what you are asking. Are you able to drink the cup that I am about to drink?" They said to him, "We are able." [23] He said to them, "You will indeed drink my cup, but to sit at my right hand and at my left, this is not mine to grant, but it is for those for whom it has been prepared by my Father." (Matt 20:20–23)

Many worldly people led by inclinations alone do not know what they are asking God. They enjoy the idea of their requests given to Jesus Christ, yet the requests are harmful, ridiculous, or selfish. Some requests are even ungodly, asking for vengeance against those they hate or for success for their evil designs. We do not know what is appropriate to ask or even how to ask what is good. As St. Paul says, *For we do not know how to pray as we ought* (Rom 8:26). The Holy Spirit helps us in our weakness to learn how to pray. We abandon ourselves to God and trust he will give us what is needed. If we want to ask God for something, we ask what his Son taught us, *Your will be done, your Kingdom come.*

To ask Jesus to *share his Kingdom with us* is an ignorant prayer. To ask to share his Kingdom, they want their own will, which is convenient to nature. They control what they consider virtuous. Their desire seems good and holy to them. However, their requests are denied out of God's great mercy, because if they were granted, it would be to their detriment and against God's glory. In place of asking to live the way they want and to be seated *next to the throne of Jesus Christ* to share his power, they should ask that he alone reign, for all glory and his Kingdom is only for God. The divine Master asks them, *Are you able to drink the cup that I am about to drink*? This is the incomparable and greatest grace. Following the sons of Zebedee's example, many want to be affiliated with Jesus Christ but do not think about drinking his chalice. To have this great grace, they must think about this.

These young men, inexperienced at glory, answer with presumption: *We are able*, because of the passion they have for their glory. However, they were incapable of suffering with faithfulness because they were far from meriting what they desired to obtain. Jesus said to them that he was willing to *share his chalice with them* and give them the strength to *drink his cup*, but to reign with him, *this is not mine to grant*, because these are the rights of the Father. Jesus Christ came to repair the injury that people had made to his Father by wanting to be like him and to share his wisdom and power. The Father gives the Son the right to lead and govern human beings, establishing the Son as their Savior and Master. Hence, the Son could not associate any person with his Kingdom without usurping the rights of his Father, who has prepared his Kingdom by his eternal decree. The Father communicated this design to the Word in his divine birth and engraved this in the heart of the Word made flesh at the moment of his incarnation. This invariable resolution will never change. It is not in Jesus Christ's power to take this gift away from those for whom his Father had reserved it to give it to those disciples whose mother with superficial simplicity had asked for it. All this teaches us that we must discern even what we think are the holiest demands, especially when they elevate us. Instead, we must think of *drinking the chalice of our Lord* by faithfully carrying our cross, by reposing in the will of God.

> When the ten heard it, they were angry with the two brothers.
> [25] But Jesus called them to him and said, "You know that the rulers
> of the Gentiles lord it over them, and their great ones are tyrants
> over them. [26] It will not be so among you; but whoever wishes to
> be great among you must be your servant, [27] and whoever wishes
> to be first among you must be your slave; [28] just as the Son of Man
> came not to be served but to serve, and to give his life a ransom for
> many." (Matt 20:24–25)

It is impossible to love Jesus Christ and to suffer someone who wants to usurp his Kingdom. The ten apostles are justly indignant at the sons of Zebedee's self-interested passion, which may appear as pure zeal. Yet the other apostles could not allow these two brothers to lead them as if they were part of the sovereign domain of Jesus. The apostles have tasted Jesus's Kingdom with so much sweetness and followed him faithfully. Whoever has tasted the adorable conduct of Jesus will not let himself be led by other humans. Jesus Christ asks that our soul follow him. The Kingdom of God is sweet, and the soul will find this Kingdom to be pure and natural to him. All the rest feels like a violent state opposed to the Kingdom because it keeps us away from God and attached to amusements and other creatures. Instead, Jesus Christ carries us to our fulfillment and end.

Jesus *said* more to his apostles, *The rulers of the nations dominate them*, God having given them this external empire over human beings. *But it will not be so* among interior persons, represented by the *disciples*, since he himself will rule them. For those who have authority over others, humility is the surest sign of elevation. Once a soul is abased and annihilated, the greater she becomes. Once a soul is elevated, she must be small and subdued. The Savior still shows that the truest mark of advancement is to work with humility to help others and to assist them in their salvation.

> As they were leaving Jericho, a large crowd followed him. [30] There
> were two blind men sitting by the roadside. When they heard that
> Jesus was passing by, they shouted, "Lord, have mercy on us, Son
> of David!" [31] The crowd sternly ordered them to be quiet; but
> they shouted even more loudly, "Have mercy on us, Lord, Son
> of David!" [32] Jesus stood still and called them, saying, "What do
> you want me to do for you?" [33] They said to him, "Lord, let our
> eyes be opened." [34] Moved with compassion, Jesus touched their

> eyes. Immediately they regained their sight and followed him. (Matt 20:29–34)

As Jesus Christ was always followed by a large crowd of people, the leaders made many efforts to prevent this. Jesus Christ still lives in large numbers of interior people, despite the controversy aroused against them because of this. In this interior kingdom, he draws them by a secret attraction to follow him.

There are at times the *blind* who remain in public places and who repose in their blindness. They are in the way of perdition and seem to stop and enjoy it. However, when Jesus Christ draws near, he gives them a secret desire to be delivered from their blindness. As soon as these blind minds and hearts are willing to be healed, the Son of God has compassion on their state and asks only one thing of them, which is to want to be healed.

The people who were already following Jesus Christ prevented the blind from crying out to him instead of encouraging them. That is, as new converts, they do not have enough compassion for sinners. But far from being rebuffed, the blind *double* their courage and faith. They ask for mercy, even as more obstacles appear and less appearance of getting it. Ah! Soon the blind will be converted! They call him *Lord*, bringing their faith to him. Next they call him *Son of David*, hoping to move him to compassion. They beg him by reminding him, *Since you came out of this illustrious penitent, spread over us the mercy that you have done to him*. So *Jesus stops* to *call them*. Here are the conversion and the return, which is soon done when we have a little faith. Then he asks them, *What do you want me to do for you?* He asks them for their consent to bring them into a more advanced state. So they beg him to touch them with the light of truth. He touches them in their will and with a passing impression gives them enlightenment. They welcome the entry of the divine light, for as soon as one consents to this, the divine light is very ready to penetrate.

But what does this enlightenment ask from them? They follow Jesus Christ wherever he leads them. A soul touched and enlightened by Jesus Christ must follow him, abandoning all the rest to him. This is the sign of a true conversion.

> When they had come near Jerusalem and had reached Bethphage, at the Mount of Olives, Jesus sent two disciples, 2 saying to them, "Go into the village ahead of you, and immediately you will find

> a donkey tied, and a colt with her; untie them and bring them to me." (Matt 21:1–2)

The donkey represents the captivity of nature subject to sins by the demon. The colt also represents this, because all productions of nature are as linked and enslaved as she. Jesus Christ gives power to his apostles and to his priests to *untie* them and *bring them* to him. That is what they can do to take human nature out of sins. They *untie* by forgiveness and *take them* to Jesus Christ by the way of prayer.

> If anyone says anything to you, just say this, "The Lord needs them." And he will send them immediately. (Matt 21:3)

When someone finds resistance in the conversion of a sinner or when someone stops her nature from being freed from captivity, it must be said, *The Lord needs* her *to be brought to him*. Using the authority of the Word of God surmounts the difficulties of those who are held in captivity. Jesus Christ cannot take possession of a soul not delivered from captivity to sin and not separated from external occasions that hold them. Priests use the authority that has been given to them to take the captive nature to Jesus Christ with an admirable facility. When we consent to leave the occasions, these occasions leave us. Once a person begins to convert, the world has nothing but contempt for her who moves gradually away from the world. God permits this because of her weakness of nature who would not have the strength to leave a thousand things at once yet has the strength if these same things leave her.

> This took place to fulfill what had been spoken through the prophet, saying,
> [5] "Tell the daughter of Zion,
> Look, your king is coming to you,
> humble, and mounted on a donkey,
> and on a colt, the foal of a donkey." (Matt 21:4–5)

Once the detachment and first conversion are done, we must assure the soul who has come into the interior that she is *the daughter of Zion* and that *her King comes* to reign within her but that he comes *mounted on a donkey*, without anything rough in his domination. Being gentle and merciful, he is powerful and strong. The soul must surrender herself entirely to such an amiable Sovereign and let herself be completely led. He is *mounted on a donkey* because he himself subdued human nature, which will always be captive to the demon and corruption of Adam unless Jesus

Christ is mounted on it and holds captivity captive, subjecting her who was previously subject to her enemies. It also teaches us that Jesus Christ reigns over us when he subjects our nature. After he tames our nature, he is mounted on us. So let him be our King and do not resist him as he subjugates our rebellious and criminal nature. He also mounts *on a colt, the foal of a donkey* (he mounts successively first one and then the other). This shows that it is not enough for nature to be submitted to Jesus Christ. Our productions and operations must also be subjected to him as Master so that nothing may oppose his reign. These are the effects of a true conversion.

> The disciples went and did as Jesus had directed them; [7] they brought the donkey and the colt, and put their cloaks on them, and he sat on them. (Matt 21:6–7)

This mysterious manner show how spiritual directors must lead souls whom God has sent them. The disciples are content to carry out their mission, which is to untie their nature or sin or anything else that stops them from coming to Jesus Christ. *They brought the donkey*, which means the soul; they *put their cloaks on it*, which means their vestments, as is represented by what they did to the *donkey* and the *colt*. They exercised on them an external authority based on a rule but which is also based in obedience. But for the interior, the wise director must take them to Jesus Christ, who mounts and takes possession to lead them himself, which is only the proper domain of Jesus Christ. This is important for directed souls to understand so they do not amuse themselves with the confessor instead of going to Jesus Christ and abandoning themselves. But alas! The director is the spiritual head of this little church, which is the soul. In this way, he must rule the exterior. Like *the mouth of the Lord* (Jer 15:19), the director must discern in the conduct the good from the bad and the true from the false. But in the interior, he must leave this to the motion of the Holy Spirit, observing the steps the soul takes without leading the soul through his own understanding and not destroying the work of God in his own sanctuary.

> A very large crowd spread their cloaks on the road, and others cut branches from the trees and spread them on the road. [9] The crowds that went ahead of him and that followed were shouting,
> "Hosanna to the Son of David!
> Blessed is the one who comes in the name of the Lord!
> Hosanna in the highest heaven!" (Matt 21:8–9)

These people, although in good will, do not do everything that a true convert must do for their conversion to be solid and long lasting. They are content to follow only the external laws of Jesus Christ, which is to *spread their cloaks on the road* under his feet, and they do not give their hearts absolutely to his Kingdom. This means that after praising and applauding him, soon after, they crucify him in a mortal fall and sin. For the conversion to last, they must return and submit their heart to God, allowing him transcendent authority in their interior hearts and not only in exterior lives. Because *rending* only *your garments* and not your heart (Joel 2:13) is so crude and useless a gesture that God reproached the people about this through a prophet. If Jesus is the master of the interior, he will infallibly also be the master of the exterior. But if he is master only of the exterior, it will only be for a short while. A sensible servant will not offer the Savior only his cloak but his heart as well. Without this, we see only a few solid conversions and witness people leaving their regulated faith and life to return to involvement in the world. If our virtues are practiced only in the exterior without roots in the interior, the virtues will not last.

We must notice that these people do not give all that is due to Jesus Christ and by doing this remove what is greater in him. They greet him only as the Lord's messenger instead of calling him the Lord. Not knowing the greatness of his power, they do not submit entirely to his dominion. Some Christians, even spiritual ones, also imitate and do this. They treat Jesus Christ as a Messiah *sent by God* in that they want to be saved and enriched with celestial gifts by him. But they do not want to treat him as God and surrender entirely to his conduct by the renunciation of all propriety.

> When he entered Jerusalem, the whole city was in turmoil, asking, "Who is this?" [11] The crowds were saying, "This is the prophet Jesus from Nazareth in Galilee." (Matt 21:10–11)

When Jesus comes into a soul, he enters into the emotions. The senses and the powers, which are not accustomed to this, say, *Who is this?* We have never experienced anything like this. This is the presence of the Creator making himself sensitive to the soul while moving to her center. The grace of the Redeemer moves to purify her, shaking all her faculties. Reason believes it should know where this great goodness comes from but is ignorant and attributes this to works of external charity or austerities. They judge by what is most apparent, which is why the good people say that *Jesus* was *from Nazareth in Galilee*. Instead, this goodness came from Bethlehem, the smallest, and from the soul who receives him in good will.

With the coming of Jesus Christ, the will tastes some rest, and the heart is penetrated by living joy. All nature is in fright because this way does not accommodate nature and sees well that this will cost her painful retrenchments. Nature would try to stop this entry if God did not take her by sending her sweets and drawing her gradually from her emotions. Something similar happens when apostolic people come to a city. The demon puts everything in trouble. Everyone is surprised by this novelty and wants to know what this means. Many judge wrongly, though some understand them favorably but initially have a bad opinion. The devil uses his puppets to describe the apostolic people badly to others under the cover of zeal done by people of authority. However, those people sent by Jesus Christ come from Bethlehem, and they have a real mission for interior souls, which is manifested by their fruits.

> Then Jesus entered the temple and drove out all who were selling and buying in the temple, and he overturned the tables of the money changers and the seats of those who sold doves. 13 He said to them, "It is written, 'My house shall be called a house of prayer'; but you are making it a den of robbers." (Matt 21:12–13)

Once Jesus Christ *enters into* a soul as the *temple of God*, he chases out all *money changers* and banishes all commerce with creatures. The den of robbers fills the heart with unregulated self-interest and ambition. This traffic in the temple of God occupies the soul only with the spirit of the things of the world, the affairs of others, noises from the world, and a thousand amusements.

Everything that tears us away from God and attaches us to the creature is a traffic, and we exchange the things of God for this nonsense. Then we are occupied only with other people and not our own vocation. Jesus *drives away* all this bad trade *from his holy temple*. O God! This is admirable! Most who serve in the temple sell simple and docile souls to turn them away from God. This is why they are driven out of their ministry as profaners of the temple. When Jesus Christ comes into the temple, he chases away self-interested people, taking away from these simple and trusting people the confidence they had in them, so they will no longer follow and imitate them. Then they will be attracted to the interior life. Then he tells us that our interior is his *temple* and the place where he will inhabit. We must be *a house of prayer* with a free and continual prayer, as the Spirit of God suggests and operates in the hearts of those who are subject to him.

We *make* this holy temple a *den of robbers* when we have a thousand proprieties and tear away from God his right to conduct, govern, and possess the soul, holding God captive under the domination of the human being. All interior occupations that do not point to God alone, however good they may appear, are robberies. All people who are not interior and have not learned to take care of our one and unique necessity are filled with useless things, however important they may appear. These are injustices, because we have taken from God what he is due: know him as the only occupation of our heart and the sovereign preference of all our views. All other things must be chased from the soul, and the soul must remain empty, so that God remains there alone. Otherwise, this house will never be a house of prayer.

> The blind and the lame came to him in the temple, and he cured them. [15] But when the chief priests and the scribes saw the amazing things that he did, and heard the children crying out in the temple, "Hosanna to the Son of David," they became angry. (Matt 21:14–15)

As soon as Jesus *drives* everything out of the interior temple, the believer's blind spirit and lame will that leaned toward the creature *go* to Jesus. At the same instant *he heals* the spirit of its blindness, enlightening her with the light of faith, which makes her discover God alone in her heart. Everything else departs before God. The will, which had participated in a thousand exterior things that made it *lame* and falling from side to side, is also *healed* and straightened. Her Savior brings her back to the one point of pure love and the will of God. By this the soul is made straight and simple, and her powers cry out like *children crying out praise God* but very conformed to the Spirit of truth. The *doctors* and human directors who *see* such a great change accomplished by praises, yet do not participate in praising, *become indignant.*

> And said to him, "Do you hear what these are saying?" Jesus said to them, "Yes; have you never read, 'Out of the mouths of infants and nursing babies you have prepared praise for yourself'?" (Matt 21:16)

The doctors of the law are not content to blame Jesus Christ for the healings he made; they condemn him also for the *praises* that the *children* said. These innocent souls spoke sincere praises to God. The impression of the divine truth revealed that everything is God, and they sincerely offered glory, honor, and praise to him in all things. These infants acted without reflection and without turning the praises toward themselves, which made these praises valuable. We too, like simple and innocent children, must give God *perfect praise* and honor him. Perfect praises take nothing for ourselves but like children follow their instincts. In acting in this way, *they give God perfect praise* by abandoning their will to him and not deviating from it.

The perfect abandonment of childlike simplicity consists in being reduced to the entire nudity of God alone. The soul rests in no other power than the will of God and follows only the way of providence, which accomplishes from moment to moment the revelation of eternity in time. Finding their support in the world of creatures prevents them from perfect abandonment because they seek assurances about their state in the world. But finally, being penetrated by divine truth, she realizes her folly, namely to seek some greater assurance than trusting in God alone. Finally established in the freedom that God gives to his children after they have gone through many deserts, abysses, precipices, deaths, and losses, she cries out with ravishment that truly the *Lord guides the righteous* who trust in him *on straight and safe paths*, however oblique and dangerous they seemed. In the end, God *shows her the Kingdom of God*, which is the immense freedom in which God places her through real joy in God. He teaches her the wisdom and science of the saints, *knowledge of holy* things, which is hidden with the saints in God (Wis 10:10).

Therefore, only spiritual children may offer God perfect praises. These children do not reason or reflect but walk in the simplicity of their heart without malice. Children abandoned to the guidance of their father do not even ask where they are being led. They do not reason about what they are to do. O childlike state! State entirely divine! *Out of the mouths of those* who are blessed *God performs his praise.* Since God praises through them, their phrases resound like echoes as when received from God.

> He left them, went out of the city to Bethany, and spent the night there. [18] In the morning, when he returned to the city, he was hungry. [19] And seeing a fig tree by the side of the road, he went to it and found nothing at all on it but leaves. Then he said to it, "May

> no fruit ever come from you again!" And the fig tree withered at once. (Matt 21:17–19)

O God! What was your hunger? Human beings may bear fruit within you, but you are not satisfied with only leaves. However, most people are content to produce grand *leaves* and show their greenery, so they do not appear as a dead tree. They focus only a little on the body of the Christian religion and neglect the Spirit altogether. But when Jesus will come to us to see if we have any fruit he may eat, if he finds none, he will give us a *curse*. Whatever grand and brilliant things we can do by ourselves, if they are not done according to Jesus Christ, these are just leaves and not fruit. Far from meriting his approval, this attracts his indignation.

What is this fruit, O divine Master, that you want us to feed you? *My food*, Jesus said to them, *is to do the will of him who sent me and to complete his work*. God asks of human beings the fruit of doing his will. Whoever resists God's commands is not fit to be the nourishment of Jesus Christ and to be transformed into him. But we are only fruitless *fig trees*, bearing only leaves, if we do virtuous actions made only by our own will. The divine Master will strike us with his own curse, taking away our vigor. This is the way that God deals with proprietary people who follow their own will. He gradually takes away the spirit of their life that supported them and consists in a certain ease in doing things and a secret taste to do this. They also get upset and die by their own actions, but this could help them live in God if they would make use of it.

> When the disciples saw it, they were amazed, saying, "How did the fig tree wither at once?" [21] Jesus answered them, "Truly I tell you, if you have faith and do not doubt, not only will you do what has been done to the fig tree, but even if you say to this mountain, 'Be lifted up and thrown into the sea,' it will be done." (Matt 21:20–21)

Those who are in the apostolic state have received Jesus Christ with such great power that everything these people say concerning other souls happens. Many experience this. If they talk to a self-interested person, they see they have only *leaves* and say to them, You will never *bear fruit* in yourself. Their own self-life must be changed, and they must enter into the nudity of faith. If the apostolic soul commands someone who is like a *mountain* with great living love and ardor *to be thrown into the sea* of death and annihilation, he will enter into this state. Faith operates great things by those with the apostolic spirit whom God has chosen for the interior ministry. But to do these wonders and miracles, we need, as our Master says, *to speak with faith and without hesitation.*

> Whatever you ask for in prayer with faith, you will receive. (Matt 21:22)

The Spirit of God makes us ask *with faith* for fulfilled prayers. Oh! If we know the greatness of this prayer of faith flowing from the will of God. Jesus Christ made an infallible promise to accomplish these prayers with miracles and wonders. These saints themselves are miracles both in their interior and exterior.

> When he entered the temple, the chief priests and the elders of the people came to him as he was teaching, and said, "By what authority are you doing these things, and who gave you this authority?" [24] Jesus said to them, "I will also ask you one question; if you tell me the answer, then I will also tell you by what authority I do these things. [25] Did the baptism of John come from heaven, or was it of human origin?" And they argued with one another, "If we say, 'From heaven,' he will say to us, 'Why then did you not believe him?' [26] But if we say, 'Of human origin,' we are afraid of the crowd; for all regard John as a prophet." [27] So they answered Jesus, "We do not know." And he said to them, "Neither will I tell you by what authority I am doing these things." (Matt 21:23–27)

Bishops, theologians, religious, and people following worldly standards see those with apostolic grace doing good for souls. Yet they question, *By what authority are you doing these things, and who gave you this authority* to speak as you speak? Seeing the great effects of grace, the Pharisees question in perplexity if this is divine, for the apostolic souls may not have social position or may be females working in the service of souls. Those watching become scandalized.

The Pharisees, who see Jesus Christ teaching and performing miracles with such success, ask by what *authority he does them.* They do not recognize Jesus Christ as author of all things and the source of all authority in the church. Similarly, some people take offence at those working for Jesus's Kingdom without knowing that Jesus works through them. As creator of both male and female sexes and source of all graces, God calls both sexes to speak to others about the Kingdom of God. Because they speak the truth, encourage love, practice justice, inspire holiness, and testify to God alone, we accept that they received a secret mission to help souls. Fruits so divine can be born only from a tree well established in God.

These people thus sent by Jesus Christ to work for his Father do not need to respond to their adversaries. In hypocrisy, the Pharisees do not recognize John the Baptist's authority. Because their pretended ignorance has made them unworthy, Jesus Christ does not explain this to them.

> "What do you think? A man had two sons; he went to the first and said, 'Son, go and work in the vineyard today.' [29] He answered, 'I will not'; but later he changed his mind and went. [30] The father went to the second and said the same; and he answered, 'I go, sir'; but he did not go. [31] Which of the two did the will of his father?" They said, "The first." Jesus said to them, "Truly I tell you, the tax collectors and the prostitutes are going into the kingdom of God ahead of you." (Matt 21:28–31)

Some people enter the ways of God with repugnance and annoyance yet succeed well. At first they resist and reject what they are told, yet when they reflect on it, they are persuaded to give themselves with much delight to the will of God. Others, though, promise to do things yet will do nothing difficult and so do nothing. Without doing anything, they cannot advance. Jesus Christ says that only those who act and not those who *promise* are doing the will of God. How many people feel a few crosses and then experience appalling revolts and temptations to leave Jesus? However, following Jesus Christ is the best thing, and we should suffer faithfully even while feeling nature's resistance. Some fear this temptation. They cry out to God to cover them and implore his help. Expecting nothing from themselves, they pray that God destroy their own will. Others, though, consume themselves in promises and resolutions but have only a small fire leading them to do good, and because of this, they advance almost not at all.

Jesus says, *The tax collectors and the prostitutes are going into the kingdom of God ahead of you.* O superb doctor, the Pharisees depend on their own prudence and so become blind and hardened. But sinners, so destroyed by their own weakness and experience, continually have no faith in themselves and instead abandon themselves to God and do what pleases God. This is why they go ahead of the philosophers and the wise men who esteem themselves. And where they do advance? *Into the Kingdom of God*, the interior Kingdom. Learned people with exterior lives have much opposition to the interior Kingdom. The sinner with self-woundedness arrives more easily at the Kingdom of God than these strong people. If Jesus Christ himself had not said this, we would not believe it. We need docility, smallness, self-distrust, and trust in God. With these we arrive easily at the Kingdom of God.

> For John came to you in the way of righteousness and you did not believe him, but the tax collectors and the prostitutes believed him; and even after you saw it, you did not change your minds and believe him. (Matt 21:32)

Jesus works marvels in penitent souls. In these solid conversions, the sinners turns inside to open the door to Jesus Christ's light. In taking the interior route, they make rapid progress. Yet when others use the multiplicity of many spiritual practices, they languish in the same state. Continuing in multiplicity, they do not become captivated by this happy experience of interior conversion.

> Listen to another parable. There was a landowner who planted a vineyard, put a fence around it, dug a wine press in it, and built a watchtower. Then he leased it to tenants and went to another country. [34] When the harvest time had come, he sent his slaves to the tenants to collect his produce. [35] But the tenants seized his slaves and beat one, killed another, and stoned another. (Matt 21:33–35)

God gave us all the necessary power to bear fruits of grace, yet this power was abused. Yet through God's mercy, this mystical *vine* will bear great fruit for the glory of its master. As soon as we enter into the spiritual way, God gives us graces, covers us with his protective wings, and surrounds us with the care of his providence like a *fence*. God stops the tempestuousness of temptations so they do not harm or disturb us. We live in our state of sweetness and peace. He then gives birth in the midst of this person to excellent *fruits* of virtues and all the best of good practices, enriching us with his gifts. God rewards her with admirable ease and success in everything she undertakes. All this is enclosed by a fence. The Master is *owed* his fruits. God alone owns the glory and rich possession with the creature returning everything she has to God, preferring his will to any imagined goods and profits. This being given, the great *father of the family* goes away for a time, giving her freedom to cultivate his vine. This remoteness sweetly tests our faithfulness.

When the time to receive the fruit of the vine has come, Jesus Christ sends his ministers of justice, wanting to ground the faithfulness of his lovers by stripping away her gifts that she has enjoyed. But what has happened? His guarded vineyard has rebelled and become its own owner. Against all justice, she wants to keep all the fruit and wealth. The master then sends other servants, who more intently request that she give back to the owner what is his and request that she remember the agreement they had. But she insists on wanting to lose nothing of all that she has unjustly appropriated and despises these actions and servants of God, beating one and stoning another with specious reasons why she does not owe anything. This unfaithfulness happens to many when they appropriate God's gifts, refusing his fruit at the right time. Without giving the fruit, there is no way forward.

> Again he sent other slaves, more than the first; and they treated them in the same way. [37] Finally he sent his son to them, saying, "They will respect my son." [38] But when the tenants saw the son, they said to themselves, "This is the heir; come, let us kill him and get his inheritance." [39] So they seized him, threw him out of the vineyard, and killed him. (Matt 21:36–39)

Jesus Christ himself comes and urges them by feelings of his presence to give back to him what is his. But the unfaithful *tenants*, far from respecting and submitting to his Kingdom, from their infidelities chase him away from his ground and, through mortal sin destroying their soul's life, they finally kill Jesus Christ. We must watch for the first infidelities in lesser things so as not to fall into extreme unfaithfulness, which leads into final ruin. Lovers of themselves easily become the murderers of Jesus Christ.

> "Now when the owner of the vineyard comes, what will he do to those tenants?" [41] They said to him, "He will put those wretches to a miserable death, and lease the vineyard to other tenants who will give him the produce at the harvest time." (Matt 21:41)

Several had been called to the grace of the interior life yet made themselves unworthy by their usurpations. They have abused the celestial gifts to idolize themselves, instead of using them to give rise to the reign of God. Because of this, they are precisely deprived of them, and their happiness will be granted to others, who will have a better use of it.

> Therefore I tell you, the kingdom of God will be taken away from you and given to a people producing its fruits. (Matt 21:43)

This threat is terrible! Faith, which makes God reign in the church, is often taken away from entire nations and passed from one Kingdom to another because of the corruption of morals. This is the harshest punishment God can give them. It also means the grace of the interior is taken away from those who reject it to be given to others.

> Anyone who falls on this stone will be broken to pieces; anyone on whom it falls will be crushed. (Matt 21:44)

He who falls on this stone must necessarily be *broken* either by justice or by mercy, as well as he on whom it falls must be crushed. We are *broken* by justice when, for having refused to submit to divine power, we fall into the hands of the living God, who arms this very life against those who refused it. If they do not want to allow themselves to be animated by it, life takes horrible revenge. One is *broken* by mercy when, abandoning oneself in its arms, the criminal nature is destroyed and annihilated by an infinitely advantageous fall. The weight of God's love and goodness falling on us not only breaks us but crushes us and annihilates us. Blessed are those on whom this annihilating operation of God falls! God crushes them only to give them a new life in him.

> And again Jesus spoke to them in parables, saying, [2] "The kingdom of heaven may be compared to a king who gave a wedding feast for his son, [3] and sent his servants to call those who were invited to the wedding feast, but they would not come. [4] Again he sent other servants, saying, 'Tell those who are invited, "See, I have prepared my dinner, my oxen and my fat calves have been slaughtered, and everything is ready. Come to the wedding feast."' [5] But they paid no attention and went off, one to his farm, another to his business, [6] while the rest seized his servants, treated them shamefully, and killed them." (Matt 22:1–6)

We are all invited to the wedding feast of the Lamb in this life and in the next, but those who refuse to do so in this life are in danger of being excluded in the next. The feast is always ready. The victim is still there. It is up to us to go there, and yet we are so insensitive to our happiness that we refuse. God is not content to have invited us himself to this wedding feast of his Lamb by many inspirations, although it is an honor and an advantage that we should prefer to a thousand lives. He also sends his servants, who are the ministers of the Word to whom he has given a mission to invite many people to his feast; however, they refuse. This feast is very close to us, the table is always ready, not only at the holy Eucharist, but within us, where we are invited to the communion of our spirits with the Spirit of God, and where David says, *And let the just feast, and rejoice before God: and be delighted with gladness* (Ps 67:4 Douay-Rheims). In a continual feast with an unfailing joy, they can at any time feed on this celestial manna that God constantly communicates to them with the intention of filling them with himself. However, almost all of them, far from going there and responding to such pressing invitations, become all the more attached to the earth and strengthen themselves even more. Instead of returning to the divine table, they move away from their foundation where the table is set to participate in the commerce of creatures. They cannot bear the instructions by which they are urged not to lose so great a good. They treat with contempt those who render them this good office. They are even irritated against them to the point of destroying their reputation and depriving them of the life of honor.

> The king was angry, and he sent his troops and destroyed those murderers and burned their city. [8] Then he said to his servants, "The wedding feast is ready, but those invited were not worthy. [9] Go therefore to the main roads and invite to the wedding feast as many as you find." (Matt 22:7–9)

God first calls to his feast the most important of the people: priests, monks, scholars, and persons eminent in dignity. However, they make themselves unworthy of it by their refusal. What does God do? He sends his most faithful and most apostolic servants to invite sinners to his wedding, inviting those who did not think of him or know him. He does not look at the standing of these persons, because the important people, although distinguished by their character, have made themselves unworthy of this happiness that had been offered them. They are deprived of it. Instead, those who did not think of it are made worthy of it by the very one who invites them. Now because of their docility they allow themselves to be led where God wants to lead them.

> And those servants went out into the roads and gathered all whom they found, both bad and good. So the wedding hall was filled with guests. (Matt 22:10)

It only takes submitting and letting yourself be carried away without resistance to be introduced to this feast. Jesus Christ *shows no partiality* (Rom 2:11) and receives both sinners and righteous if they want to go to him. O poor sinners, who are so often detained and prevented from going to the feast of your Savior by leaders who allege that you must wait until you are good and holy to become familiar with him! Go there freely as soon as you are invited there, for you will never begin to be good and holy until you set out to go there. Do not fear being familiar, for he wants the sinner's love and praises and for sinners to throw themselves at his feet and embrace and kiss him. The more familiarly we communicate with him, the more we come into the respect and love that we owe him. Jesus Christ invites us as friends and in conversations gives us his divine virtues. He calls us to unite with him, repeatedly telling us that he loves to be with us and in us. Not only does he allow us to eat with him at his table, but he gives himself for us to eat. Ah! If we know even a little the love that Jesus has for human beings and how he is the true remedy for evil! Far from letting our sins, imperfections, and miseries prevent us from going to Jesus Christ, because of them we have the reason we must run to him. The remedy for our evils can be found only in him. However clever or holy we are, we need Jesus Christ, and we immediately have recourse to this Savior of human beings. Men and women can speak good words to us, but at the most they can make us know the will of God. Jesus Christ alone can give the grace and fidelity to accomplish God's will and grant us conversion and salvation. John 1:17 says, *For the law was given through Moses; grace and truth came through Jesus Christ.* This should make us understand the wrong that we do to souls who want to convert, stopping them through fears and embarrassing them in a heap of human inventions instead of sending them straight to Jesus Christ.

Convert, O sinners! Leave the *wide road* you are on and go to Christ's table. You will undoubtedly be admitted, because it is made for you. You will not cease to be bad until you have eaten at this table. Go there with confidence. But you may ask, Where do we go? Luke 17:21 says, *For lo, the kingdom of God is within you.* For it is there that you will hear the divine inspiration that invites you to this feast, and where you will soon find your heavenly Father, who shows himself to you full of goodness, always ready to receive you. With this, you burst into tears of relief, tears of compunction protecting you from evil. Through giving you the kiss of peace and reconciliation, you will enter true penance and will experience the consolations of his grace. It is a great mistake to seek conversion outside of ourselves in certain people in certain places and practices. We must seek within us to find God in the interior. When we love a person, we naturally do not want to offend them. Without love, we do not heal from evil. God asks us only for our heart, because as soon as he has the heart, he soon has everything else. However, we do otherwise: we want to oblige souls to give their treasure without giving their heart: yet, their treasure is their heart, and their heart is their treasure. Our heart and treasure cannot be divided. In conversion, we want to begin to detach them from their external vanities and their inclinations. This is impossible since their whole heart is in it. Turn this heart to another object, and you will see that everything else will fall apart. The heart will no sooner be won than everything that depends on it will be too. We easily give all things to a person to whom we have given our heart. Everything I have just said is based on whom the King invited to his son's wedding, both the good and the bad, and people of all kinds of constitutions.

> But when the king came in to look at the guests, he saw there a man who had no wedding garment. [12] And he said to him, "Friend, how did you get in here without a wedding garment?" And he was speechless. [13] Then the king said to the attendants, "Bind him hand and foot and cast him into the outer darkness. In that place there will be weeping and gnashing of teeth." [14] For many are called, but few are chosen. (Matt 22:11–14)

This place seems to be contrary to the previous section. If the good and bad are invited to the feast, how does the king complain that a man who has been led from the high road to the banquet table does not have the nuptial robe, since he was led in? Moreover, among so many guests at a banquet, there is only one repulsed man, says the King, for *many are called, but few are chosen* and come in a manner insulting to the King. First, all those called to the feast are called to conversion, which covers us with the nuptial robe. To be presented, we need to be cleansed from present and actual. Who remains in this disposition to sin cannot convert and merits the indignation of God. But our past sin, which our will no longer wants to commit and which we hate, must not prevent us from approaching Jesus Christ. Actually, these sinners have left the sin of will and go to Jesus Christ to take part in his feast. Because they have returned to God, the King orders that the nuptial robe be given to them at the entrance of his palace. We must have grace to commune with him and return to his heart, because one cannot enter his heart unless one is converted. The conversion happens when we enter the King's heart.

Second, our Lord says, *Many are called, but few are chosen*. This regards all those who had been invited, and not with regard to those who were at the table. Many people filled the seats at the banquet, yet there was only one who had no nuptial robe. If there was a Judas among the apostles at the table of the Lord, it is not surprising that there is a man in willful sin. But it must be noted that there is only one and that it would have been cruel to deprive all the others of the feast. Because he alone was guilty, we must not remove the souls from Jesus's table on the pretext that there are some who abuse it. In the same way, although some interior people only seem to be interior, and nevertheless use this cloak only to cover their sins, it must not be said that the way is not good. Isn't the feast of the King of kings good? But the wicked disposition of some subjects prevents them from taking advantage of it.

> Then the Pharisees went and plotted how to entangle him in his words. [16] And they sent their disciples to him, along with the Herodians, saying, "Teacher, we know that you are true and teach the way of God truthfully, and you do not care about anyone's opinion, for you are not swayed by appearances. [17] Tell us, then, what you think. Is it lawful to pay taxes to Caesar, or not?" [18] But Jesus, aware of their malice, said, "Why put me to the test, you hypocrites? [19] Show me the coin for the tax." And they brought him a denarius. [20] And Jesus said to them, "Whose likeness and inscription is this?" [21] They said, "Caesar's." Then he said to them, "Therefore render to Caesar the things that are Caesar's, and to God the things that are God's." (Matt 22:15–21)

Nothing is greater or more instructive to us than this place of the Gospel. The incarnate Word uses the occasion of the malice of the Pharisees to give us in a few words the perfect rule of our conduct. Jesus wants to see *the image of the coin* before deciding to whom it is due, and as soon as he sees that it bears the image of Caesar, he orders that we *render to Caesar the things that are Caesar's and to God the things that are God.* Similar to the image on the literal coin, all humans bear the image of God, which has been engraved on us by our creation. Because of this, we belong to God.

Yet we want to retain the tribute that we owe to the Creator by appropriating his image and claiming ourselves as belonging to ourselves. Like the coin must return to him whose image it bears, we too must pay our tribute to God, giving him full possession of ourselves, so that God may dispose of us as he pleases. In the same way, Caesar disposes of his financial coins.

Let us also render to Caesar what belongs to him, applying ourselves in our exterior lives and rendering to father, mother, and spouse what we owe them, as well as to all the lay superiors and clergy. But we do this in such a way that our interior preference is always reserved for God and that our soul, which bears his image, is only for him.

> When they heard it, they marveled. And they left him and went away. (Matt 22:22)

Many people agree on the truth and justice of this passage, which asks us to give God what we owe him and also to give to our neighbors what is theirs. But even as they admire what Jesus says, they withdraw from him without embracing this reality. Everyone wants to do what they want and claim for themselves what belongs to God or to our neighbors.

> The same day Sadducees came to him who say that there is no resurrection, and they asked him a question, 24 saying, "Teacher, Moses said, 'If a man dies having no children, his brother must marry the widow and raise up offspring for his brother.' 25 Now there were seven brothers among us. The first married and died, and having no offspring left his wife to his brother. 26 So too the second and third, down to the seventh. 27 After them all, the woman died. 28 In the resurrection, therefore, of the seven, whose wife will she be? For they all had her." 29 But Jesus answered them, "You are wrong, because you know neither the Scriptures nor the power of God. 30 For in the resurrection they neither marry nor are given in marriage, but are like angels in heaven." (Matt 22:23–30)

All the difficulties that we have in the interior life are caused by two reasons. The first is we do not *know the* holy *Scriptures*. The second is we doubt the *power of God*. If we understood the Scripture and consulted it attentively, we would see that all the interior states are described there. For the Holy Spirit gives us what it is essential for us to know. Speaking of the body of Christ, he gives us what is needed for the sanctification of souls. In relation to Jesus Christ, he gives the greatest of graces deserved for souls with whom he will unite in marriage: the purification of his spouses, the trials showing their fidelity, the consummation of their love, and their eternal marriage with the King of glory. All that God operates secretly in souls is written about in the divine books and is included with all its principles and examples. When God is pleased to lift the veil that covers the symbolic figures, we cannot admire them enough. God draws aside the veil only as one advances through the experience of these spiritual states that are depicted in this table of truth. Already there are a thousand places that convince us of the reality of these states that even those with a mediocre understanding can witness in the word of God. The particular goal of this work to prove the interior life as solid truth is advanced in this place. The adversaries of the interior life *are in error* because they do not *know* and consult *the Scriptures.*

Moreover, if we trusted divine power, we would find nothing impossible or difficult. We would abandon ourselves to God without any reservation. Yet our hesitation to abandon ourselves reveals that we doubt his power. Our lack of abandonment shows we think it is dangerous to side ourselves with God in his power and goodness.

Jesus Christ teaches us another truth, that the state of mystical resurrection is an entirely angelic state. A soul who has experienced this *resurrection* and the death that precedes it finds herself in a state entirely *angelic*, not only for the functions of the spirit but also for the weaknesses of the body. She is not exempt from the miseries and infirmities of the flesh, but they seems as foreign and outside of her as if she had no body.

> "But regarding the resurrection of the dead, have you not read what was spoken to you by God: 32 'I am the God of Abraham, the God of Isaac, and the God of Jacob'? He is not the God of the dead, but of the living." 33 And when the crowd heard it, they were astonished at his teaching. (Matt 22:31–33)

There are three kinds of death: natural, mystical, and criminal (the death of sin). There are also three kinds of *resurrections*. God is not properly the *God of the dead*, since death opposes the reign of life. He is not the God of the dead of those in sin, because they have revolted against him instead of submitting to his Kingdom. He is the God of the natural dead as regards the dependence of their being resting in him, but he is *their God* only as long as they are *alive in him*. When their bodies are reduced to dust in time, they must rise to be reunited with their souls, always alive, which the Sadducees doubted, just as the sinner who died in his crime must be resurrected through grace, so that the God of those who sleep in the tomb of mystical death must be resurrected by grace. In the experience of mystical death, God seems to have lost his memory of them and to have rejected them from his hand with the dominion of his scepter. While this state of mystical death lasts, the believer still has some opposition to the divine kingdom, because the remnants of the creature's proprietary life are not sufficiently annihilated to give rise to the divine life without any resistance. Since death is not completed until the resurrection, there is no longer any resistance but only impotence and inaction. God does not yet animate with his life-giving principle what the poor, dead, and buried person tries to do. So in mystical death the person is not in action, but rather in powerlessness to act in deprivation and death. He must therefore rise again so that God in perfection may be his God. And this being done, he moves in animation as God pleases. God is the *God of Abraham, the God of Isaac, and the God of Jacob* because they all experienced this mystical resurrection and in the states represented by the patriarchs' characters that lead to it, as we saw in the Old Testament.

> But when the Pharisees heard that he had silenced the Sadducees,
> they gathered together. 35 And one of them, a lawyer, asked him
> a question to test him. 36 "Teacher, which is the great command-
> ment in the Law?" 37 And he said to him, "You shall love the
> Lord your God with all your heart and with all your soul and
> with all your mind. 38 This is the great and first commandment."
> (Matt 22:34–38)

This is your great commandment, which contains all the others and without which all the others would be useless! O commandment of commandments! Whoever practices you, keeps all the law! O God of Love! You command us to love you! Do you not have charms to attract hearts without pressing them further by this pleasant precept of giving oneself to you? You allow us to love you without obliging us to do so further under pain of your indignation and our misery. You command all these hearts, which you have created, redeemed, and filled with a thousand blessings, to love you, and they do not fail to defend themselves against it! Or will they find a law softer than that of love and also stronger, since love makes everything easy and finds nothing difficult?

But to love God with all our heart, we must be entirely for God, because we love God only as much as we give ourselves to all his wills for us. The whole heart must be turned towards him to completely unite with him. Then everything transforms in love in order to be completely changed into God. If we hold back some things with reservations, we do not love God with all our heart. What makes us give our whole heart to God is what makes us obey this commandment, which is recollection and prayer of the heart. We need to pray from the heart to fully satisfy this commandment. Even more, perfect love consists in loving God with all the heart, *since whoever abides in love abides in God, and God abides in him* (1 John 4:16). Arriving in God, we have perfect charity by the flow of our entire being into that of God. To be in God in a consummated state requires work and trials to fulfill this commandment in all its perfection. I say that strictly speaking, it is enough for salvation to love God and prefer God to all creatures, but who are those who really have this love? We are content to prefer God to the devil by abstaining from sin, but who are those who prefer God to all their own interests, not only for goods, honors, and life but also for salvation and eternity? Yet we need to love God with our whole heart, because if we love only as we love as some created good, whatever it might be, we could still love God more. Namely, we love God with our most sovereign love, reserving nothing and sacrificing everything to God.

Love God with all our soul means to consecrate our whole soul to him with our faculties so only God possesses our soul. A soul cannot obey this command better than by giving herself to love him with all of herself and by sacrificing all of herself to God. She gives herself to the one she loves and flows into and loses herself in God. She no longer finds herself in herself, but only in God, in which she becomes all love.

To love God with our whole mind is to apply everything to God without reserving anything for ourselves. When this is done by a consummated sacrifice of this same spirit, we yield ourselves to the Spirit of God, allowing all of our own activities to be overcome gradually by the divine operation until God's Spirit becomes our spirit, as well as the heart of our heart and the soul of our soul.

To love God with all our heart, therefore, is to give our whole heart to God and everything that depends on this. To love God, the whole soul unites and attaches to God. To love God, the whole spirit gathers up and turns towards God, submitting to his operation. Now none of this can be done perfectly except by the central union, which is the fruit and the end of the whole interior journey. Outside of this, everything is more or less only self-love, *for they all seek their own interests*, both in time and in eternity, *not those of Jesus Christ*, as St. Paul deplored (Phil 2:21).

> And a second is like it: You shall love your neighbor as yourself. [40] On these two commandments depend all the Law and the Prophets. (Matt 22:39–40)

The second commandment expands our understanding of love to include our neighbor. To love our neighbor means to help in time of need and to not cause any evil. Instead, we desire the good that we would want for ourselves for our neighbor. Those in pure love and in perfect charity by loving God and our neighbor are in the consummation of the law.

Those who love God in this way without thinking of the law fulfill all the law perfectly.

> While the Pharisees were gathered together, Jesus asked them,
> 42 "What do you think about the Messiah? Whose son is he?"
> "The son of David," they replied.
> 43 He said to them, "How is it then that David, speaking by the Spirit, calls him 'Lord'? For he says,
> 44 'The Lord said to my Lord:
> "Sit at my right hand
> until I put your enemies
> under your feet."'
> 45 If then David calls him 'Lord,' how can he be his son?" 46 No one could say a word in reply, and from that day on no one dared to ask him any more questions. (Matt 22:41–46)

David fathered Jesus Christ according to the flesh, but Jesus Christ is the Lord of David according to eternal generation. Jesus is also the Lord of David as the great King in his interior, as was seen in his life. The Spirit of the Word guided David in his mystical journeys as well as in his prophecies. Moreover, David was the living figure of Jesus, and his relationship with the Lord made him like the most exact copy of the Lord.

This also makes us understand that Jesus Christ can be both the Lord and the Son of interior people. He is their Lord since he rules and governs them. He is their Son when they produce him in hearts.

> Then Jesus said to the crowds and to his disciples, 2 "The scribes and the Pharisees sit on Moses' seat, 3 so do and observe whatever they tell you, but not the works they do. For they preach, but do not practice. 4 They tie up heavy burdens, hard to bear, and lay them on people's shoulders, but they themselves are not willing to move them with their finger." (Matt 23:1–4)

We must obey people of authority who are seated in the courts of the church. But alas! How many are there who make strange rigors for sinners that they would not want to have for themselves if they were in the same weaknesses? The divine Master reprehends the bitter behavior of the Pharisees towards the people after having given the true rule of charity, *love your neighbor as yourself.* Because of this principle of love, we must treat weak souls with gentleness and empathy. Yet we censure others with zeal and rigor, while we indulge and justify ourselves. We see people's faults without reference to God. We interpret sins according to our own meaning; and we impose on the weak a *yoke that we would not want to bear*. Yet God gives the desire to the pure soul to communicate with angelic dispositions obtained only by communion with God. Yet these Pharisees call others monsters for the slightest faults, while they tolerate in themselves intolerable choices. Do not follow the behavior of these people. Let us sit with more fairness towards our brothers and sisters, and yet let us not stop obeying the good things said by those who have authority over us.

> They do all their deeds to be seen by others. For they make their phylacteries broad and their fringes long, [6] and they love the place of honor at feasts and the best seats in the synagogues [7] and greetings in the marketplaces and being called rabbi by others. [8] But you are not to be called rabbi, for you have one teacher, and you are all brothers. (Matt 23:5–8)

Jesus Christ, the Judge and the Doctor of justice, makes these severe rebukes to the scribes and Pharisees. All who hold a rank in the church similar to the rank these people held in the synagogue must consider them attentively and look in the Savior's mirror of truth. How many are there who still imitate the Pharisees and are concerned only about appearances? They want their exterior to look good and receive the esteem and approval of humans, yet they do not trouble themselves about the rest. If a fault is noticed by other human beings, this causes abjection and makes them inconsolable. Their extreme vanity makes them always want to have the preference.

Jesus Christ does not want the apostle or the directors to adopt this quality of pretense and phony elevation that these teachers have. Only God can lead us in the interior by his inspiration. Leaders must help us to follow God's conduct and bring us to abandon ourselves to God, but they must not be interested in wanting to lead us themselves as they please. It is up to them to observe and follow the movements of the Spirit of God on souls.

> And call no man your father on earth, for you have one Father, who is in heaven. [10] Neither be called instructors, for you have one instructor, the Christ. [11] The greatest among you shall be your servant. [12] Whoever exalts himself will be humbled, and whoever humbles himself will be exalted. (Matt 23:9–12)

We all have only one Father, who is God, and this Father is jealous that we treat only him as a father. We must have perfect trust in God as

Father and share our trust with no one else. We deny God's loving quality if we do not trust him blindly. Only our Master Jesus can instruct us. We listen only to him, or if we listen to humans, they must speak as Jesus would to us. Any other language must be foreign to us.

Our Lord then gives us a lesson on the rules of perfection. Grace moves us towards abasement, humiliation, and annihilation through the weight of love, the order of justice, and the proof of fidelity. This center of peace unites us while providing a refuge against all illusions. The character and Spirit of Jesus Christ protect us. Let us despise everything that promises us elevation. Let us hold on to love our abjection. The measure of our abasement and annihilation will be that of our subsequent elevation, and the deeper the humility, the greater the elevation in God. The true elevation is therefore the deepest humiliation. It is to this that we must tend as to our center.

We must not seek abasement, though, as a means of attaining elevation in God based on what he has promised those that *humble themselves will be exalted*. This uses humility to make it a passage to one's own glory by humbling oneself not for the glory of God, but for human beings. Jesus Christ commands us not to pursue wrong goals. He tells us we must seek and love our lowliness only for the glory of God. We must devote ourselves through eternal resignation to the will of God. Let us fulfill what God commands us without pretending to surrender to God's will while truly seeking our own human glory. For the slightest interest in receiving crowns from him one day for our abasement would be far removed from perfect humility and pure charity.

> But woe to you, scribes and Pharisees, hypocrites! For you shut the kingdom of heaven in people's faces. For you neither enter yourselves nor allow those who would enter to go in. (Matt 23:13)

This passage is frightening, not only for the doctors of the law but for all in the Gospel. Those church leaders close the interior Kingdom to human beings by preaching superficially, talking only of external matters without letting them know that God dwells in their depths. Christians need to seek God's Kingdom within themselves. Since Christians can be instructed in the interior only by their leaders, are they not closing the door to them by not allowing them entry? They stop souls from entering the interior Kingdom. They persuade believers to refuse the interior Kingdom, because Pharisees do not want to enter it themselves. Ah! What an account will these interior persecutors render to God for so much glory that they have stolen from him and for so many crowns that they have stolen from souls. They do not want to let them walk in the freedom to which the Holy Spirit called them. They even unite to cry out against the interior ways that Jesus Christ came to teach by his word and by his example. They leave in peace many great sinners who are the disgrace of Christianity, yet people everywhere decry spiritual persons who only try to do the will of God and to teach others to do it!

> Woe to you scribes and Pharisees, hypocrites: because you devour the houses of widows, praying long prayers. For this you shall receive the greater judgment. (Matt 23:14)

Both the literal and spiritual meaning here can be applied to the interior life. Injustice means the usurpation of the good made by hypocrisy. These hypocritical and proprietary people, under the pretext of a false exterior, devour the interior life of simple souls who, like widows, find themselves devoid of all support. As soon as these souls fall into the hands of hypocrites, they absolutely hold them back and destroy their interior house by their bad advice.

> Woe to you scribes and Pharisees, hypocrites; because you go round about the sea and the land to make one proselyte; and when he is made, you make him the child of hell twofold more than yourselves. (Matt 23:15)

These hypocrites deserve *hell* because they have no interior faith but only external actions while teaching others to do the same. If we are content to convert only the person's exterior, we work only with the exterior bark of religion without entering into the Spirit. These imperfect conversions prevent them from giving ourselves entirely to God, according to the expressions of the Holy Spirit. As the prophet Jeremiah says, *Yet for all this her treacherous sister Judah did not return to me with her whole heart, but in pretense, declares the Lord* (Jer 3:10).

Jesus Christ says the Spirit of God inspires holy freedom. Without this, we convert others to put them in inconceivable discomfort, ending the desire to become faithful. These unhappy conversions teach difficult austerities and practices of which few are capable. People of good will cannot support the yoke imposed on them. Then only a few people use religion for their own purposes as food for self-esteem, which puffs up and fattens them as if they had done something great. Our Lord condemns the virtue of bodily constraint done out of human pride. Instead, with a converted heart, the soul learns to give herself to God without reserve. She loves and seeks God within her heart, entering gently and wisely into external penance only according to her strength. Then the exterior depends on the interior. Thus, she applies herself to loving God, living in the exterior without embarrassment or constraint. Because of this, she lives without being shy or constrained. On the contrary, she is gentle, humble, and peaceful, whereas in the other way of life, one is aggressive, worried, and anxious.

> Woe to you, blind guides, who say, "If anyone swears by the temple, it is nothing, but if anyone swears by the gold of the temple, he is bound by his oath." 17 You blind fools! For which is greater, the gold or the temple that has made the gold sacred? (Matt 23:16–17)

This *blindness* still exists today because the *gold of the temple* is valued more than the temple itself. The external good works of gold can have value or merit only from the temple of the interior soul. If the temple is holy, it sanctifies everything else; otherwise, the good works are a very small thing. The holiness of the exterior must therefore start from the interior, and not the reverse order of making the interior depend on the exterior.

> And you say, "If anyone swears by the altar, it is nothing, but if anyone swears by the gift that is on the altar, he is bound by his oath." 19 You blind men! For which is greater, the gift or the altar that makes the gift sacred? (Matt 23:18–19)

Our heart is the *altar* on which we must make the sacrifices, and the sacrifices take their value from this altar. This is what makes the external sacrifices so small compared to the interior ones. Our offerings must be immolated on the altar of our heart to be considered by God. However, being *blind*, we swear only by the gift, making everything consist in the exterior; instead, everything has to start from our interior altar.

> Woe to you, scribes and Pharisees, hypocrites! For you tithe mint and dill and cumin, and have neglected the weightier matters of the law: justice and mercy and faithfulness. These you ought to have done, without neglecting the others. (Matt 23:23)

Some people cling in a scrupulous way to *small things of the law* which are nothing. They go to confession frequently with strange fears of omitting an outward trifle, and yet they *neglect what is more important in the law, namely, justice, mercy, and faithfulness.* In *justice* we render everything to God and give him all our heart and love, returning all things we have taken from God and possess with propriety. In *mercy* we procure primarily the good for our neighbor, above all their spiritual good. In *faithfulness*, we keep our promises to God and other humans. The heart of the law is the spirit of justice, mercy, and faithfulness. Without omitting the rest, when we do well in these three essential points, we do exactly what is our duty.

> You blind guides, straining out a gnat and swallowing a camel! (Matt 23:24)

Those exact in these small things strain a gnat and swallow a camel. Their propriety of monstrous size endangers them. Propriety bears the fruit of infidelities and crimes. We believe we act for God, yet we corrupt almost everything by self-love. Ah! How blind we are! We do not follow the gospel counsels, which speak to us only of the cross, renunciation, poverty of spirit, loss, death, and annihilation. The gospel counsels teach us to let God act. We abandon and entrust ourselves to God because of our profound blindness. The Savior of our souls uses the penetrating ray of his wisdom and zeal to give us both the knowledge and the remedy, instructing Christians at the same time as he corrects the carnal hypocrisy of the Pharisees.

> Woe to you, teachers of the law and Pharisees, you hypocrites! You clean the outside of the cup and dish, but inside they are full of greed and self-indulgence. [26] Blind Pharisee! First clean the inside of the cup and dish, and then the outside also will be clean. (Matt 23:245–26)

Our Lord instructs us about our exterior's futility if it is not animated from the interior. Therefore, he complains of the abuse that still persists in our days. We *clean the outside*, while leaving the interior full of *greed and self-indulgence*. We steal a thousand things from God without scruple. However, true purity found in the *interior* cleanses the exterior naturally. All purity not coming from the heart is only imaginary. Also, the divine Master says that those with a pure heart will see God. The foolish virgins, even though they are still virgins, do not fail to be rejected from the celestial wedding. Reform the exterior as much as you please, you will never be pure unless you are exempt from propriety which usurps the role of God.

> Woe to you, scribes and Pharisees, hypocrites! For you are like whitewashed tombs, which outwardly appear beautiful, but within are full of dead people's bones and all uncleanness. (Matt 23:27)

When we cleanse the outside and neglect to apply ourselves to the interior, we are *whitened sepulchers* who appear composed well, while the inside is full of rotting corruption. The less we feel this corruption, the more dangerous it is. We know this by a rare mercy of God, who opens our interior to show us what we thought of as great virtues were only great faults. The sins of the Pharisees have this peculiarity that, hidden in the spirit, they are the most unrecognizable and without remedy, except for an extraordinary stroke of the finger of God.

> So you also outwardly appear righteous to others, but within you are full of hypocrisy and lawlessness. (Matt 23:28)

In their blindness, the Pharisees judge themselves full of virtue. They give value to what God rejects and condemn what God approves. Yet they will understand one day that they deceived themselves, having paid heed only to living and exterior virtues, whereas God esteems infinitely the interior virtues.

> Woe to you, scribes and Pharisees, hypocrites! For you build the tombs of the prophets and decorate the monuments of the righteous, [30] saying, "If we had lived in the days of our fathers, we would not have taken part with them in shedding the blood of the prophets." [31] Thus you witness against yourselves that you are sons of those who murdered the prophets. [32] Fill up, then, the measure of your fathers. (Matt 23:29–32)

After the death of saints, we approve in them what had been condemned during their life, yet those who praise them after their death persecuted them cruelly in their lifetime. In reading the lives of the saints, we notice with astonishment the persecutions they suffered, yet we have saints among us who are treated similarly, but we do not stop this. Far from it, even as we condemn the persecutions other saints endured, many are even more heartless to those who live in their days. So they actually blame themselves when they rise up against those who mistreated the saints.

The Pharisees' strange lives dwell in blindness. They believe they are doing justice when they spark an unjust persecution. The Pharisees honor the saints of heaven by building monuments to them and preciously enshrining their relics yet tear the saints from the earth with great cruelty. Yet God consummates the saints through hidden ways. Just God! Who can avoid the Pharisees' dangerous mistakes? None other than the one who refrains from *judging before the due time* (1 Cor 4:5) and who, being persuaded that we cannot penetrate the interior, will abandon to you judgment which is reserved for you alone.

> You serpents, you brood of vipers, how are you to escape being sentenced to hell? [34] Therefore I send you prophets and wise men and scribes, some of whom you will kill and crucify, and some you will scourge in your synagogues and persecute from town to town, [35] that upon you may come all the righteous blood shed on earth, from the blood of innocent Abel to the blood of Zechariah the son of Barachiah, whom you murdered between the sanctuary and the altar. [36] Truly, I say to you, all this will come upon this generation. (Matt 23:33–36)

Jesus Christ's condemnation of the Saint's persecutors should make us all tremble in fear of being a persecutor. As we believe in our own just zeal, we only persecute holiness. Jesus Christ declares that those who now persecute the saints are also guilty of the former persecutions of the saints, since their innocent blood must fall on them and attract the indignation of God. Sooner or later, the persecutors will receive strange punishments. What kindles the anger of God in persecutors is that they attribute to the evil spirit what is the gift of his Holy Spirit. The world treats saints as the dregs and excrement, yet God takes his delight in these souls. God shows the Pharisees his excess of fury by calling them serpents and a brood of vipers. These human snakes cover themselves with their prudence to hide their great injustices. As a brood of vipers, they seek to kill those who would give them life.

> O Jerusalem, Jerusalem, killing the prophets and stoning those who are sent to you! How often would I have gathered your children together as a hen gathers her brood under her wings, and you would not! [38] Behold, your house is forsaken and desolate. [39] For I tell you, you will not see me again, until you say, "Blessed is he who comes in the name of the Lord." (Matt 23:37–39)

This passage shows us the goodness of God, who wants to save all people, and the resistance that people show to God's salvation. Jesus Christ speaks to all Christians under the name of Jerusalem. He desires to gather them all under his wings for salvation if they abandon themselves to him, but they do not want to, preferring to walk alone and dispersed, ready to be devoured by their enemies, than to let themselves go under the wings of his protection. The prophet-king who had experienced the confidence of being thus protected by God said, *Hide me in the shadow of your wings* (Ps 17:8). Oh, how confident we are of such protection! What could we fear? God calls forth from the soul's center both powers and senses to bring us back into his unity, but we defend ourselves against it, living in continual diffusion, unable to return within. Most of those whom God draws find many persecutors who do not want them to listen to Jesus Christ within or the apostles and prophets who speak in the exterior. So what happens to these souls not desiring reunion with Jesus Christ? Their house becomes deserted and uninhabited. They experience within themselves only a terrible desert.

Alas! How empty a heart is when God does not dwell there! And how could God live where no one wants to allow him to be the Master? And how would he be in the heart since he is always kept at the door? And how could he reign within when he is given only the exterior? Also, because those people never go into the interior, Jesus Christ disappears and hides from them until, recognizing their fault, they receive him by some stroke of providence when they learn about the interior life. And then, convinced of the wrong they have done, they praise Jesus Christ for his goodness in seeking them.

> Jesus left the temple and was going away, when his disciples came to point out to him the buildings of the temple. [2] But he answered them, "You see all these, do you not? Truly, I say to you, there will not be left here one stone upon another, that will not be thrown down." (Matt 34:1–2)

Jesus Christ gazed into this temple in Jerusalem, the interior temple. The soul in the state of light and love is like a superb edifice: there is nothing more beautiful to see, and it inspires admiration in the whole spiritual world. But this building must be destroyed that there remains only stone upon stone. Everything must be demolished to the foundations. Figures of Scripture speak of this as much for the interior of souls as for the exterior of the church! O God, how hard it is to suffer this destruction! However, Jesus Christ swears by his truth that this must be a strong destruction, and the extreme strippings are good to see.

> As he sat on the Mount of Olives, the disciples came to him privately, saying, "Tell us, when will this be, and what will be the sign of your coming and of the close of the age?" (Matt 24:3)

Jesus Christ sits on the *Mount of Olives*, a mountain of anointing and peace. Needing instruction, his disciples ask him what sign there will be of his coming and the end of the world. Jesus Christ takes his place when the world is at its end. This *world* is what there is in us of sinful and corrupt Adam. It must necessarily end before the advent of Jesus Christ, who, after the mystical death of the soul, comes to revive the soul and to receive new life.

The soul no longer has a world because once Jesus became her life, the world is over for her. Everything is given to Jesus Christ in God in eternity.

> And Jesus answered them, "Take heed that no one leads you astray.
> 5 For many will come in my name, saying, 'I am the Christ,' and
> they will lead many astray. 6 And you will hear of wars and rumors
> of wars; see that you are not alarmed; for this must take place, but the end is not yet." (Matt 24:4–6)

Many people want to seduce souls and interfere in the work of Jesus Christ by drawing them away from God so they live according to human invention. But whoever understands the path of Jesus Christ will easily know the contempt of these seducers, because everything Jesus prophesied must happen before he himself comes. First, many wars have to be endured. In the beginnings of conversion, the person must war by the vigor of love against external things in order to detach himself from them. A believer must also war against their senses and passions, to mortify them and repress their movement, which could prevent their perfect return to God. Paul speaks of this war when he says, *For the desires of the flesh are against the Spirit, and the desires of the Spirit are against the flesh; for these are opposed to each other, to prevent you from doing what you would* (Gal 5:17).

In a more advanced state, a superior force makes the second and passive war. Then person gives a simple acquiescence by accepting failure and the poverty of dying love. His self-loving nature suffers and receives deadly blows. Previously the soul enjoyed a long peace and nearly won victory in the first war. In the second war, the same enemies whom he believed to have defeated and exterminated are reborn and revolt. But having exhausted his active forces in the preceding combats, he knows very well that his remaining courage and vigor cannot repulse these harshest attacks. He wants to leave to his Beloved all the care for the fight, so the Beloved receives the honor of victory. The person only supports, feels, and sees in part these last fights in which God himself fights against propriety. Of this passive war, God inspired Moses to say, *The LORD will fight for you, and you have only to be still* (Exod 14:14). All of this must happen before the end draws near. Those therefore who believe that God has come into them but have not experienced these things are greatly deceiving themselves. Some of his gifts as forerunners may well have come; but God did not come himself.

> For nation will rise against nation, and kingdom against kingdom, and there will be famines and earthquakes in various places: [8] all this is but the beginning of the birth-pangs. (Matt 24:7–8)

Jesus Christ will come to earth in an invisible way, pouring out his Spirit on many holy souls before coming as Judge in the last advent. These signs happen in the world, although they are not understood. Certainly, the bloodiest war ever will precede the most universal of all peace.

This conflict also happens in each destined soul who finds consummation with God in this lifetime. First, she experiences in faith the revolt of one people against another people, which is the uprising of the flesh against the spirit. In this battle, an infinity of thoughts and reflections rise up against each other, striking down and killing each other. Romans 2:15 reads, *They show that what the law requires is written on their hearts, while their conscience also bears witness and their conflicting thoughts accuse or perhaps excuse them.* The more you believe you have destroyed corruption, the more it recovers. The self-will, which appeared dead and extinguished, now awakens and wants to revolt against the will of God. The empire of the demon comes to fight that of Jesus Christ, and in the commotion, the troubled soul experiences what Paul says, *For I do not do the good I want, but the evil I do not want is what I do* (Rom 7:19). She then enters into that terrible famine that David experienced, a terrible hunger through the deprivation of that which can satisfy her. The longer her deprivation is prolonged, the more her hunger increases: and the more the only object that can satisfy her moves away from her. Her hunger doubles until she despairs of ever being satisfied.

Few experience these states, and they experience them differently. First, those in deprivation without suffering hunger are those without love of God and no desire to possess him. Some experience this in the state of death. Others have arrived in God as their end and can no longer desire anything. Yet God wants their consummation and advancement so causes them to feel some privations of the sweet presence and divine life.

Second, some hunger without deprivation. Even as they experience hunger, they are full. Not yet real possession of God, the soul always has a secret hunger for something it does not have. This state precedes that of death and naked faith, being a passiveness of light and love. Following this, there arises a secret hope of the satisfaction of this hunger called a state of purgatory.

Third is the most terrible state of spiritual hell where the soul experiences this strange hunger as in the state of purgatory without the hope of ever being refreshed and satisfied. The more this hunger increases, the more extreme becomes the privation and despair. This is the cruelest torment here.

Fourth, after having known both deprivation and hunger, the soul also loses this hunger. All that remains is the sight of the loss of the secret hunger of God without having been either satisfied or possessing God. Then we know that the torment caused by hunger itself is a sensible sign of love and tenderness. But when this hunger is lost, and all that remains is the sight of this loss, the state becomes unsupportable. The state of pain is much more supportable than the state of nothing. As self-love understands how much he must suffer, the suffering itself consoles him. The loss of this brings the perception of nothing to lean upon; this brings desolation and agony.

After this state, or perhaps before it, comes that of *plague* where contagion mixes everywhere, gradually corrupting and spoiling. This plague attacks formerly exempt places, and *earthquakes occur in various places*. Fear and fright fill the inferior part, which loses the health and peace it formerly enjoyed. In the superior part, the soul shakes with fear of infection from sin and by the sight of the loss that seemed to her inevitable. Those who have passed through these states will see that they are here expressed very naturally. But these strange fears and frights are *only the beginning of the pains* that must follow.

> Then they will hand you over to be tortured and will put you to death, and you will be hated by all nations because of my name. [10] Then many will fall away, and they will betray one another and hate one another. (Matt 24:9–10)

All true servants of God, the dear delight of his heart, must be treated in this way. Those who should protect instead betray and deliver them to human justice. This external persecution reveals that God has placed designs on these souls whom he tests. We do not judge these souls by the grandeur of the gifts of God but by their cross and the profundity of their annihilation. God purifies these faithful souls through these harsh and insupportable ways while the light of affliction leads them. As God's will rules from eternal order, God delivers souls of faith differently, and always as he pleases to the ministers of his justice. Certainly, many experience terrible things from the demons.[2] People who pass through this comprehend this easily. They know through their consolations that they are not alone. Only God's most cherished souls experience this. This is not said easily in writing. I beg them to make use of their pain and not torment and defend themselves, which only augments and prolongs their torture. Instead, they need to abandon themselves to suffer this pain fully as God's purpose and know the full duration of their martyrdom. No sooner do they abandon themselves with courage without turning away for a moment than the devil will leave them in repose, because he cannot bear such generous abandonment. May they remain steadfast in the midst of the most extreme tests, strongly persuaded that the ministers of hell may do no other thing than what God permits. The demon sees the faithful soul's firmness, withdraws in rage, and does not come to attack these souls who have become so strong in their abandonment. Abandoned souls defy all of hell without fear, for hell fears them. In such strength, they become masters of demons. If the faithful soul fears, the devil sees this and uses this to his advantage and prolongs the torments. God allows because the soul has only a small resignation and little trust in his divine protection.

Spiritual directors who guide people who have suffered much from demons must support them by offering grand compassion. Vocal prayers or penances will not deliver them, for the sufferer will be delivered only in this way: by abandoning everything to God without any reservation.

2. Guyon's note: See Angela of Foligno, *Life*, ch. 19 ["Likewise, devils pursue and harass me in many ways, and almost continually persecute me. They have power over me because God has placed my soul and body in their hands. But no matter how much they may be able to afflict my body, they cannot torment and inflict pain on my soul to the same extent, for the soul is more closed to their attacks than the body. It seems to me that I can almost see them in bodily form with their horns set to assail me" (Angela of Foligno, *Complete Works*, 204)].

All who experience this must do the same. God does not deliver because they have doubled their ministries and activities. To the contrary, God delivers them through their annihilation and trust during this. In the exercise of their faith, God carries them to total abandonment and hope in every situation. When on the point of leaving, the demon tricks people by increasing its torments against poor souls who have resigned themselves courageously. But without fear, they double their faith and abandon, even when tempted to quit because of the increased pain.

External crosses almost always accompany interior crosses. We must expect persecutions and venomous hatred because of the name of Jesus Christ. People who do only evil stir up the bloodiest persecutions against us. Why? For the name of Jesus Christ, the cause for whom we work, to make him known and loved. Many are horrified to see his loving name like an aromatic oil spread everywhere. These faithful hearts of whom we speak find themselves in love with his love.

> And many false prophets will arise and lead many astray. [12] And because wickedness is multiplied, most men's love will grow cold. [13] But he who endures to the end will be saved. (Matt 24:11–13)

The interior wars and persecutions caused by demonic people would be little to suffer if beyond this there did not rise false prophets. And who are they? These false prophets seduce and persuade many simple people that they are not on a good path, causing them to submit to worldly ways. These false prophets greatly damage the sheepfold of Jesus Christ by joining their firm opinions with extraordinary actions.

Many will leave God throughout the world, and *wickedness will be multiplied*. Yet the time of great mercy lies close. The pure charity and ardor of faithful souls living in the interior rule of Jesus Christ must be sustained during this flooding of crime. Instead they must redouble their courage. Genesis 6:12 reads, *And God saw that the earth was corrupt, for all flesh had corrupted its ways upon the earth.* We need a deluge and fire to purify us. O deluge of interior grace! O sacred fire of pure love! Only you can stop and arrest this corruption. Do this therefore for the glory of the Father of mercies.

At this time, O spiritual directors, you must open all hearts to love and practice prayer. No other way causes deliverance. Sacred love banishes the love of the profane which poisons all hearts. Human beings naturally love. Without exercising their fire by loving God, they become involved with external things. We must love God in our interior life. Love seeks the presence of the Beloved. Love wants the knowledge and the taste of whom he loves. Love wants conversation and familiarity. We find intimacy with God only in the profound place of the heart. O fathers of souls, conversion never happens with external rules. Engage with the human heart, and people find conversion and a natural reformation of exterior life. When a person finds their heart, they will soon be given the love of God. To have God in love, we seek within ourselves and turn toward God with all the power of the heart. Ah! When conversion is done in this way, soon people feel love for God and lose a taste for all the rest. The will tastes and attaches to God with strength because what God gives ravishes us delicately and infinitely more than anything creatures can give. Then we naturally persevere in God's love without ever leaving because only those who persevere find salvation.

> And this gospel of the kingdom will be preached throughout the whole world, as a testimony to all nations; and then the end will come. (Matt 24:14)

O interior Kingdom! Mystical gospel! The time will come when you will be preached throughout the world. And though now few preach this, you will be preached to all the corners of the world! When our Savior's prediction is perfectly accomplished, there will be only *one flock and one shepherd* (John 10:16). All hearts will love. As all people reunite with the Savior, the church will extend throughout the world. This prophecy of our Lord will be accomplished in both the exterior and interior world.

The world will not end until this happens. O Love! Our hearts are lifted up when we think of you ruling everything and engaging all hearts! O why do you not come sooner? Why do you delay? But this kingdom is already beginning to expand. In this last age of the church, which is at hand, Jesus Christ must absolutely triumph. Because of this, the demons, hell, and all wicked or carnal people arm themselves with all strength to fight and prevent the growth of interior faith, but Jesus will be the strongest. All persecutions raised to destroy the interior Spirit will serve to kindle and ignite the Spirit more. Before the world ends, we must express and honor particularly the childhood of our Savior called the Child Jesus. Up to now we have honored and imitated the other states of the Savior. With our imitation of the Savior's childhood, grace becomes not only strength and bodily austerities but also great innocence and pure love, indeed the Spirit of Jesus Christ. In recent years, the Holy Spirit has given birth in the church to this singular devotion and adoration of the Child Jesus to give us a new disposition. This offers us a peaceful and happy state of being, revealing the worldwide Christian communion. Predicted by many saints, the Scriptures repeatedly express this clearly. The state of the Child Jesus is one equally innocent and interior though under a common exterior. Jesus Christ wants all Christians to imitate his childhood through perfect simplicity and innocence.

O priests, who by your character are elevated above others to such an eminent degree, let yourselves be penetrated by the interior Spirit and spread this throughout the earth! Infernal spirit, you stifle this Spirit from its birth, but you enchant and infect souls with your poison only for a time (Rev 12)! Then the prophecy of St. John on Patmos will be accomplished. The church is this woman pregnant with the interior Spirit: under her feet she has the inconstancy designated by the moon, yet she is crowned by the twelve fruits of the Holy Spirit like so many stars. Ready to give birth, the church brings forth its fruit, but the infernal dragon makes every effort to devour it but may not overcome the woman. Instead, this fruit will be taken into the bosom and center of God as a place of repose where it spreads on all the faithful. The rivers of persecution and heresies will attack this woman, but they will not drown her, for God keeps her under his protection. The earth opens to swallow up all her enemies.

> So when you see the abomination of desolation spoken of by the prophet Daniel, standing in the holy place (let the reader understand). (Matt 24:15)

This abomination in the holy place has already come. This prophecy has already been fulfilled and is still being fulfilled every day. It must come more fully before the world ends in its malice and abomination and before the interior Spirit is spread everywhere. Before the particular soul reaches divine immobility, it must experience this abomination. And the general church is experiencing it now. Whoever reads this, let him hear. O truth of the prophecies! You are shown for the mystical coming of the Son of God in souls. And although all this concerns the last judgment, it is nevertheless certain that Jesus Christ did not say a word that did not have several meanings. For how could he who was foretold by the Law and the Prophets not speak more profoundly than the Law and the Prophets? Therefore, speaking of the last judgment at the end of the world, this designates also the coming in souls of the interior reign. O day of glory and triumph for my God, for whom I am passionate!

> Then let those who are in Judea flee to the mountains. (Matt 24:16)

Some souls have long experienced the sweetness and the peace of the interior, as in Judea where they lived. Now in the time of such a hard test, they must strengthen themselves and quickly leave this land of *abomination* to flee to the mountains. This means they must be lost in God by a total abandon where they live in assurance. In these states of the greatest abjection, we must stay in God.

> Let the one who is on the housetop not go down to take what is in his house. (Matt 24:17)

Those who have arrived in God at the highest point of the Spirit are lost in God and must not descend to reflection to see what is happening under the pretext of *taking what is in his house* that which he believes is needed. He must remain in God, for he does not need anything from his house. All that is dearest to us we must leave and abandon without reservation if we want to pass into God, whom we cannot enter if we retain anything.

> And let the one who is in the field not turn back to take his cloak. (Matt 24:18)

The one in the fields has already been set free, being naked and stripped of what once concerned him. Hence, he does not go even with good reasons to take his cloak by returning to the exercises and practices that previously served him. Now he abandons himself to God and remains in this liberty without borrowing from means or anything created to take back those that he had.

> And alas for women who are pregnant and for those who are nursing infants in those days! (Matt 24:19)

The pregnant and nursing women will then have exterior and temporal misfortune and interior and spiritual misfortune. Along with persecution, their suffering may be like Jesus Christ's terrible suffering. These people represented by pregnant and nursing women pass through states more terrible than others.

These are two types of people and a very rare, third type that contains the other two. The pregnant women are those who must give birth to the souls of Jesus Christ. The nursing women are those who must breastfeed the spiritual children. The first type are the mothers and the second type nourish. Both types go through tragic states for both the exterior and interior, more than others not destined for this. The third state of being both mothers and nourishers will cost them much misfortune and suffering.

> Pray that your flight may not be in winter or on a Sabbath. [21] For then there will be great tribulation, such as has not been from the beginning of the world until now, no, and never will be. (Matt 24:20–21)

Both of these states must happen in the general church before the interior state is spread everywhere. This has happened already. At the same time, these souls experience strange states within themselves. Our Lord wants that we *pray* then because souls passing through such a harsh and rigorous winter instead of *fleeing* to God flee to exterior things, abandoning the interior. Even more, there are two winters, one interior and the other exterior. If we flee during an exterior winter before it passes, we will infallibly get lost. This is why the Bridegroom invites the spouse to follow him, saying, *The winter has already passed* (Song 2:11). We must pray to God to not let us run away during winter, because we would run and throw ourselves back into the world of creatures.

The *tribulation* of the state of death that precedes the renewal is *so extreme* that all other pains that precede this are only a shade of pain in comparison to this. But if they are strange in the time we suffer them, there is something to console us; as the Savior assures us, there will never be anything similar, this last pain ending all the other interior pains and the excess of misfortunes ending all misfortunes.

> And if those days had not been cut short, no human being would be saved. But for the sake of the elect those days will be cut short. (Matt 24:22)

If God had not cut short these days of these terrible tribulations, *no human being would be saved.* Corruption would go beyond all that could be said. But God's goodness does not permit that we are tempted beyond our strength; all that may touch our senses cannot reach the Spirit. If the continuation of temptation or the pain would cause an entire shipwreck, God puts an end to it and does not allow any similar ordeals. It is therefore of great consequence to abandon oneself to God, because he never fails to help in the favorable time.

> Then if anyone says to you, "Look, here is the Christ!" or "There he is!" do not believe it. [24] For false christs and false prophets will arise and perform great signs and wonders, so as to lead astray, if possible, even the elect. (Matt 24:23–24)

When a soul is in great desolation, many people want to make her leave the way, assuring her that Jesus Christ is not there but that he is assuredly in another way. However, when she follows the counsel of Jesus Christ by trusting God and abandoning to his will, human reason deems it a horrible loss. In opposition to them, she walks in the good way of the interior path of the righteous. The way of the righteous is prayer, abandonment, and faith. All of this is Jesus Christ himself. We must be firm to stay in God's way and abandon ourselves into his hand, even when the world disapproves. We see that many *false prophets* can do *great signs and wonders* before the eyes of the humans, so people follow and commune with them. The false prophets do not want the secular persons to pray, and because of this, they persecute the prayer of the heart. In our century, they dare to threaten the innocent with sin and refusal of absolution if they persist in doing what Jesus Christ recommended, namely, *to worship the Father in spirit and in truth* (John 4:24). The faithful choose as much as they can the *better part*, which is to *sit at the Lord's feet* and listen to God's word (Luke 10:39–42). And those who threaten these faithful ones occupy with brilliance and applause the pulpits and the courts of the church. But those who open Jesus Christ's treasure of Christianity to the faithful remain firm in the path and find strength in these contradictions.

Make no mistake: Jesus Christ is the same as he was on earth with his interior life. Let us know his words and his examples. Was he not in continual annihilation, having no support or sustenance except in God, and letting divinity move him in his works? And as God lived only in God and of God, he also calls us to be children of God, living his annihilated and divine life. Those true prophets who preach this interior state of Jesus Christ and who lead us to give everything to God speak by his Spirit. But false prophets fight prayer and the interior while giving too much to humans and remain in the exterior and the material world. They lack both the soul and the life of religion and the true Spirit of Jesus Christ. The life of Jesus was a continual prayer, a life of death and annihilation, poverty, detachment, and separation. This teaches us self-denial, division from the world, the faith to carry our cross and to follow him like this. We learn that the Kingdom of God is within us. The true apostles of Jesus Christ choose this life. But those living in the exterior life, who flatter nature and self-esteem while not living the life of Jesus Christ, I say, are made by a particular spirit and not by the Spirit of Jesus Christ or of his church, though they appear outwardly religious.

> See, I have told you beforehand. [26] So, if they say to you, "Look, he is in the wilderness," do not go out. If they say, "Look, he is in the inner rooms," do not believe it. (Matt 24:25–26)

Jesus Christ told us beforehand that there are people who do extraordinary signs and will be found *in the desert*, and we will be told to go, but we should not go. Instead, we find Jesus Christ in interior recollection, not in the desert. Interior recollection is the true solitude, the solitude of the heart disengaged from all strange affections. I believe that the exterior solitude supports the interior solitude, but the interior solitude precedes the exterior solitude. Otherwise, the exterior solitude would bear no fruit and expose us to great dangers. This is why Jesus Christ was in the desert only when he began preaching and then lived three years in a communal life in the exterior, although separated in his interior and in entire retreat from all things, teaching us that Christians must sanctify the common life.

I wish with all my heart that we understood we must be sanctified to an eminent degree in the communal life. We do not leave it without a particular order from providence or a well-recognized vocation. Because if we believed it firmly, each one would try to sanctify himself in the state where he is. But the false persuasion says, to be religious we must lead an extraordinary life, and so they abandon perfection. Ah, my friends, whoever you are, kings, princes, magistrates, soldiers, nobles, merchants, artists, laborers: all of you may find great holiness if you remain faithful to your vocation. God made saints visible to his church to encourage everyone to perfect themselves as *established, and exercised by the principle of justice and charity.*

Jesus Christ sanctified all states, honoring them with his presence, edifying them by his examples, and blessing them with his graces. No one is excused from becoming holy in the rank he holds among the faithful. So Jesus Christ is for you in a place where you are. Jesus Christ is in you. Strive to make yourselves holy in your state.

John the Baptist, the first announcer of the Kingdom of heaven, preached this to all sorts of people, Pharisees, publicans, soldiers, and generally all people, telling them to enter the Kingdom of heaven. He did not tell them to come out of their state, but he taught them to sanctify themselves each in his state. The law of Jesus Christ, however perfect it may be, does not prevent us from doing what is our duty; on the contrary, it urges us to do so. Whoever who will have his Spirit will acquit himself in the condition in which God has placed him. Some people are always looking for new ways to save themselves. They need to content themselves with what they have in the providence of their state.

> For as the lightning comes from the east and shines as far as the west, so will be the coming of the Son of Man. (Matt 24:27)

When God deigns to visit a soul, he appears in the foundation *as lightning*. He reveals himself to her by a divine light, which makes him appear alone. He hides things from the soul, like she who is struck by the bright spark of lightning cannot at this moment perceive anything other than the very light that dazzles her. This flash passes from the east to the west, penetrating all the capacity of the soul, surpassing even its extent. But it is only a flash that passes in an instant, without it being in our power to make it come or to hold it back when it appears. So it is with the liveliest touches of God in this life.

> Wherever the corpse is, there the vultures will gather. (Matt 24:28)

As the vultures gather near a dead body, so the elect must be *reunited* in Jesus Christ. But this is done only by the price of his death and by the living power of his flesh and blood. This also unites the powers in the foundation where in a union of spirit God is revealed and where he manifests his Son. Finally, the purest souls, elevated like *vultures* by the sublime flight of their prayer, *gather* around the body of Jesus Christ reposing in the Eucharist in a state of mystical death to adore and praise him, eat this, and unite themselves more and more to the source of their life.

> Immediately after the tribulation of those days the sun will be darkened, and the moon will not give its light, and the stars will fall from heaven, and the powers of the heavens will be shaken. (Matt 24:29)

These signs preceding the last coming of Jesus Christ on the earth arrive in a like manner in a soul before it is renewed. After its tribulations, he has said, *the sun will be darkened, and the moon will not give its light.* The soul enters into dreadful darkness. The true light of Jesus Christ, the divine *sun*, has previously led her there, hides himself, and does not let her feel the sweet effects of his presence. The small remnant of light from the *moon*, which still served her for guidance during the night of faith, is also taken away. The *stars* of illustrations of the mind and knowledge fall in the same way *from* heaven. The mind seems to be reduced to stupefaction. But all this would be little if the *virtues of heaven* were not shaken, when such a soul, after having led long years of an entirely celestial life, finds itself shaken by strange accidents and weakened without use of any virtue, everything being withdrawn and hidden in its most supreme parts. Everything is shaken within her and appears in disorder.

> Then will appear in heaven the sign of the Son of Man, and then all the tribes of the earth will mourn, and they will see the Son of Man coming on the clouds of heaven with power and great glory. (Matt 24:30)

In the reduction to such a deplorable state, when the loss is complete, one begins to see the *sign of the Son of Man*. This sign shows the division of the superior part from the interior done by the cross, accompanied by a secret and inexplicable operation of God. Then all the peoples of the earth, that is to say, all that belongs to the lower parts, deplore their distress, because nature being stripped of all the support is reduced to extreme desolation. But at this point, this neglected soul begins to perceive the *Son of Man*, who comes little by little to restore her life. He first appears to her through all these clouds, but they diminish as he advances. They dissipate on his arrival as one sees the sun rising from the bosom of the night and dissipating little by little this same night. But at this unexpected return, he appears with so much power and majesty that the soul loses all will and power, until finally he alone remains powerful, glorious, and reigning in her.

> And he will send out his angels with a loud trumpet call, and they will gather his elect from the four winds, from one end of heaven to the other. (Matt 24:31)

After the Son of Man begins to appear, he *sends his angels*, who gather together all the soul has lost, or so it seems. Certainly, the loss was real in external practices. She had the real advantage, although hidden in her foundation, everything is collected and reduced to unity. Like a net reuniting everything lost, all his gifts, graces, and favors, and the practice of virtues are returned. God gathers and brings back to himself all that he has chosen and recognizes what is his, even though he had seemed as distant from this person as the *four winds* separated from one another. Alienated from her state of misery, yet nothing that is chosen for God perishes, although it appears to be annihilated for a time as one extremity of heaven is from the other. He to whom all things are present does well to find everything when the time has come.

> From the fig tree learn its lesson: as soon as its branch becomes tender and puts out its leaves, you know that summer is near. [33] So also, when you see all these things, you know that he is near, at the very gates. (Matt 24:32–33)

These passages confirm and support that the coming of Jesus Christ, or the mystical incarnation, will be made clear, as the Scriptures in the Old Testament say. *The comparison* of this with the fig tree is admirable, because truly it shows that the winter is past and that the eternal spring of the spiritual resurrection has arrived. The soul has then taken on a new life and must *put out its leaves* of renewal of the virtues as the interior incarnation of Jesus Christ comes as the principle of her actions. The soul truly participates in his states. Like the fig tree's fruit, the coming of Jesus Christ shows that the immortal summer is near and that the autumn will infallibly follow, since these seasons will remain in an invariable order, as was declared in Song 2:11, *For behold, the winter is past; the rain is over and gone.*

But Jesus Christ's second coming leads us by his truth back to our Origin to find life in our source. Following this, he gives grace to the soul to communicates this life to others without the soul's losing her own permanent life. She participates in the life of Jesus received from the Father. Jesus possesses a perfect union of essence with the Father, and he communicates this to humans. His life becomes our light, and his light gives us life. As John 1:4 says, *In him was life, and the life was the light of men.* Such a person feels a great fullness of life that she must communicate to others. She must spread this fullness to others and possess this not only for herself; she possesses this to help others.

Some are destined to bear apostolic fruit in souls while remaining in repose, possessing their hidden treasure in great peace and solitude, exercising only an apostolate hidden in God, which consists in obtaining from God by their prayers, labors, and love very great graces in favor of souls. Others do the same but also engage directly with others and not only consummate their lives in this very sweet, fruitful, and tranquil rest continually in God but have a fullness of abundance for others. This grace floods them so they may give life to others. This Spirit overflows from the source that Jesus Christ confessed of himself when he said, *Someone touched me, for I perceive that power has gone out from me* (Luke 8:46). Paul experienced this in his heart when he expressed his great desire to communicate this apostolic grace by comparing it to the pains of childbirth. *My little children, for whom I am again in the anguish of childbirth until Christ is formed in you!* (Gal 4:19). At the beginning, Paul made them Christians, and now he ardently desires that they become perfect. But those called to the apostolic work and the grace of the divine mission participate equally in the fullness of pregnancy and the suffering of childbirth. God gives these persons a part in his secret power in proportion to their union with the divine source and the design of their vocation.

> Truly I tell you, this generation will certainly not pass away until all these things have happened. 35 Heaven and earth will pass away, but my words will never pass away. (Matt 24:34–35)

The world *will not end* until the truth of the gospel and the life of the Word have been spread throughout all the nations of the earth, and all people have been able to learn to live only the life of Jesus Christ. Each soul will not come to his end until after all these predicted things have happened to him, at least, according to the ordinary ways by which God leads souls. God's only rule is his will. God chooses from certain passages or journeys as means to bring about the death of the soul. However, some indispensable characteristics are the renunciation of ourselves, the loss of all propriety, and the death of all created to enter into the sharing of divine life. All souls called to salvation may not enter until they have passed through these states, either in this life or the next, where a terrible purgatory will serve only to purify the souls from obstacles that prevent the life of the Word in them. The Word *has life in himself* and is given to him to communicate this, and it also flows back upon him in principle (John 5:26).

Ah! That souls are destined for great things! O terrible misfortune to use all life in trifles and be filled with the life of the demon or remain in nature instead of living the life of God. O terrible loss! Who will understand you? What regrets, what pains will tear at the end for these souls, who will not have let themselves be taken in by the Word's Spirit! If we understand, we have lost the opportunity to be possessed by this treasure, which we cannot acquire by our own effort but only by the loss of all things. O hearts so noble and so great! Why do you not allow yourselves to be possessed by him who offers himself to you? Alas! You will see one day that what you consider great is only baseness. Being created for such a sublime end, why do you amuse yourself with deceptive goods? O nobility, O dignity of humans! To the blind some make themselves a slave to the goods, honors, and pleasures that are below him, instead of making himself master of them by looking at them with a generous contempt! O human! You are created with such a capacity, that nothing less than God is worthy of you, and yet you profane yourself and prostitute yourself, making yourself the subject of glory as Phil 3:19 says, *They glory in their shame.*

Ah! If one could express what one understands of it! But the brilliance of these truths penetrated inwardly passes all expression.

Jesus Christ adds, *Heaven and earth will pass away, but my words will never pass away.* All the greatness in the soul represented by heaven must pass away; this is a thing assured. All of the sinner Adam, designated by the earth, unmistakably also passes away. Only one thing exists eternally, to know the *Word of Jesus Christ*, which will last forever, as the Son of God is the Word of the Father, and in Jesus Christ the Word is life and the life the Word. He has no other life but the Word, nor any other Word but the life. Within the Trinity, this life of the Word flows and communicates eternally with God the Father but also flows externally, where it spreads in favor of human beings. Every human must live the divine life and receives the life of this life of the Word. Jesus says he was incarnated for this reason: *I came that they may have life and have it abundantly* (John 10:10). This Word of life subsists and remains always in souls because they may not live in all eternity except in this Word.

> But concerning that day and hour no one knows, not even the angels of heaven, nor the Son, but the Father only. (Matt 24:36)

Only God the Father knows the *day and hour* of the coming of the Son and his generation in souls. In his eternal generation, there was no hour or moment, but in his mystical generation there is a moment that is known to the *Father only.* This does not however exclude the Son nor the Holy Spirit, who have one and the same knowledge with the Father. This instant is also the annihilation of the soul, because from then on God engenders from all eternity the adorable flow of the Trinity taking place in the soul as soon as no obstacles exist between the soul and God by one's own will and propriety. When the operation of God finds no resistance from the side of the creature, this is the beginning with the manifestation of this Word in a pure heart. In the measure that the soul leaves the self, she enters in communication with the ineffable commerce of the Trinity. The Father communicates the Word to this soul to communicate to others. Therefore, she carries the life of this Word to other souls dwelling in annihilation, so the divine Persons make in the soul a permanent residence, according to the promise of Jesus Christ. *If anyone loves me, he will keep my word, and my Father will love him, and we will come to him and make our home with him* (John 14:23).

> For as were the days of Noah, so will be the coming of the Son of Man. [38] For as in those days before the flood they were eating and drinking, marrying and giving in marriage, until the day when Noah entered the ark, [39] and they were unaware until the flood came and swept them all away, so will be the coming of the Son of Man. (Matt 24:37–39)

According to the literal meaning, certainly this means death and the last judgment. But truly in the spiritual sense the grace of the *coming of Jesus Christ* happens suddenly, so that we must allow ourselves to be carried away by its sweet impetuosity or be overthrown and destroyed in the wrath of the Lord. Those carried away by his love, promptly obeying his inspiration, enter, like *Noah*, into the ark of assurance, but those not carried by the torrent of his charity will be consumed by the fire of his fury. People who lovingly belong to Jesus Christ must live with sinners, who think only of sensual satisfaction in the life of this century. These see the interior souls enter the ark of resignation and trust in God without wanting to follow them. On the contrary, they act with amused contempt, but they will know soon and suddenly, according to their merits, either the fire of purgatory in the mercy of justice or the fire of hell in the fury of justice.

> Then two men will be in the field; one will be taken and one left. [41] Two women will be grinding at the mill; one will be taken and one left. [42] Therefore, stay awake, for you do not know on what day your Lord is coming. (Matt 24:40–42)

We learn here that exterior work does not sanctify us, since regarding *two people* who also work in the same job, *one is taken* for salvation, and the *other is left* for perdition. Vigilance to God and gentle attention to his presence keep the soul always ready to receive him with whichever surprise he comes. Those in the interior life continually watch for the coming of the Son of God and even always converse with him interiorly as if he had already come. O advantage of the interior life! When the Son of Man comes, the interior person will be conceived, and his fearless heart welcomes the arrival of the Judge, held in deep respect and distrust of ourselves through annihilation. Whoever in his work keeps attentive to God, always having him in view and desiring only to please him, will undoubtedly be *taken* by the Lord and be carried away by the force of his love. But those in the middle of their work and occupied only with themselves and their interests *will be left for perdition*. No, it is neither solitude, expressed by the *field*, nor the externals of business, signified by the *mill*, that can save and unite us with him so we can faithfully accomplish all his will. We watch like a servant watches for his master to know his orders and carry them out. One should not vigilantly apply one's self to so many useless things and forget God. To know the *coming of the Son of God* who arrives with surprise, we must take *care* of him and *care* only for him, because if we care for many things, however good they seem to us, this will pass so quickly that we will not see it. The Savior gives us two examples. The first example is two persons who are in a *field*. One watches her field, and that one is left; the other watches over her God, and she is taken by him. If we knew the moment at which Jesus Christ must come as our Way to lead us to his Father, we would not watch over anything other than him, because in confidence we think we can watch for only an hour before his arrival. But since we do not know this moment on which all our happiness depends, we must constantly watch.

> But understand this: If the owner of the house had known at what time of night the thief was coming, he would have kept watch and would not have let his house be broken into. 44 So you also must be ready, because the Son of Man will come at an hour when you do not expect him. (Matt 24:43–44)

Those in the hour of death found in this *watchfulness* for God will be blessed. They pass from waiting to a clear and perfect joy. But how much happier is the one already so close to God and taken up in him that there is no need to watch! However, we must always be vigilant and never tire of being attentive until the master takes us away. The whole life of the Christian until he is caught and taken away from God should be a continual expectation, done by a simple openness before God, trying to do all things under God's eyes purposely to please him. If that were so, we would not be long without the Son of God, who became the Son of Man to take us with him into God and make us children of God. If we taught children from a very young age to remain attentive to God, in a very short time they would be led to their end. This vigilance soon wins the heart of Jesus Christ and obliges him to lead those who are faithful to him into the bosom of his Father with all the impetuosity of his love.

> Who then is the faithful and wise servant, whom his master has set over his household, to give them their food at the proper time? [46] Blessed is that servant whom his master will find so doing when he comes. [47] Truly, I say to you, he will set him over all his possessions. (Matt 24:45–47)

Our Lord speaks here of the apostolic state in which the faithful receives absolute power over those God calls him to help and to provide the spiritual food they need. If he works faithfully in this great and holy ministry that God has entrusted to him, O God! what glory will he not receive from it? Faithfulness in helping souls makes us a steward of heavenly gifts and graces to distribute them according to God's order and design. Those who partake of this nourishment feel good about the effects.

> But if that wicked servant says to himself, "My master is delayed," [49] and begins to beat his fellow servants and eats and drinks with drunkards, [50] the master of that servant will come on a day when he does not expect him and at an hour he does not know [51] and will cut him in pieces and put him with the hypocrites. In that place there will be weeping and gnashing of teeth. (Matt 24:48–51)

Christian is the servant who gives God his heart for purification and becomes ready to receive God to dwell in his heart as his own good. God sustains and elevates him. We should apply ourselves to the Lord, who gives our souls the nourishment we need in the right time by employing ourselves in reading, prayer, tending to divine union and holding ourselves in God's presence.

But what happens? Most people though, instead of using the supernatural aids and free will God gives are, on the contrary, like the people of the world and the sinners, who do not want to do what God commands. Instead, they abuse their freedom to commit crimes. But if they use it that way, *the Master will come when we least think about it.* Death will surprise. God will separate them from his faithful servants, whom they will have mistreated either by bad examples or by insults. God will give them the share of the hypocrites, which is hell.

If we do not pay attention to these words, God will put us in the rank of hypocrites. It seems that hell is properly more for hypocrites than for serious sinners because the just Judge hates hypocrisy more than any other sin. However, in this world, hypocrites reign, because most of them want to pass for servants of God rather than to be one. The negligent and unfaithful servant works only when his master sees him, because hypocrites do good works only when they are seen by people.

Likewise, even some spiritual humans live almost as if only people witnessed and judged their actions, and so they try to create a reputation for themselves in the world and try to live without reproach in people's eyes. They would also like to please God to avoid his punishments and to be rewarded by him, but most fill themselves with seeking glory from other people and opinions from the world, so they have only a little corner for God. Almost everyone is infected with this kind of hypocrisy. We save the outside, and we neglect the inside.

> Then the kingdom of heaven will be like ten virgins who took their lamps and went to meet the bridegroom. [2] Five of them were foolish, and five were wise. [3] For when the foolish took their lamps, they took no oil with them, [4] but the wise took flasks of oil with their lamps. (Matt 25:1–4)

All Christians are called to unite and experience the ineffable commerce flowing between the church and God. They participate in the pure and grace-filled interior, looking forward to the Spirit of love and union. All souls can and should aspire to the happiness of becoming the Beloved of Jesus Christ.

To show this, our Savior gives us the example of two sorts of ten virgins, all equally virgins, who aspired to the marriage of the Lamb and presented themselves to be admitted there. They all had, moreover, a similar exterior, regular and well composed, signified by the lamps. Their exterior was the same except for this difference. Some carried *oil in their vases*, that is to say, had the oil and the sacred balm from within, which maintained light and the fire in their lamps. The others, having failed to make the same provision, found themselves without light and fire at the arrival of the Bridegroom. They all desired to go to the marriage feast of the Lamb, the marriage of the church with her Spouse, yet only half of them participated in the marriage. Thus, the actions done by a life-giving principle of life hidden in the interior in God are very different from those that are done only in the exterior without drawing their life and nourishment from within. Those with exterior actions have only lights ready to extinguish. The eyes of the Bridegroom do not look at appearances as people do, but instead his look penetrates even into the most intimate part of the soul. Those sustained by interior anointing always maintain the light needed to see the Bridegroom on his arrival and enter with him into the wedding. For this reason, the external behavior of these interior people is always equal and united without fluctuation, as is seen in those who, being completely exterior, are sometimes like servants and sometimes in drought.

I do not speak here of advanced souls in the state of faith, because even though they experience continual alternations of light and darkness, abandonments within, and strange stripping of the exterior, yet these are not highs and lows. Instead, they always follow the principle in their foundation, which is to be equally content with the state in which God holds them, caring only for him, finding and possessing him in all things, and invariably contenting themselves with him alone, allowing their self to be filled and emptied at will. This conduct is the same and uniform in all interior persons. All the difference is that some go further than others.

Our Savior wants us to see in this comparison that the exterior is nothing without the interior. The interior is the oil that must give life from within to all the actions that appear outside. Now this interior is Jesus himself as the oil of life, as the bride declares when she says to him, *Your name is like an oil poured out* (Song 1:2). To see these virgins in the exterior one takes them all to be similar. However, Jesus Christ assures us that *some are foolish and others are wise*. The foolish virgins have no interior oil yet pretend to have oil so they can enter with the Bridegroom. Just as oil serves to light the lamp and gives it life, only those who have Jesus Christ acting and operating in the interior as the life-giving principle are the souls who can aspire to the wedding feast of the Lamb. All the others will indeed be virgins and servants, but they will never be married until they have their vessels full of oil; to aspire without the interior life to this happiness is folly.

> As the bridegroom was delayed, they all became drowsy and slept. (Matt 25:5)

All slept, the wise as well as the foolish: but how their love, which appeared quite similar on the outside, was very different on the inside! Some slept through ignorance, succumbing to the drowsiness of common souls. Their sleep comes only from lack and not from plenitude. The others, on the contrary, slept in truth, resting in abandonment, and in fullness between the arms of God, waiting for the happy moment when they were to be introduced in the room of the Bridegroom. But their sleep was a rest of love and trust by which they could say, *We sleep, but our heart watches* (Song 5:2). The body succumbs to the need of sleep, but the heart never ceases to watch over her God, and even while sleeping she rests in him.

> But at midnight there was a cry, "Here is the bridegroom! Come out to meet him." (Matt. 25:6)

When the Bridegroom is to come, as long as we watch, he makes himself heard. This cry of joy made in the depths of the soul announces the King of kings, all being returned to God and participating in God, since by the loss of all propriety the faithful lover enters into the interests of the Bridegroom. Also, the same prophet adds that this cry of the King's victory is heard from the bottom of the heart only when he has become the true Israel, that is to say, raised to the contemplation of God alone, beyond all the most pious imaginations and all shapes and figures, even though holy. O who could describe this cry! But it can be understood only by those who have the experience. It is a powerful cry and yet a mute cry; a cry that is heard by the whole soul, and which nevertheless has neither voice nor word; a cry that is a concentration of the deepest silence, and yet which is an assurance that penetrates to the marrow, that the Bridegroom is coming. It is then that there is a great silence in the interior sky, and at the same time we hear a voice crying out. O cry! O silence! O silence that cries out! O cry that is made without noise! And what does this cry say? It says the Bridegroom is coming. O happy news! But what else does it add? That you have to get up and go to meet him. You have to come out of yourself, which is the last step in order to be admitted to the wedding. The soul is no sooner out of itself than the Bridegroom appears.

> Then all those virgins rose and trimmed their lamps. [8] And the foolish said to the wise, "Give us some of your oil, for our lamps are going out." (Matt 25:7–8)

All the virgins *rose*, but their rising differed from one another. Some arise by renouncing some propriety (desire for that not of God) that remained in them, and strengthened by this, they are in a condition to enter with the Bridegroom. The others get up with the effort of a passing servant who ignites in them a fiery desire to go to meet Jesus Christ, but because this fire is not being sustained by interior oil, it lasts only a few moments, after which, far from these dissipated virgins coming out of themselves to pass into God, they sink deeper into themselves. *All prepare their lamps*, which is the common light found in the church. Maybe all have charity but in different degrees, but the charity deprived of interior unction languishes and withers away. Unlike these, the virgins drawing their sustenance from God through their intimate union enjoy continual progress through their constant and durable interior union with God.

The foolish virgins finally ask for oil from the wise. People who have no interior are like this. They feel little desire to belong to God, or rather, they feel that God belongs to them. Because their love is self-interested and seeing that their charity is ready to die out, they ask others for prayers and instructions, trying to share their good dispositions, because they want to enter with them. But there is a long way to go before it comes to that. A state so pure and elevated as that of virgins ready to be admitted to nuptials cannot be given by the creature or quickly acquired when it is time to enter. They need to prepare for it for a long time by the works and exercises of the interior life.

> But the wise answered, saying, "Since there will not be enough for us and for you, go rather to the dealers and buy for yourselves." (Matt 25:9)

This wise and judicious answer should serve as an instruction for all souls of this degree, including as a rule for beginners. The prudent virgins do not want to give their oil, foreseeing that they have been given what they needed, and at this time they should not distribute this to others. Unless one is placed in the state to make an apostolic gift, they will pour out what they need. Not being made a source yet, they will suffer from the diminution of themselves. That is why those who are not in a vocation called to help others should never interfere, even under a good pretext, because they cannot give to others without emptying themselves. They have no mission and place themselves in the wrong by acting. But when one is obliged by their spiritual state to instruct, then they receive protection by God's order, and this grace for mission makes up for what is lacking in their own perfection. Therefore, we need to learn from these virgins not to give the needed oil under the pretext of charity, since it is a ruse of the devil to bring souls to communicate before the time in order to ruin their interior and cause them considerable harm. But also, when

God wants someone to communicate himself because the communicative Spirit of the Word has been given to him in full, it would be an evil and a propriety to want to hold back.

Obliged by their character and mission to help souls, pastors and priests must do so but with this precaution. They need to pray while remaining recollected as much as possible in order to speak in the Spirit of God, drawing what the Spirit says. Ah! If they were used to speaking in this way, what good would these communications produce! But ordinarily, the one who speaks has neither prayer nor an interior full of the Spirit of God. Without speaking or listening to God in his heart, he can no longer speak of God or for God without some anointing of grace to the hearts that hear him. The minister of the Word of Jesus Christ must learn for himself through prayer and recollection what he must announce to his people by God's order. But for lack of this anointing of the Holy Spirit, he who believes he has received something finds himself even more empty than he was. And these communications are almost always fruitless.

The wise virgins therefore gave good advice to the foolish, which was to *send them to buy oil* from those who can give it and which God has established for that purpose. But what happens?

> And while they were going to buy, the bridegroom came, and those who were ready went in with him to the marriage feast, and the door was shut. (Matt 25:10)

All of these circumstances are very remarkable. First, the Bridegroom comes at midnight, in the time of nature's greatest silence when you do not think to hope for such a great blessing. Yet suddenly you see him coming. The coming of Jesus as Bridegroom in a soul sufficiently prepared to receive him resembles his coming at midnight into the world by his birth when everyone was in the deepest silence. This mystical entry into the soul resembles the entry of Jesus Christ into the world at his birth, as was said by the sage: *When peaceful silence lay over all, and night had run the half of her swift course, down from the heavens, from the royal throne, leapt your all-powerful Word* (Wis 18:14–15). Let us understand these profound words well: for in the mystical sense the Word of God comes in the soul when all is in silence, in rest, in the darkness of faith, and in the destitution of perceived gifts, which is plainly expressed by the likeness of night at midnight and the rest we are in at that hour. The divine Word comes into the soul only when the soul rests in silence to listen to it. We must lose our own word to give rise to the Word of God. O happy exchange! Why do we find it so difficult to agree to this?

Souls therefore who are *ready*, being lifted out of themselves, are taken and received: they *enter the wedding feast with the Bridegroom* and are received in God with Jesus Christ, who hides them and encloses them with him in the bosom of his Father. Therefore, the door is closed: for no witness is needed of this admirable commerce and ineffable union of the soul with God. This essential union and the spiritual marriage spoken about in the Song of Songs is the superessential union of the creature with its Creator, which imitates humanity's union with the divinity by the incarnation and of which the church sings with delight: O admirable communion! But let us not pretend to penetrate what is happening in the divine wedding chamber since the door is closed to us. Let the Lamb command if this be opened to us.

> Later the other young women came also, saying, "Lord, lord, open to us." [12] But he replied, "Truly I tell you, I do not know you."(Matt 25:11–12)

These foolish virgins come too late. When the natural life is over, there is no longer time to apply oneself to the interior life, for the soul's hour of judgment has come. All this tells us that the great desires and pious designs that we have for the end remain useless. Like the eagerness of those unfortunate virgins to go and buy oil, this was of no use. For while they were going, the Bridegroom came, and the reunion was closed. We must aspire to the happiness of the interior when we have time! They believed that because they said, *Lord, Lord, open to us*, he would open to them immediately and let them enter. But has he not declared, *Not everyone who says to me, "Lord, Lord," will enter the kingdom of heaven, but only the one who does the will of my Father in heaven* (Matt 7:21). Only those enter who do his Father's will and consequently have no longer have a will of their own. To enter into God, one must be of this kind.

These foolish virgins contented themselves with praying outwardly and asking to enter, but they did not trouble themselves to have the necessary dispositions to be admitted. Almost everyone imitates them. We want to enter with interior people into the room of the Bridegroom, but one does not want to captivate one's senses by recollection or to return to one's heart to seek God there through interior exercises. Whoever asks for this grace without being disposed to receive it will hear these words of the Bridegroom, *Truly I tell you, I do not know you.*

> Keep awake, therefore, for you know neither the day nor the hour. (Matt 25:13)

Through recollection we hold ourselves in the disposition to accomplish all of God's will.

> For it is as if a man, going on a journey, summoned his slaves and entrusted his property to them; [15] to one he gave five talents, to another two, to another one, to each according to his ability. Then he went away. (Matt 25:14–15)

God divides his goods among us according to his designs, knowing our different capacities, giving his interior and exterior talents, more to some than others.

Our principal talents are our capacity for participation in the being of God. He places us in this purpose to the end of reunion with God. This moves us and carries us to do whatever is needed to get there, having entrusted to us the Kingdom within until God comes to take possession of it.

> At once the one who had received the five talents went off and traded with them and made five more talents. [17] In the same way, the one who had the two talents made two more talents. [18] But the one who had received the one talent went off and dug a hole in the ground and hid his master's money. (Matt 25:16–18)

He who has received more must give more, but he who does not give must return even the fruit entrusted to him. To make profit on our talents, we cultivate our interior life in our heart, mind, and soul to return this to God. We exercise our heart in acts of love, according to the degree we are given. We do this with all the vigor and fidelity of our soul until the Master himself comes in our foundation to enjoy his treasure and the gain we have made by using his treasure. All must be done for the Master and his profit.

Yet the person with one talent contents himself with hiding it and leaving it useless. Many do this with their talent. They are not, they say, called to these great ways; they dare not aspire to them. They say they are not called to profound humility and to pure charity. They do not want these great virtues, or consequently, they do not desire the divine union, because that is what they are being offered under the name of the interior Kingdom. Their laziness and infidelity stop them, because they do not want to make use of this God-given talent.

> After a long time the master of those servants returned and settled accounts with them. [20] The man who had received five bags of gold brought the other five. "Master," he said, "you entrusted me with five bags of gold. See, I have gained five more." [21] His master replied, "Well done, good and faithful servant! You have been faithful with a few things; I will put you in charge of many things. Come and share your master's happiness." (Matt 25:20–21)

All perfection depends on this *faithfulness* of a soul in making use of little things, either for the interior or exterior. We use and are content in following the small movements of grace in the interior without expecting extraordinary things. We follow all that is given to us moment to moment, experiencing a little cross, an inspiration, or some contempt. For the exterior life, we do not neglect worldly virtues and must be faithful to the smallest duties of our state. We acquit ourselves exactly of our least employments, practicing good works when opportunities are given to us. We neglect nothing of what presents itself and lies in our power. We will never have the ability to practice virtue in great things if we do not practice them in small ones. Continual opportunities to form lofty ideas of transcendent things will never be unless we lose ourselves in ordinary things that God wants from us in the present time. This is why the Son of God declares, *You have been faithful in small things, and I will establish you in large things*. Faithfulness to one grace attracts a greater one, because it quickly leads the soul to Jesus Christ. When we gradually approach our good Master, he sees us, the faithful servant, doing our best according to our ability, takes us, and carries us into the bosom of his Father, where he brings us into his own joy. One cannot be intimately united to him unless one participates excellently in all his attributes.

> And the one with the two talents also came forward, saying, "Master, you handed over to me two talents; see, I have made two more talents." [23] His master said to him, "Well done, good and trustworthy slave; you have been trustworthy in a few things; I will put you in charge of many things; enter into the joy of your master." (Matt 25:22–23)

The two sorts of people who receive diverse talents also apparently receive the same recompense by equally entering the *joy of their Master*. This teaches us that they begin in the same states that increasingly develop such as servant, misery, renunciation, death, and plague. They have differing degrees, with some more eminent than others. For example, two people have arrived in God, both have entered into the joy of their Lord, but one is much deeper in it than the other. As the talent of the first person was greater than the other, so the fruit that she brought back by her faithfulness is more abundant and of greater worth. So she enters much further into the happiness of joy than the second can. All of Benjamin's brethren were well entertained by Joseph in Egypt, and each had his share of the feast, but the greatest share came to Benjamin. Remarkably, though he was but one person, his portion was five times larger than that of the other brothers. Genesis 43:34 reads, *Portions were taken to them from Joseph's table, but Benjamin's portion was five times as much as any of theirs.* Thus, the annihilations of two souls are both annihilations, but there can be a very great difference between them as to the emptiness of the creature and as to the fullness of God who fills it.

> Then the one who had received the one talent also came forward, saying, "Master, I knew that you were a harsh man, reaping where you did not sow and gathering where you did not scatter, [25] so I was afraid, and I went and hid your talent in the ground. Here you have what is yours." [26] But his master replied, "You wicked and lazy slave! You knew, did you, that I reap where I did not sow and gather where I did not scatter? [27] Then you ought to have invested my money with the bankers, and on my return I would have received what was my own with interest. [28] So take the talent from him, and give it to the one with the ten talents." (Matt 25:24–28)

In these verses, Jesus Christ describes to us the state of an idle soul who does not make use of the talent that God has entrusted to him for the benefit of others rather than himself. God does not ask everyone for this kind of work, otherwise so many holy anchorites who have consumed their lives in solitude would have incurred his disgrace and deserve to be treated like this wicked servant. Even being useless can be wicked, according to the testimony of Scripture, since this servant had not committed any crime to be called *wicked.* The only harm he did was not to take advantage of this talent that God had placed in his hands for this purpose.

To make use of the *talent* that God has entrusted to us is to reach out through purity of heart to the end of our creation. Why are we created? To know, love, and serve God.

But how do we know this? *No one knows who the Son is except the Father or who the Father is except the Son and anyone to whom the Son chooses to reveal him* (Luke 10:22). We must try to know God through

Jesus Christ, abandoning ourselves to his guidance, since *this is eternal life, that they may know you, the only true God, and Jesus Christ, whom you have sent* (John 17:3). Without doubt, through divine light we know you, O Father and O Son, who are one. You, O Father, are truly the principle of your Son; and you, O Son, are truly the Word and image of your Father. Consequently, no effort of human reason can give us this knowledge. We can have this only by *admirable light*, which is faith, which, drawing us from our darkness, places us in *your truth* (1 Pet 2:9).

And how do we serve God? The principal way is in our interior life, because God wants to be served with a *pure heart and a righteous spirit* (Ps 50:12). This righteous spirit is given through faith, hope, and charity by grace. The gifts of the Holy Spirit by the efficacy of his Word are all spirit and life (John 6:64). By the observation of the law, he wants to be engraved in our souls. All that we preach should be the interior, and in the words of Paul, we must *live according to the Spirit* (Gal 5:16).

Finally, we are created to love the infinitely lovable God. But we can advance in his love only by loving him and by making a habit of loving him by acts renewed an infinite number of times until we have learned to love him purely, and loving him in perfect repose, we never cease to love him. But is there anything more interior than love?

We must serve God in this manner and not in another. We use this talent so we can reach the end of our creation of knowing and loving God. To enjoy him by knowledge and by love, God wants our *interior worship* as our first and primary occupation. We may never know or love God unless we seek his face. Psalm 105:4 reads, *Seek the Lord and his strength; seek his presence continually!* Establish an interior conversation with God, and do all things under his eyes, in his sight, and in the pure desire to please him. This is what we are called to: to occupy ourselves with him. We invest ourselves in holiness and make use of the talent. Outside of this, we are useless, even though we work much. Those who love God more are those who work to advantage. Their simple repose in God makes them bear more fruit than those with much activity. Unenlightened people call these interior souls idle, but they are very wrong. All the work of the exterior does not equal the work of an interior life. This activity is not felt with anxiety and confusion! On the contrary, more active than all the eagerness of multiplied persons, interior life is a peaceful and almost imperceptible repose, full of rest. Through excellent participation in the divine, *wisdom is more mobile than any motion; because of her pureness she pervades and penetrates all things* (Wis 7:24).

The fire of love consumes all opposed to it. After that, the heart inflamed by the peaceful enjoyment of the sovereign good communicates continually without ceasing either to act or to love. She acts all the more nobly as she loves with more purity. Mary, who has taken the part of love, according to the testimony of Jesus Christ, has chosen *the better part* (Luke 10:42). *He who abides in love abides in God* (1 John 4:16). He who dwells in God can only be very active, since he acts in God himself and God acts divinely through him (John 5:17). We must not condemn contemplative people as if they are useless and love only repose, since it is not an empty, sterile, and idle repose but a very full, fruitful, and active repose. The person united to the truth of God through faith hopes uniquely in God with all her strength, has joy in her well-being, rests in the will of God, remains abandoned to all God's commands, and subjected to God's Kingdom. This is the contemplative. She who applies herself to love is not idle. She occupies herself only with God in the greatest and most noble of all actions by tenderly working toward the goal of creation. To be occupied only with the world around us is idle.

> For whoever has will be given more, and they will have an abundance. Whoever does not have, even what they have will be taken from them. (Matt 25:29)

God takes away the interior vocation and grace from those who abuse it and gives it to those who have an abundance. In spiritual communications, when a person instructs but lacks reception by the intended person, everything returns to them. Our Lord wants us to hear this with clarity, *And if the house is worthy, let your peace come upon it, but if it is not worthy, let your peace return to you* (Matt 10:13). If we do not have the love of God, we have nothing: and everything outside of divine love is very little. It might seem like we possess much and yet have nothing but the appearance of things. We do not have the assurance of eternal love. The little we have is torn away at death with the removal of the temporal. Even during life, the interior cold communicates itself to the external instead of the invigorating heat of love, which gives vigor to all of life.

This can very well be applied to the state of interior stripping. God always gives more gifts, graces, and favors to those whom he leads by his gifts. He deprives those whom he despoils in order to give himself. The more they are stripped, the more he takes pleasure in impoverishing them.

When Jesus Christ comes as life into a soul by his second coming, he comes there *in his majesty*. This person carries for a long time the mortal states of the Savior, namely of poverty, suffering, infirmity, deprivation, and humiliation; she then carries the state of the glory and the triumph of Jesus Christ. He himself comes into her with his court and all his greatness, and by the life of the Word communicated to her. She begins to breathe an air of paradise and immortality. It is then that he asserts himself and rests *on the throne of his glory*.[3] Ezekiel 1:26 reads, *And above the expanse over their heads there was the likeness of a throne, in appearance like sapphire; and seated above the likeness of a throne was a likeness with a human appearance*. What is this throne? It is the center of the soul that God prepared for the throne of his Son when he *ruled in the midst of his enemies* (Ps 110:2), that is to say, all that opposed in this soul to his absolute empire, *until I make your enemies your footstool*, subjugating them to him, so that he reigns there in divine majesty and in eternal repose.

> Before him will be gathered all the nations, and he will separate people one from another as a shepherd separates the sheep from the goats. 33 And he will place the sheep on his right, but the goats on the left. (Matt 25:32–33)

On the great day of the Lord, he will no sooner be seated on the throne of his majesty than he will render his judgment and will give to each what his works will have deserved. The same happens in the soul as in life, that he exercises an admirable judgment, which is, he places *the sheep on his right and the goats on his left*. He takes for himself all that is his; all that there is in this person that is good, sweet, supple, and pliable, all that emanates from God and all that is marked by God's character, as the shepherd marks his sheep to recognize them. Having therefore thus separated all his productions and all that came from him, he sanctifies them and brings them into himself. But all the production of the demon or those of the corrupt nature are separated, like so many infamous goats, from all that is God's, without there ever being any reunion or mixture. We leave to the demon what is his from the devil or from Adam, a sinner. We give to God what is his. So that after this judgment, nature remains in a total stripping, naked of all evil. Now the purified soul who served as the foundation and principle of all his impressions is taken up again in God and reunited most intimately with his Origin. God has reclaimed

3. Guyon's note: See Macarius the Great, *Spiritual Homilies*, homily 1.

what was his and evacuated what had come from the demon and what this evil spirit had communicated to the sinner Adam.

This state is difficult to bear because the soul perceives that it has been emptied of evil. Having lost scrupulosity, she now does and says things she had not done before. Without knowing how, she has no pain and might even try to force herself to have pain because she thinks she might be in a state of impenitence or hardness. Nevertheless, she cannot have pain unless she does herself great violence or through infidelity stops too long to look at herself. The struggle between good and evil has been taken from her. She clearly sees the deprivation of good, and she can no longer see in herself any good, virtue, or facility to use virtues. God has taken her to a different spiritual place and has taken virtues away from her. God abhors propriety and all self-attachment to created things. Therefore, the soul needs to give all her virtues and glory to the Savior; her deprivation cannot be perfect unless she does this.

It is a hard ordeal to suffer this general stripping by which the person finds himself reduced to nothingness of all good and all evil. Formerly through a love of his own abjection he could still make use of annihilation and welcome the suffering. He carefully hid the graces and workings of God within him. He did not allow himself a useless look or even the search for a single word to relieve oneself. Now nothing is capable of humiliating him or confusing him. He speaks indifferently of everything. What he *cannot touch has become his food* (Job 6:7) without his being able to have any pain or scruples about it. What was before his principal virtue is now what he possesses less. In the beginning this causes extreme suffering because one feels one's loss most keenly, especially when one has been careful and exact in the practice of the virtues. However, if one thinks of representing all this and of imitating those who succeed in it, alas! Into what state do we reduce ourselves? One is instantly rejected from God in such a strange way that it equals the pain of hell. Until then, we must abandon and by a prompt resignation consent to the eternal privation of all these great goods in the will of God so that it is necessary to remain dead to all good, as empty of all evil. But God who is in this soul thus deprived is in this void of virtues as an incomprehensible source of virtues. Now virtues are not given to us, but the practice of divine virtues is undertaken in the very being of God. These works done in God are as Jesus Christ said, *But whoever does what is true comes to the light, so that it may be clearly seen that his works have been carried out in God* (John 3:21).

Such a soul being annihilated cannot humble itself. If she says something that is partly to her advantage, she has no view of herself in saying it. God makes her say it for the good of others, but she says it with such simplicity and disinterestedness that she takes nothing for herself in this. Those doing ridiculous spiritual practices are scandalized by the naivety with which these people explain themselves, taking for pride what they say. God speaks through the annihilated soul, yet they are often corrected, whence it happens that these annihilated people, wishing to convince themselves that there is a defect in themselves, pressure themselves to conform to how others practice the virtues, yet their spiritual torrent carries them away in a different direction. God, however, uses their simplicity to rediscover the mercies they receive through abandonment to his eternity. Paul says this in several places in his epistles and even says, *I am talking like a madman* (2 Cor 11:23), which he was obliged to do. However, do we doubt his profound humility or annihilation? The greatest humiliation for a soul of this kind is to no longer find any humility in himself, after having desired with all his heart this dear virtue of Jesus, who is his love, and after having practiced humility for a long time with all his strength.

These persons speak naturally without thought or reflection. But if someone comes to praise or criticize them, they find themselves questioning themselves, hating themselves more than the devil and not understanding that they could have said these things. What they have said in simplicity scandalizes those who do not know the simplicity of this state. But if what they have simply said scandalizes those who do not know the simplicity of this state, the faithful have no trouble unless they had spoken it by voluntary reflection. However, they have a great joy that God has allowed this. Certainly they never practice the virtues more purely than when, after having acquired them all, they have been deprived of them; now they practice them without thinking of them.

> Then the King will say to those on his right, "Come, you who are blessed by my Father, inherit the kingdom prepared for you from the foundation of the world." (Matt 25:34)

The King Jesus, debonair King, will say to those over whom he reigns absolutely, *Come*, you whom I have separated from the rest of humanity so that you have a particular commitment to me: Come, *inherit* my *kingdom prepared for you from the foundation of the world.* As you let me reign in you, I want you to reign with me. As you want only to share in my Kingdom with me, my Kingdom is yours. You have been *blessed by my Father*, because all that is in you bears the mark of my royalty. The Father has blessed you, so that you will bear much fruit in me. Come, share in my Kingdom. I share it with you only because you fully gave yourself to me.

> For I was hungry and you gave me food, I was thirsty and you gave me drink, I was a stranger and you welcomed me, [36] I was naked and you clothed me, I was sick and you visited me, I was in prison and you came to me. (Matt 25:35–36)

All these works of charity can be practiced either with regard to Jesus Christ himself or towards his members. We can exercise this charity towards our brothers and sisters spiritually and bodily.

Jesus *hungers* for our soul. He has an extreme desire to eat with us on Easter and to enter into an entire communion of his Spirit and states of being within us. If we let him act fully and to communicate absolutely within us, without making an obstacle, we give *him something to eat* and satisfy his hunger. He *thirsts* for our salvation and for the possession of our soul, which he came to redeem. But what does he thirst, O Love? As Jesus said to the Samaritan woman, *If you knew the gift of God, and who it is that is saying to you, "Give me a drink," you would have asked him, and he would have given you living water* (John 4:10). He thirsts that we ask for a drink, so he has the pleasure of giving this. Whoever wants to receive his divine waters, which he offers to everyone, quenches the thirst of Jesus Christ, because he has more desire to communicate his graces than humans have to receive them. This is why Jesus said to his disciples after the Samaritan had received the flow of his graces, *I have food to eat that you do not know about* (John 4:32). This is to say, he loved to feed on other food than the disciples wanted to give him.

We *welcome* Jesus Christ when we give him entry into our heart. It is an astonishing thing that this divine Word, who wants to make us live with his life, appears to us as a *stranger*, and he is indeed so if we do not become familiar with him again or do not give him entrance in our interior. But as soon as we open the door to him, we give him great pleasure in lodging him. He is *naked*, stripping himself of his own glory for our sake. No interior *poverty* can ever equal that which Jesus had. Jesus reduced himself, *stripping himself of all things to enrich us* (2 Cor 8:9). Now, as long as we possess these riches of our own, which he has stripped himself for us, we live in continual usurpation, and we like to see him naked. But as soon as we restore everything to him, and as soon as we content ourselves with total deprivation, then we *clothe* him with the same things with which he had clothed us. He cares for our pains and *sicknesses* to give us health. Therefore, we *visit* and participate in his sufferings to help carry his cross. Finally, Jesus is a *prisoner* in two ways, first in the soul and second in the holy sacrament on the altar, since he is held captive there for love of us. So when we love him in our depths, trying to stay there in his presence and captivate ourselves to stay with him, we accompany him with his sufferings. Or in the church, when we keep him company with the holy angels, who are the court of the King, and we pass hours in adoration and prayer, we *visit* him in the prison of love where his goodness holds him captive.

We can have this same ministry to Jesus Christ when we serve the poor, for he gives us apostolic power to do acts of corporal mercy. Soon though he might deprive us of the means and inclinations to continue these temporal charities, yet we resist stopping these beautiful exterior acts of charity. These ministries are not incompatible with the apostolic state, but we need to be purified from the attachment we had to them to arrive at the apostolic state. Many people stop at this stage in spiritual development, not wanting to depart from what is so visibly good and so delicious in the spiritual sense, yet then they cannot be admitted to what is better without this deprivation, with more spirit and charity in the next stage.

In the spiritual realm, to *nourish* Jesus Christ is to provide souls with his knowledge and love to lead them to this life and his Spirit. Housing him in our souls prepares hearts to open to him with perfect resignation. To *dress* it is to make one strip oneself of sin to give rise to one's grace, and thus for the rest. As many spiritual goods as we do to souls, Jesus takes them all into account.

> Then the righteous will answer him, saying, "Lord, when did we see you hungry and feed you, or thirsty and give you drink? [38] And when did we see you a stranger and welcome you, or naked and clothe you? [39] And when did we see you sick or in prison and visit you?" [40] And the King will answer them, "Truly, I say to you, as you did it to one of the least of these my brothers, you did it to me." (Matt 25:37–40)

There is hardly anyone who knows how to exercise the most sublime works of charity, which belong to Jesus Christ himself, because his operations, which tend to stripping, are not known to the soul who suffers them. At the beginning the soul acts with passion and fervor, but then these acts of mercy turn into a habit. She feels less the fervor but still continues doing these works. Jesus Christ still accepts them as done to him, because her motivation is love for him, though hidden and less apparent.

> Then he will say to those on his left, "Depart from me, you cursed, into the eternal fire prepared for the devil and his angels." (Matt 25:41)

As our sovereign good is to be united with God, also our sovereign evil is to be separated from God. Jesus said to the elect, *Come, be united with me*, and to the wicked, *Go, depart from me*. Our rejection of God makes hell of this world and the next, just as on the contrary, our reception of God makes happiness in this world and the next. *Depart*, word stranger than hell itself! It is like saying, "*Depart*, you who did not want to reach your center and who stopped before the fulfillment of your creation, although I had given you a participation in my being, capable of being reunited with my all! Since you wanted to live in division from me, and to die in this opposition, you will be forever separated from your center and banished from my being; you will even be separated from all beings who have some goodness. Only sin and its torment will be your portion and your life. For not having wanted to give birth to my life, you will live the life of the devil, and because you did not want to burn with the fire of my love, you will burn eternally in the fire of hell."

God our Savior creates us to be united with him to participate in his celestial Kingdom and *desires all people to be saved* (1 Tim 2:4). This is God's joy and happiness. He never wants to lose us, as Ezek 18:23 says: *Have I any pleasure in the death of the wicked, declares the Lord God, and not rather that he should turn from his way and live?* God does not want to lose them, but if they get lost, they are responsible. The great Judge will say to the good, "*Come*, you who are blessed by my Father, because all your works have been done in me. Possess this Kingdom that I destined for you from your creation. I had prepared this good for you since your creation, and I give it to you because you let me act in you to make you worthy of it through my graces." But he says to the wicked, "*Depart* from me you who were cursed, because you want to do only earthly works." The earth was cursed through the work of the sinner Adam. Genesis 3:17 reads, *Cursed is the ground because of you*. In the same way they were cursed in their work, because they did not allow Jesus Christ to operate in them and through them. Only the works of Jesus Christ and those done in Jesus Christ are blessed by his Father, because as Gen 12:3 says, *In you all the families of the earth shall be blessed.*

Then to show that hell was prepared only for the devil and his angels, he adds, *Depart, into the eternal fire prepared for the devil and his angels.* This fire was kindled for the rebellious angels and not for people until they, joining their rebellion, had taken part in their fall. Having sinned like the wicked angels, humans entered into a share of their punishment. The just Judge had not prepared the fire of hell for them, and it had not been kindled from the creation of the world. Instead, through his goodness God had made the Kingdom of heaven for all people from the creation of the world and by the desire he had that all should be saved. But God caused death, hell, and the punishments only because our crimes deserve this and as having been forced to do so by the rebellion of angels and humans. As it is written in Wis 1:13, *Because God did not make death nor does he rejoice in the destruction of the living.*

Human beings have two kinds of faults: one that merits hell and the other purgatory. One is rebellion, and the other is resistance. The rebellious will does the mortal sin. The heart that resists commits the venial sin, greater or lesser depending on whether the resistance is greater or less strong. There is also a voluntary resistance by which we do not let God do what he wants in us and of us, because we stand proudly in our own judgment or in our will. This resistance makes sin venial.

There is another resistance, which is not in our will but only in nature, which is reluctance to allow oneself to be stripped and destroyed and to make the transition to the being of God by the loss of all that it possesses. This is an imperfection and an effect of sin but not a sin. Nevertheless, in order to be exempt from purgatory, all these properties must be consumed, both those of imperfection and those of sin. For no one can enter into God, who is the true Kingdom of heaven, with anything that may have the slightest opposition to him or that is not entirely subject to him, so that God does not find there a shadow of resistance. This would suffice to convince of the necessity of purgatory, even if we had no other authority for it. Purgatory is indispensable so that rebellion be removed to avoid hell.

The one who dies in rebellion is necessarily damned, because the moment of his death unites his sin with eternity and makes him fixed in this cursed state and unconvertible forever. If he were received in paradise, he would still have there the same division that the rebellious angel had and for which he was expelled from paradise: for he would bring with him the firm and obstinate spirit of an eternal revolt against God, and consequently he would put hell into paradise.

The one who dies in resistance dies in that which is voluntary from either ignorance or weakness rather than malice. For every sin of malice belongs to the rebellious will; they are not able to be admitted into heaven without being purified, since this rebellion prevents the full penetration of the Spirit of God and the perfect union. However, natural resistance is a certain hardness and a narrowing of the soul, which prevents the soul from sinking back into its origin and being fully submitted to God. We need for the fire of purgatory to devour both of these resistances, because we have not allowed the fire of pure love to do. If the resistance is strong, it takes a long and terrible purgatory to consume it. No one can judge this better than those who know how much it costs them in agony and death to be purified of it in this life. If the resistance has already been greatly diminished in this world, it takes little trouble to complete it in the other, and sometimes it ends in an instant, or shortly before death, or in the last breath, or soon after, according to whether it pleases God to announce his mercies or to reward the labors and the sufferings that his friends have suffered to acquire such a great good. But however that happens, all resistance being melted and dissolved, the soul remains all pure and fit to flow into God. Nothing can any longer prevent this spirit from returning to its Creator, since it arrived at the purity of his creation.

> "For I was hungry and you gave me no food, I was thirsty and you gave me no drink, 43 I was a stranger and you did not welcome me, naked and you did not clothe me, sick and in prison and you did not visit me." 44 Then they also will answer, saying, "Lord, when did we see you hungry or thirsty or a stranger or naked or sick or in prison, and did not minister to you?" 45 Then he will answer them, saying, "Truly, I say to you, as you did not do it to one of the least of these, you did not do it to me." (Matt 25:42–45)

As the just Judge assures his elect that they are blessed and rewarded because of so many good offices they rendered to him, he says in proportion to the wicked that the defect of these same works is the cause of their loss. However, we see that predestination includes the necessity of good works. The words of the Spirit are full of meaning, that they would suffice to solve any difficulty, if one wanted to be content with them and seek understanding of them by blind faith and entire submission to the truth of God. The Kingdom of heaven has been prepared for all people by great mercy and will be given by true justice to those who have deserved it by good works. He plans and designs both the ways and the end. If therefore we want to enter into life, let us keep the commandments. We will never get there by any other road, and through this way we shall enter it infallibly. The humble disciple of Jesus Christ is content with this theology.

> And these will go away into eternal punishment, but the righteous into eternal life. (Matt 25:46)

At the time of the great judgment, this eternal division will suddenly be executed, for there will be no more ways or middle between these two states or purgatory. But the particular judgment that is given at the moment of death precedes the general and final judgment. This judgment of the sovereign Judge is also executed during all the centuries in this way, that those who die in rebellion will go immediately to hell. Those who die only in resistance are not immediately in the enjoyment of life, although they truly enter life as a child enters life as soon as life is given to him, although he is not unable to use it until after birth. In the same way, the soul enters into eternal life as soon as it receives its favorable judgment, which confirms it in grace and puts it in no condition to ever lose this life: but one can enjoy the advantages of this life before purgatory has finished making her worthy of it. Then she enters not only into life but also into the perfect enjoyment of life.

> When Jesus had finished all these sayings, he said to his disciples,
> 2 "You know that after two days the Passover is coming, and the Son of Man will be delivered up to be crucified."
> (Matt 26:1–2)

The apostolic life does not cease with the passage to the last and natural death. In this small interval, it is necessary to suffer many evils and to end finally with the cross. The original divine must be in this, as in everything else, imitated by its most faithful disciples. Jesus ceased to preach two days before dying, because now he needed to accomplish through the shedding of his blood the redemption of the world, which he had just announced by the outpouring of his word. He exercises imposing silence before his killer, and by the eloquence of his cross he fulfills the oracles of all the prophets. This teaches us that the apostolic life must cease in order to enter into the consummation of his sacrifice made by the death of the cross, after having sacrificed oneself for the salvation of people to the sovereignty of God. Whoever penetrates with anointing this conduct of Jesus Christ finds in it something to instruct all apostolic persons and something to correct the natural eagerness of those who want, without knowing it, to mingle their glory and their satisfaction with the glory and the good pleasure of God.

Jesus preaches only about three years and has little time to do his work. Jesus made few conquests by his prediction, even though it was divine, and backed up by many miracles. Who will be saddened because he does not win souls for God? Jesus is silent, *in whom are hidden all the treasures of wisdom and knowledge* (Col 2:3). The eternal Word no longer speaks. Who will still want to hasten to preach and run for this bishop's chair when the order of God does not call him there? Or run boldly where he is neither sent nor called? "In two days," says the Savior, "Easter is going to take place: I am going to pass from the apostolic state to the consummation of my sacrifice: the cross must end my missions and my life."

> Then the chief priests and the elders of the people gathered in the palace of the high priest, whose name was Caiaphas, [4] and plotted together in order to arrest Jesus by stealth and kill him. (Matt 26:3–4)

When Jesus declares to his disciples that he will die, he gives himself up to death and gives power to humans over his person. His enemies *plotted together* ways to *arrest* him and make him *suffer the death* to which he himself has committed.

Nothing escapes the providence of God: everything falls infallibly into his order and serves his will, even with what the most wicked of men do. The eternal Father wants the sacrifice of his Son for the salvation of humans. This beloved Son wants to immolate himself. Those who are impious believe they will surprise him and make him die in spite of himself. If you opened the entrance to this sanctuary to us, O Holy Spirit, we would discover marvels there that would transport us! Let us see what you please, yet we will still adore and love what we do not penetrate!

When the mission is finished, he is delivered to death, and the power is given to the ministers of God to consummate the sacrifice. No longer able to speak on earth, there is nothing left but to suffer extreme evils for a little time and then to die, as did the sweet Savior. Having finished talking as much as he should in the world, he must cease living in this world.

> But they said, "Not during the feast, lest there be an uproar among the people." (Matt 26:5)

These evil magistrates changed their plans from putting their Savior to death at the time of the greatest feast with many witnesses. This was needed to accomplish the will of God, who had ordained that his Son was immolated to be our Passover and that an infinite people witnessed both the innocence of Jesus Christ and the redemption of world. The one who died *to reconcile to himself all things, whether on earth or in heaven, making peace by the blood of his cross* (Col 1:20), should not raise an uproar among the people.

In spiritual paths, we must not let our sin isolate us from Jesus Christ through the demon, especially in the first and dangerous privations. For then, feeling deprived of sensible forces and without the sweetness of grace, one returns easily to sensual pleasures and nature. Instead, we faithfully stand with Jesus Christ in drought, keeping our eyes on him.

> Now when Jesus was at Bethany in the house of Simon the leper,
> 7 a woman came up to him with an alabaster flask of very expensive ointment, and she poured it on his head as he reclined at table. (Matt 26:6–7)

This celebrated action by Mary Magdalene towards Jesus Christ happened six days before Easter, according to the report of St. John. But Matthew places it here to show what gave rise to Judas's betrayal of Jesus, which begins the history of his passion. Magdalene, already purified by her perfect conversion that the almighty gaze of the Savior had operated and carried into her soul, became like an *alabaster* by its candor and purity, the *precious perfume* of the interior, and divine anointing, because Mary was not only converted from sin to grace but from exterior to interior. She was put first into interior silence and a profound recollection by her excellent participation in the anointing of Jesus Christ. But what is she doing? She comes to restore everything to Jesus Christ himself and to cause this outpouring to flow back into its source. Spreading her fragrant liquid on the head of our Lord, she declares by this action that she recognizes that because everything comes from the Word, everything must flow back into the Word: if humans retain this for themselves, they steal it. As Magdalene is the figure for contemplatives, the *vase full of perfume that she carried* is the figure of what was happening within her. The vase is *white, polished alabaster*, free from all voluntary stains, but although it is beautiful and pure, it is has a small capacity. This vase must be broken, as St. Mark writes, *she broke the flask and poured it over his head* to show that God, who wanted to make a miracle of this lover, broke and began to annihilate her soul to help her power expand immensely in order to communicate with God (Mark 14:3). The same happens to the souls of this character. After their purification, the souls become larger; this new capacity extends in proportion as God wishes to communicate himself to them.

The small stream receives from the source and returns to the source. This is the same with souls occupied with God alone. They receive passively divine communications and faithfully let them return to God. To understand this, we look at the difference between a living channel (which cooperates vitally with all that it receives) and an inanimate channel (which does not contribute to it by any action). Now God has an infinite pleasure in seeing such a soul so passive in all its operations and so disinterested that although treasures of inestimable graces flow through it, it retains nothing of them for self.

> And when the disciples saw it, they were indignant, saying, "Why this waste? For this could have been sold for a large sum and given to the poor." [10] But Jesus, aware of this, said to them, "Why do you trouble the woman? For she has done a beautiful thing to me. [11] For you always have the poor with you, but you will not always have me." (Matt 26:8–11)

Interior people remain with God alone, occupied with God in the interior, so that one can no longer think of anything else. Some torment them because they do not use their time and their grace in favor of the *poor*, for there comes a time when one can no longer apply oneself to works of charity except in duty. Let not these dear friends of God be tormented for this under the pretext of serving the poor; for Jesus, who does all and who judges according to the truth, defends and excuses them all in the person of Magdalene. "*Why*," he said, "*do you murmur against these souls?* What they are is a good work and supremely good among the best. They care for me alone, because I do not apply them to other things. They restore to me the greatest glory that I can receive, applying themselves only to my love, concerned only with love." Then to show how faithful they must be to enjoy his presence, when it is granted to us by his grace, he adds, "*For you always have the poor with you, but you will not always have me.* So take advantage of these precious moments in which I make you feel my presence, and make good use of them." One cannot believe how important it is to be attentive to God and repose before him when he gratifies us with his joy. We receive rare perfume in these happy moments, giving him back joy for joy and love for love, letting him have joy in us without detour or resistance as he deigns to let us enjoy him. As he said to his saints, *My joy may be in you, and your joy may be filled* (John 15:11). If we spread this interior balm on other than Jesus Christ, we lose it. But if we reserve everything for him, he will preserve and return it to us with an infinite increase.

> In pouring this ointment on my body, she has done it to prepare me for burial. (Matt 26:12)

How should this be understood? It does not mean only the burial of his body but the burial of his whole being in souls. Jesus buries himself in them in order to bury them with him in the bosom of his Father. He also teaches us by this that the most suitable disposition to receive him worthily is Magdalene's disposition. He has the intention of burying himself alive within us by communion with his body. He asks us only to prepare ourselves for it by imitating the pure passiveness that Magdalene had. We return to him through a general disappropriation that his perfume gives us. This disposition is the one that most brings Jesus Christ to come and bury himself in our hearts, where he lives and operates in a very hidden but very real and completely divine way.

> Truly, I say to you, wherever this gospel is proclaimed in the whole world, what she has done will also be told in memory of her. (Matt 26:13)

The gospel message in Magdalene's outward actions has been preached everywhere, but there will also be a time when the interior disposition of this lover will be preached. Then everyone will understand and enjoy the advantage of this state. O God! Make that time approach! O Love! In the future, the interior gospel will be everywhere published, known, and practiced.

> Then one of the twelve, whose name was Judas Iscariot, went to the chief priests [15] and said, "What will you give me if I deliver him over to you?" And they paid him thirty pieces of silver. [16] And from that moment he sought an opportunity to betray him.
> (Matt 26:14–16)

There is nothing so bad as a person who, having tasted the way of God, comes to leave it. Such a person makes himself the persecutor of his Master and seeks only the means of betraying and delivering him up to his enemies. He who had been united to God by a great grace goes far away from God by a heavy fall. He becomes an apostate minister of Satan to decry the interior Kingdom and turn many souls away from it. He even becomes a demon, as Jesus declared when predicting that Judas, one of the twelve, should betray him. *One of you*, he says, *is a devil* (John 6:71). All interior people engaged by providence to instruct will experience this passion of the Lord. Those who have done the most good will stir up the bloodiest persecutions. This happens because the interior person is conformed to Jesus Christ in the preaching of the gospel of Spirit and life. Yet there are also some Judases among the followers of the interior person who by slander and ill treatment make him still more like the divine Master. Wonder not, fathers and mothers of souls, when this happens to you. If a fallen disciple has betrayed, sold, and delivered the Son of God, it is no wonder that you are treated the same way by some of your spiritual children, especially since he himself predicted it to you. Expect this as soon as you declare yourself for the interior. He says to you, *If they persecuted me, they will also persecute you* (John 15:20). This persecution is the most unbearable, not only because it comes from an unexpected side but much more because of the insult this does to the Holy Spirit. The betrayer condemns truth as falsehood and charity as hypocrisy. However cruel it is, this must be suffered with all the others, and God will also know how to draw his glory from it.

Jesus is sold for thirty pieces of silver. Misers who cling to the creature sell both their soul and their God for a very low price. Judas sells his Master, which is so vile an action that the prophet Amos says this is to sell the righteous for money and the poor for a pair of shoes (Amos 2:6). But we often sell it for less than that, preferring a small good, honor, and pleasure to the reign of Jesus Christ. Anyone who attaches himself to any creature for pleasure or enjoyment offends God and sells Jesus Christ for this same thing.

> Now on the first day of Unleavened Bread the disciples came to Jesus, saying, "Where will you have us prepare for you to eat the Passover?" [18] He said, "Go into the city to a certain man and say to him, 'The Teacher says, My time is at hand. I will keep the Passover at your house with my disciples.'" [19] And the disciples did as Jesus had directed them, and they prepared the Passover.

This Passover had often been prepared during all the centuries since it was ordained to Moses, but no one could consummate it until Jesus came to fulfill it by himself, filling this with truth from the bosom of the church. Now the time of the true Passover is at hand, because our Passover Lamb is going to be slain for us. Therefore, it is as if our Lord had said: "Not only is the time of my death near, but also the time when I must myself be the Passover, which gives peace and value to all the Passovers that have been celebrated before my coming into the world; and to all those who will be celebrated until the end of the centuries. This is the time when the figure must yield to reality, and the shadow to truth; and where I myself must be my Easter, making myself yours."

> When it was evening, he reclined at table with the twelve. 21 And as they were eating, he said, "Truly, I say to you, one of you will betray me." (Matt 26:20–21)

Jesus *sits down at table* in the evening to begin his sacrifice in order to show that he consummated by this sacrifice all the other sacrifices, all being finished and accomplished in this sacrifice. After therefore having sat down to table, *as his disciples ate with him*, he warned them before making his testimony that one of them was to betray him and procure his death. Why, O Savior! do you tell the future that he will betray you since he has already betrayed you and that he has agreed with your enemies on the price of your blood with a promise to deliver you into their hands? This prediction was to serve the great purposes of God: it bears witness to the truth of Jesus Christ. It was to instruct the whole church and tended singularly to touch the treacherous disciple with some repentance, his betrayal not yet being performed, for there is always some hope for a sinner until he has consummated his deed. Moreover, Jesus Christ did not want to confuse him by naming him openly; but on the contrary, to bring him to penance, addressing his crime not yet committed in order to give him courage to withdraw from it.

> And they were very sorrowful and began to say to him one after another, "Is it I, Lord?" 23 He answered, "He who has dipped his hand in the dish with me will betray me. 24 The Son of Man goes as it is written of him, but woe to that man by whom the Son of Man is betrayed! It would have been better for that man if he had not been born." (Matt 26:22–23)

The Son of God consoles his good apostles. The perfidious Judas knew well that Jesus spoke of him. However, far from repenting, he resolved still more strongly to execute his unfortunate design. His master's mild warning cannot save him from his crime. Let no sinner apologize for the lack of the grace of God, whose help abounds for those who are willing to receive and cooperate with it. But how inconvertible is a heart that has fallen from great grace! Jesus will not stop pursuing him again. Jesus calls Judas his friend in the very act of his black betrayal. Jesus receives Judas's kiss and presses him inwardly by his inspirations. Yet nothing will be able to remove Judas's hardness! Let the ministers of the word of God and of his sacraments neither wonder nor complain that they cannot convert all the sinners they undertake. This example should instruct and console them.

> "The Son of Man goes as it is written of him, but woe to that man by whom the Son of Man is betrayed! It would have been better for that man if he had not been born." 25 Judas, who would betray him, answered, "Is it I, Rabbi?" He said to him, "You have said so." (Matt 26:24–25)

How far the hardening of a heart goes! Everything that should touch him the most serves only to make him even more inflexible. Judas, instead of allowing himself to be enlightened by the advice of his good Master, asks him with inconceivable audacity if it is he who should betray him. The other apostles ask it only while trembling with fear, because they distrust themselves and love their Master. This treacherous Judas asks it with as much boldness as if he did not know that Jesus penetrates to the depths of hearts, and although Judas declares, *Is it I*, he persists in his evil design. O the true *woe of the man by whom the Son of Man is betrayed!* And woe to all who imitate the perfidy of this apostle. Woe to all those who, imitating the perfidy of this apostle, still betray the Son of God in the person of his disciples and his dearest friends! When Jesus Christ said, *It was better for Judas that he was never born*, he said it in view of the feeling that Judas would have in his damnation. Jesus was anticipating what Judas himself would say in his torment, "It would have been better for me if I had not been born." This is a common thought to those who see themselves reduced to extreme misfortune.

> Now as they were eating, Jesus took bread, and after blessing it broke it and gave it to the disciples, and said, "Take, eat; this is my body." (Matt 26:26)

Here is the testament of Jesus Christ by which he leaves us his body to be our food. All that he had done and ordered up to now could be either revoked or interpreted by himself or limited by some condition. But here is the testament and the declaration of the last wishes of our Father, who confirms everything he has established so far; and that which will be authorized by his death and sealed with his blood must itself be inviolable: *For where a will is involved, the death of the one who made it must be established.* [17] *For a will takes effect only at death, since it is not in force as long as the one who made it is alive* (Heb 9:16). Jesus being in full poverty of the goods of this world, and nevertheless wishing to leave something to his children, leaves himself in an ineffable sacrament where he wishes to be for them the source of eternal goods. First, he commands that he be taken and eaten: he does not say only, "Look and worship," although no one should take or eat if he has not worshipped. But he says: *Eat*, making a precept to eat it. We are even sorry that we should offend him if we do not eat it. Then he assures us that what he gives us to eat is his body, which he gives us as a testament. Jesus makes it clear that the bread we eat is his body. These are his last well-declared wishes to accomplish what he wanted to promise us: *to be always with us until the end of the centuries* (Matt 28:20).

Jesus Christ has done us the greatest of favors by becoming man for us. He wanted to leave a memorial that contains the same promise of his love that he reminds us of here. He therefore wants to dwell throughout the centuries with humans as really as he was with them living on earth, although not visibly. This is why he finds a way to perpetuate his presence, sacrifice, and memory, remaining in his own person with men and women, although hidden under the veils of his sacrament. Now wanting to give himself to us, he made his will so clear that there was no room for any dispute. Jesus, my Savior and God, said, *This is my body.* He has already prepared hearts for this doctrine when Jesus says so positively in John 6:53–55, *Truly, truly, I say to you, unless you eat the flesh of the Son of Man and drink his blood, you have no life in you.* [54] *Whoever feeds on my flesh and drinks my blood has eternal life, and I will raise him up on the last day.* [55] *For my flesh is true food, and my blood is true drink.*

If it is not the true body of Jesus Christ or he wanted to deceive us, or he could not change the bread into his body, he was therefore not God, to whom everything is possible. He changes the bread into his body and tells us that what he holds and commands us to eat is his body. To say that he deceived us or even that he used a figure is to do him the last insult.

Coming to establish a religion, would he have deceived us in a principal point of religion, in the adoration of the true God, the unique and perpetual sacrifice, source of the greatest graces, greatest of the sacraments in his own person, in what is the foundation of all our religion? Could he deceive us in things of such great consequence? He had predicted to his disciples that he would be betrayed, delivered over, and crucified, and all this happened very truly and not in image or figure. Having promised them that he would give them his body to eat and his blood to drink, he accomplishes it very truly. And our Lord does not say, My body is in this bread, so the bread would subsist with the body; but *this is my body*. Certainly, the bread is no longer bread, and the entire substance of bread is changed to the body of Jesus Christ.

> And he took a cup, and when he had given thanks he gave it to them, saying, "Drink of it, all of you, [28] for this is my blood of the covenant, which is poured out for many for the forgiveness of sins." (Matt 26:27–28)

Jesus then takes the chalice, and giving thanks, he gives it to his disciples to drink. He communicates to all the priests of the church by a legitimate succession the power to consecrate and distribute it. Therefore, at this same time he ordained them priests, giving them the power to perform the sacrament and to offer the sacrifice of his body and his blood. He therefore assures that this wine is his blood of the new covenant that he wants to make with people. This new testament will be sealed with his blood and made irrevocable by his death. This is why he says, "It is the blood of the new covenant that I make; and as it will be true to say that I very truly shed my blood for many, it is very real that it is no longer wine, but my blood that I give to you. The shedding of this same blood, which is about to take place, will be the confirmation and the tangible proof of the truth that I advance. Let one not seem to you more difficult to believe than the other, since I prove one to you by the other. Certainly, I really give it to you to drink; it is infallible that it is poured out for the remission of your sins." Now, like our Redeemer, he gives his chalice to his apostles so that they may communicate it to the whole church and the apostles accept in the name of the whole church the testament that he has just made.

> "I tell you I will not drink again of this fruit of the vine until that day when I drink it new with you in my Father's kingdom." [30] And when they had sung a hymn, they went out to the Mount of Olives. (Matt 26:29–30)

The *fruit of the vine* is the blood of Jesus Christ. He calls himself the vine, and by his blood the church bears fruit. Jesus is the source of the life that animates us. The sap of the vine spills out when its branches are cut off, also the blood of Jesus Christ must pour out of his wounds in order to give life to all people. But the new wine, which the Savior here promises to his disciples and to all the elect in his Father's Kingdom, is the very glory that he has won for us by his wounds, on which the prophet-king spoke quite clearly when he said, *They feast on the abundance of your house, and you give them drink from the river of your delights.* [9] *For with you is the fountain of life* (Ps 36:8–9).

Our Lord says he is going to finish his sacrifice after having given us this last testimony of his love. Having sung the canticle of thanksgiving for the reciprocal acceptance of this new sacrifice and eternal covenant that he has just made with humans, he ascends the Mount of Olives, the mountain of unction and grace, the mountain of peace and reconciliation, to begin the blood sacrifice of his life and to immortalize by his death the sacrifice of himself that he has just made.

> Then Jesus said to them, "You will all fall away because of me this night. For it is written, 'I will strike the shepherd, and the sheep of the flock will be scattered.' [32] But after I am raised up, I will go before you to Galilee." (Matt 26:31–32)

The most extreme sufferings of the last sacrifice always cause some scandal, and even to interior people of good will. Everything that happened in the Passover, which was explained in Exodus, must be fulfilled in its last passage. The bread of our own being must be changed into the being of the Word, who absorbs into his life what is mortal in us, that is to say, lose in his divine unity what is proprietary in us. The wine of our strength must change to the blood of the cross, and we must suffer the last sacrifice of the utter destruction of all of ourselves, wrought by total death. But this sacrifice, although so perfect, is an occasion of scandal, even for those who are called within. Not having passed this last sacrifice, they cannot understand, and they ignore it until God makes it known to them by their experience. God makes them fall into it when they think they can avoid it the most, lest they refuse it when shown it from afar, or they counterfeit it by natural abandonment in wanting to prevent it.

The pastor smitten by both the hand of God and humans often finds the apostolic life ending. The sheep are separated and dispersed by this blow, but these deviations serve only to reunite them more strongly with their shepherd and among themselves. This scandal brought them together in the way of salvation, and this proof of their fidelity served to purify their love. If Jesus, sovereign Pastor, was struck, should we be surprised that all those whom he associates with his apostolic life are struck with him? Will you complain, O directors, of having to suffer something for the elite of souls in whose favor the Son of God was delivered and crucified? Serve with faithfulness those whom the heavenly Father gives you; and if you come to be struck on their account, do not be surprised either by your blows or by their scattering. All that will serve to give more success to your way.

But after, *I shall be raised up*, says this divine Pastor. "By my natural death, I shall have merited the mystical death for you. By my resurrection I shall have made you enter into a new life; *I will go* and wait for you in *Galilee*, which is the place where your apostolate must begin." Jesus always goes before his apostles, because he prepares their hearts for ministry and because he is always at the head of those who work or fight for him.

> Peter answered him, "Though they all fall away because of you, I will never fall away." (Matt 26:33)

This response from Peter marks the state of a soul who, still in the fervor of passiveness, has not yet experienced its weakness and its misery. However, what we believe to be a great love is only a secret presumption. Until we have experienced what we are, we often make mistakes of this nature, and we attribute to the strength of the creature what comes only from God. How many graces, O Lord, what must it cost you before we are well persuaded of this truth and allow you to tear this venom from our naturally proud hearts to undeceive those who from their childhood have breathed the air of ambition? God alone can shed this light of true humility and sincere self-distrust. No human discourse will ever be able to convince us of humility, because we are so steeped in self-esteem and blinded by self-love, even in the best things! The divine Master assures us that all his disciples will be scandalized by it, and Peter claims to be exempt from it, even though all the others succumb to it. O good disciple, how necessary it was that you felt your weakness! You, who appear the most resolute of all, will fall first and most heavily. The time is already approaching that you will now renounce your Savior and God that you now want to confess at the risk of your life.

> Jesus said to him, "Truly, I tell you, this very night, before the rooster crows, you will deny me three times." [35] Peter said to him, "Even if I must die with you, I will not deny you!" And all the disciples said the same. (Matt 26:34–35)

O poor Peter! What do you think? Your Master swears by his truth that you will renounce him; and you dare to protest the contrary! Jesus has foreseen that your presumption leads you into a precipice, because you have only a passing fervor. If we were only told this we would not believe it, yet Peter's fall provides tangible proof of this. Instead of relying on the love he had for Jesus Christ, he had to recognize his weakness. Instead of trusting in his Master's support, Peter dared to promise faithfulness out of his own constancy and generosity. Hence, this reed broke immediately under him and *will pierce the hand of any man who leans on it* (Isa 36:6). His fall must serve as instruction to the presumptuous, just as his prompt and lasting conversion is the example of the penitents.

This is how so many fervent protests we make to God usually end. We promise not to do certain things into which we fall first. Those that we have resolved to do with more courage are those that we most miss. As much as we have risen by presumption, so have we humbled ourselves by falling.

The sign that these bold protestations spring from a vain confidence is the infidelity that follows them. Our support is in God, and in him only is truth, yet Peter protested against the truth Jesus told him. Anyone who is truly humble and has experienced his weakness does not protest as Peter did. He understands his weakness and knows that if God leaves him to himself, he will fall into sin. *To you they cried and were rescued; in you they trusted and were not put to shame* (Ps 22:5). He knows he will do evil if the hand of God does not restrain him. He also knows that on his own he is incapable of good. The faithful person looks at God in a completely annihilated way, waiting and placing all his confidence in God, abandoning himself to the Spirit of his grace to avoid evil, and practicing good according to God's will. This sincere humiliation delivers us from every trap. Drawing him out of his weakness places him in the strength of God. It was good for us that Peter fell, as well as for himself, so that through him we might learn of our own true weakness.

> Then Jesus went with them to a place called Gethsemane, and he said to his disciples, "Sit here, while I go over there and pray." (Matt 26:36)

Here Jesus trains his disciples in true repose, resting before God while he himself prays. If Jesus Christ, although both man and God, and in a state as divine as one can be, took time to pray, does this not teach us in the most convincing way that there is no state in which we cannot and should not pray? We pray not by rules or in a state of impotence. Instead, we pray by the movement of the Spirit of God. In this divine state we worship in a state of resurrection and renewal in God according to the movement of the Spirit of God. We allow ourselves to be led by the divine impulse.

> And taking with him Peter and the two sons of Zebedee, he began to be sorrowful and troubled. (Matt 26:37)

The Son of God must have witnesses of the sacrifice he makes of himself to his Father. Jesus feels pain by the vivid representation of the evils that will consume him. Jesus's last sacrifice must have witnesses and comforters. How good it is then to have friends who console and be the spectators of this agony! They take part in such excessive pain. Previous sacrifices must be carried out in secret and without witnesses. The stronger the suffering, the more the suffering is pure. But in this suffering, the very power that has supported the other sacrifices is itself sacrificed. Now the man who is its victim is put in pure weakness.

> Then he said to them, "My soul is very sorrowful, even to death; remain here, and watch with me." (Matt 26:38)

Even Jesus with God's strength cannot help complaining of such terrible sadness. We who believe that we have reached the agony of the garden and yet who nevertheless carry our sadness with power are not at the level of this agony. Our sadness is still bearable to us, but the agony in the garden cannot be supported. In this inconceivable agony, the soul feels the full weight of the sacrifice through which she is going to pass. Nature itself surrenders. Finding herself without consolation, abandoned of all both interior and exterior support, and destitute of all strength to carry such a state, nature is reduced to nothingness. For if one had some strength to bear this deprivation, it would be bearable, but here weakness is equal to pain.

The interior person is shown the sacrifice through which he must pass with all the horror of this. The person's powers are dead, because the withdrawal of sensible grace is complete. This unbearable sadness without courage, resolution, and strength and with all the repugnance of nature, which neither wants nor accepts this sacrifice, the death of nature brings about his total ruin. He suffers from the cruelest of all tortures. Jesus Christ accepts the full burden and confusion of sin like a garment of reproach to him, hiding from him all the beauties of his soul. He saw himself charged with all sins, placing him in this agony. The same happens in proportion to a soul whom God causes to pass into this state. The sin with which she sees herself covered and clothed, after having seen herself all brilliant in virtues and rich in good works, horrifies her intolerably. She sees herself clothed in sin without any trace of the divinity that once shone within her. Nature cannot endure a garment that covers her with shame; and truly then, as David had experienced, such a dying person cries out,

> The cords of death encompassed me;
> the torrents of destruction assailed me;
> 5 the cords of Sheol entangled me;
> the snares of death confronted me. (Ps 18:4–5)

This martyrdom exceeds any other martyrdom, because without it, any torture would give life to the soul. The more life he had of his own, the more pain and agony must this martyrdom cost. This sadness therefore cannot be better expressed than by comparing it to a sadness of death, because life is being taken away. Indeed, the life of Adam is destroyed in him. In the destruction that took place in Jesus Christ, he bore the pain of all the sacrifices of his chosen ones and sanctified them all by his sacrifice.

Another part of the Savior's mortal sorrow was to see that very few persons would enter into this last sacrifice, although it had been deserved by all. Although he had been the first to expel all the bitterness of it, hardly anyone would be found who had the courage to follow him. He carried away the pain and the weaknesses of the martyrs, granting them the grace to suffer with strength. For the sufferings of the martyrs have for the most part been vigorously borne. The interior sacrifice takes place without any force of the creature. Only the force of God can sustain and accompany all the weaknesses and repugnance of nature to sacrifice. Thus, the sadness of Jesus in the garden was the ultimate interior sadness and pain. This intimate sacrifice caused him an incomprehensible torment, capable of reducing him to dust, if he had not borrowed the forces of divine power to prolong his martyrdom so that he would end only on the cross. It was even to make his passion more painful that he weakened himself in the garden, suspending the vigorous and sensitive assistance of his supreme part, so that the inferior was abandoned to a crueler torment. The extreme suffering of the cross was accompanied by more force than appeared in this agony of the garden. On the cross, Jesus shows no weakness; he speaks with great firmness and utters powerful cries, showing unparalleled constancy. But here he expresses his great sadness to his *disciples*, asking them to *remain with him and to watch*, asking for their vigilance. And although the Savior wanted to experience these weaknesses to console us when we too experience such a strange sacrifice, he also did it again to make it known to his disciples, as if he wanted to say to them, "Since I will hardly find anyone who wants to enter with me into this sacrifice, you at least, who are those of my apostles whom I have chosen to participate, *remain with me* in this extreme immolation, and do not refuse to bear this state one day. *Watch* with me and remain abandoned for all the rest. In entering into my agony, stay passive to the sacrifice that will take place in you. Keep me company and relieve my pain by whichever part you want to take." O how few are capable of this sacrifice!

> And going a little farther he fell on his face and prayed, saying, "My Father, if it be possible, let this cup pass from me; nevertheless, not as I will, but as you will." (Matt 26:39)

Jesus Christ wanted to experience everything that happens to those who are immolated by such a strange defoliation, in order to animate us by the sight of what he suffered and to instruct us by his example. But this interior example can be read in Jesus's book of life only as we experience what is written there.

First, in excessive pain, Jesus prostrates himself against the ground. In doing so, he offers himself as a sacrifice and abandons himself to his Father's will, but he also momentarily experiences the natural fear of his senses. In a similar way, the faithful experience a natural repugnance against the last and total sacrifice of themselves. We see in this annihilating posture the great sacrifice of the immolation of the soul. This state of voluntary immolation that precedes the sacrifice is more terrible than the sacrifice itself because the soul then receives an impression from the hand of God that makes it discover the pains, the circumstances, and the consequences of the sacrifice. This is shown to the person so that she accepts it with her own free will, consenting to what sacrifice she will be asked to make. Through her abandonment, she accepts the will of God. In the time of the real sacrifice, she is bound and carried away by the torrent of providence that she must follow. People who have not fully abandoned themselves may still experience mortal pain in the awareness of self after the real sacrifice. In this hard experience, nature seems to experience only repugnance. She sees only pitfalls of sand; mortal fear seizes her. Heat comes to her face. Death would be sweeter to her than such a terrible state, because her human nature cannot will what must follow. She knows that this must be her destruction and the eternal loss of that which she dearly cherishes. The foundation of the soul and the higher will can no longer not want this, this soul finding itself without will for anything. Yet the more the will of nature is filled with repugnance, the more the higher will becomes animated in the will of God. For here the will of the human is entirely lost in the divine will. This loss of all will causes the soul to no longer perceive the conformity of its will to that of God, and she perceives only the repugnance of nature. However, she is completely resigned to God, as she is powerless to want anything more than what God wants, not by deprivation of liberty but by a perfect love, which having consumed all its propriety, has united the will to its source and has happily sunk it in that of God.

Second, by these words Jesus Christ wanted to show us the reluctance of nature to consent to its destruction: *My Father, if it be possible*; if it can be done without contravening your divine will, let the chalice of my passion *pass from me*. However, after having exposed some repugnance of sense to his Father, even this inferior will remains submissive, as he declares with these words: *However, not my will, but yours be done*. This shows two things. First, when we enter into some new state of a more advanced sacrifice, God requires of the human a new abandonment. It is as if the person says, "I have entered by the will of God into a state of terrible pain: previously my abandonment was proposed to me in a confused and general way. After having run away because of the repugnance of nature, I immolated, abandoned, and sacrificed myself to carry this same state in a real way. Having abandoned myself in this way, I remain abandoned in this abandonment, being as if mute and dead in pure suffering as long as this sacrifice lasts. If a new sacrifice then comes to be made that I feel that God asks of me, I consent to it, and I remain abandoned there as long as it lasts." It is the same for all the others who follow them. It is not that Jesus needed new abandonment to pass the new places of his mortal life: that which he made at the moment of his incarnation was infinitely perfect and extended distinctly to all that was within him and would happen. But he wanted to be weakened in this place and overcome this weakening by a sensibly expressed immolation in order to instruct and encourage us in encounters of this nature.

The second thing that our Lord expressed by this prayer, *My Father, if it is possible that this chalice pass from me*, was that his interior martyrdom does not end with him alone but that he shares this only with his chosen. One of the greatest torments of the Son of God was to see the ingratitude of humans who would not want to drink this chalice with him and that most would oppose it.

The interior pains of Jesus were infinitely greater than the exterior ones. His passion visible to the eyes of men, although very excessive, was only like the shadow of that which he suffered within to the sole eyes of his Father. He also passes this inner chalice of inconceivable agony into his chosen souls. They suffer much more internally than externally, although the evils that come to them from without are excessive. To suffer from the impression of divine pain, to suffer without consolation, to suffer without support is to suffer as Jesus suffered. This loving Savior suffered at this moment all the evils of this kind that his chosen ones had to endure; and the excess was so unbearable that the Spirit through his evangelists said only that Jesus sweated his blood and was reduced to agony. This prodigious passion and this extreme suffering show the inconceivable weight of his interior torment since even God succumbs to it. The eternal Father here deploys the strength of his arm to overwhelm his Son, and seeing him burdened with the sins of everyone, he causes all the storms and waves of his anger to burst upon him. Nothing less than the forces of God are needed to bear the weight of this arm. All people would have been reduced to dust by the agony that the Son of God then suffered. At this moment, his Father avenged himself on him for the sins of all people and for which his justice demanded full satisfaction. Now those in whom God wishes to exercise pure justice, subtracting for a time the sensible effects of his mercy, share in this state of Jesus Christ; and no joy, peace, freedom, and nobility of soul can equal that which they enjoy through him in the serenity of their hearts, also as no pain, martyrdom, and agony can be compared to what they suffer inside to acquire perfect purity and to take part in this immolation of the Savior. This state introduces us into his consummation of all sacrifice, so that after that there is no more new sacrifice but only some reiteration of sacrifices past and already consummated, which were no longer by the combat of natural repugnance nor by the blood of pain, but with complete peace and perfect freedom, this having become as it were ordinary and natural. After the sacrifice of Jesus by the cross, there is no more other sacrifice but only a daily renewal of the same sacrifice in a very gentle and non-bloody way.

There are three states in which a soul appears to bear the agony of Jesus Christ. First, when she bears her pain in union with that of Jesus, Jesus conforms her to himself, giving her not only the sight of his sufferings but also the experience and the desire to unite with him wearing these sufferings. So this person has a great strength to suffer everything because the sight and the conformity of the dying Beloved supports her, and she is aware of her advantage in participating in the pains of the garden and Calvary. Second, when being put in the agony of Jesus Christ, she experiences the rigors of God's justice but without sight or thought of Jesus Christ. All appears to be the punishment of sins but instead should be seen as divine justice in a strong, saving reality; instead, we look at it as an assurance of our loss and an unjust excess of the wrath of God. Nothing consoles or reassures these agonizing people; and though they do carry a state of Jesus Christ, yet they do not discover Jesus Christ. Third, a state happens much more advanced than all that, and she must have become God by a most sublime participation to carry it. Jesus himself expressed this in his state of agony and death. Only God can carry such an unbearable weight. Jesus was carried into other states by the active and passive fidelity of the creature aided by a powerful grace; and he carries himself in the latter, which soon ends life.

To say what this last state is and the extent of its sufferings cannot be said. All other sorrows are only shadows compared to these, but God carries everything; the more the soul has become divine, the more Jesus is in the soul with the fullness of his states. In proportion as she bore the other two states of Jesus, so she bears this, but there are few people who wear the latter. David carried it, as we have been able to see in the history of this holy king. Paul carried it, as proven in the life of the great apostle. Both, however, carried it differently: David as a living figure and prophecy of Jesus Christ who was to come, Paul as the true expression and faithful tracing of Jesus Christ already come. We can learn from them only the truth and consummate perfection of this state. Paul being there no longer believed anything but Jesus Christ and Jesus Christ crucified. Paul had lost sight of himself, and he was no longer there. He no longer saw himself; he lived, spoke, suffered, acted, no longer in himself but in Jesus and like Jesus. And as much as he had passed into God, so much had he been transformed into Jesus crucified. This is visible in his epistles, but however vividly everything is expressed there, it can be sufficiently intelligible only to those who have the good fortune to experience it also. Let us suffer, however, for the love of Jesus Christ; let us die at all times to ourselves in conformity to his death, while waiting for him to deign to come and be our life, suffering, and all. He does not make us discover such great things, except to pique our desire to experience them, but there is no other way to arrive at the life of Jesus Christ than the death of Jesus Christ. Let us die every day with him by the continual renunciation of ourselves, so that his life flows in us and reigns there forever.

In purgatory as well as in hell, the impression that divine justice will make on souls will be infinitely more painful and unbearable than all the pain that can be caused there by the fire. Two things included in the pain of the damned will be the most terrible torture of purgatory and hell. First, the soul having been created to be united to God will eternally have a central upward slope at this meeting, which is the strongest exertion ever. We hardly feel it in this life, except that we have no real rest or conscious peace until we are united with God by his grace, because we are dissipated by a thousand things that prevent this strong feeling. But when the soul is separated from the body, then having nothing to stop or amuse it, the pain will be with violent passion, yet she will find herself powerless to let herself go, being repelled by God as strongly as she is attracted. If the soul ceased rejecting God, it would immediately reunite with its center with more haste than the stone freed from what held it back descends again to earth. Or if she ceased to be attracted, she would cease to suffer. But both are impossible since the creature was made to be reunited at its end. Only participation in the being of God leads to this reunion, so that if these impediments are of a nature capable of being consumed, they gradually become consumed. As they become consumed, the soul advances towards its end. Her hope increases as her obstacles are removed, until there being no longer any impediment, nothing stops him. This pain caused by the impediment of reunion with God is so cruel that the soul hardly feels the violence of the fire. Although no doubt she feels it very keenly, I mean in relation to the central tendency, the fire is less important. So that if it were necessary to endure an infinitely more violent fire to be freed from this impediment, she would rush into it with pleasure. Now this pain mingled with hope and accompanied by resignation is that of purgatory, where the soul, feeling every day that a few chains have been removed, approaches the divine union. Also, in great mercy, God has given to souls who depart impure from this world a place of purification, because God being so pure, he cannot suffer the least corruption or propriety. If God had not established this place of purgation, these souls would have had to be deprived forever of his enjoyment, which is the eternal pain of the damned. The difference between purgatory and hell is that in purgatory the soul has the hope of getting out and sees its impediments gradually being consumed, but in hell there is no longer any hope of ever leaving, because the impediments there are of a nature that can never be consumed. And this is what causes the eternity of hell and the strangest pain of the damned, because on the one hand, their being tends naturally to God as to its origin and to its center, and on the other hand, God repels them with the strength of his arm, because their being of sin is absolutely opposed to him. This attraction therefore being as strong as the rejection is powerful and seeing themselves forever in this most intimate conflict and torment in their being, they enter into rage and despair, which causes them an inconceivable torment.

The second pain is the gravity of the arms of God and the weight of divine justice; this weight is unsupportable. This overwhelming torrent of divine justice would consume the soul in a moment if the soul were not immortal. The abuse that the person has made of God's design to be reunited with him merits these punishments, which are even more rigorous as they are experienced in this place of torments. God mixes his justice with mercy. God is displeased by the sight of this being with whom he has shared himself and desires reunion but is separated by the malice of the creature. All people can follow the divine light, which has been communicated to them and welcomes participation in God's being. Jesus Christ announced this, as Paul says in Romans, *For what can be known about God is plain to them, because God has shown it to them* (Rom 1:19). If a nonbeliever has discovered in faith the truth of God and been instructed in salvation yet has ignored this, they will be damned to have abused the light of faith and the grace of sanctification. If they have never known Jesus Christ or his way of salvation, yet they abandon themselves to this instinct to unite back with their origin and be reunited with the source, they secretly participate in the grace of redemption that Jesus Christ has merited for all of humanity. They will be guided to God by Jesus Christ without ever having known Jesus Christ. They will flow into God through the incarnate Word, who is the only mediator and channel of communication of God to humans and through whom humans return to God. Jesus Christ became man so that we may hope in him and be saved through him. In heaven we will see the abundance of grace that God has given to those outside the Christian religion. There will surely be those with much divine power. For those who keep the law of nature, live morally well, and follow the natural tendency to his first principle and final end, God will send an angel to instruct rather than let the person perish and will assist a true contrition and a true charity by which he will be justified and saved. Receiving the grace of the Savior before knowledge, he will have joy in him before having knowledge of him. The evangelical law can expressly bind only those to whom it has been announced. This is why God frequently sends his missionaries to faraway countries.

What therefore caused extreme pain to Jesus Christ in his agony was to see so many souls being lost for lack of making use of their being and their redemption. O! If we understood well the nobility of the being of humans, we would not be surprised at the great mercies that God shows to his servants, seeing that what he gave by creating and redeeming them is infinitely greater than all that he adds to them by his graces. All his mercies tend only to make people return to their Origin; and all that is not God himself, however great and exalted it may be, is less than human, less than the capacity he has to possess God by his creation. He acquired the right to possess God by his redemption after having lost it by his fall in Adam. This is why all his graces received in the capacity of humans, however sublime they may be, are bounded and limited, since being enclosed in a human, they are nevertheless sustained in them, and yet they can always receive more. They are included in its capacity. But none of all the greatest gifts can fill the heart of a human or give it perfect satiation. What satisfies is what is received in God himself, when the soul, being lost, finds everything in God, who can fully satisfy her. Then having all God without distinction, and all having become God to her, she becomes so great, noble, and elevated that everything that is not God himself is unworthy of her. So she must go beyond everything by a generosity and an elevation as full of humility as of justice and sustained by the fidelity of love to lose herself in God.

For this reason, whatever is given to the human, however sublime it may be, cannot give him pride as soon as he has known his nobility in God and not in himself. The person is created for something greater, namely to be reunited with the sovereign being. In this state, he can no longer have pride. Nothing elevates him, because he is above everything; and nothing lowers him, because the conviction of his nothingness makes it unalterable. Pride appears to him as baseness, and baseness appears to him as pride. When a soul sees itself in distinction from God, it finds itself having nothing of itself that may be appropriated. If God takes away from her what is God, she would instantly fall into nothingness. She cannot therefore glorify herself, but she glorifies herself in her nothingness and in the weaknesses that are proper to nothingness. And her glory comes from the fact she remained in her nothingness as its origin and has learned to be content with it by God's preference from the all of God, without claiming anything proprietary as her own. Participation in the divine being reunites her with the all, mingled and transformed with God, so that this soul is God and nothing less than God is worthy of her. The world appears to her only as a point at the cost of her immense nobility and grandeur, and she regards it with as much indifference as if she had nothing at all in it. Moreover, *all are yours; and you are Christ's and Christ is God's* (1 Cor 3:22), because as she no longer sees outside of God, she would no longer be able to lose God; since God possesses her being, she naturally associates with the way God looks, possesses, and governs.

Ah! How good it would be for all persons to know their dignity and the great things to which they are called, in order not to amuse themselves with trifles! But unfortunately! Under the pretext of humility (which is a fine temptation) they hide from the great designs that God has placed on them and the means of responding to the nobility of their origin, although God has made them all common! Would to God that all people had that pride of *aspiring to the most excellent gifts* and that by a determined and vigorous courage they tend to their end and despise all the rest (1 Cor 12:31).[4]

> And he came to the disciples and found them sleeping. And he said to Peter, "So, could you not watch with me one hour?" (Matt 26:40)

The sovereign Shepherd speaks to Peter, although he also addresses the two other disciples with the same message. Jesus considers Peter as the one who should be the pastor of the pastors of his church. Through the message to Peter, he instructs all pastors about the vigilance with which they must guard their flocks. We need to watch with Jesus Christ, for nature watches with a tireless fatigue. If pastors were united and bonded to Jesus Christ by great charity and the ardor of zeal, we would see many other fruits of their vigilance in favor of their flocks.

4. Guyon's note: John 17:21–23; 1 Cor 6:17; 2 Pet 1:1; Macarius the Great, *Spiritual Homilies*, homily 14; *Life of St. Catherine of Genoa*, ch. 14 ["And in her purified union with God and the fire she felt within, it was apparent that she had seen into the mirror of her spirit and humanity and had seen thereby the state of the souls in purgatory" (Catherine of Genoa, *Spiritual Dialogue*, 136)].

> Watch and pray that you may not enter into temptation. The spirit indeed is willing, but the flesh is weak. (Matt 26:41)

Pastors must watch God and their flock while praying continually. Sadly, though needing prayer more than others, they pray the least. Most fall asleep in this double duty and fail in both vigilance and prayer. Though Jesus Christ recommends this the most, yet they observe this the least. Pastors must ask about the needs of souls. Our flocks must remind pastors of their duty. Pastors might consider even vocal prayers as too burdensome and become indifferent to all prayers. Jesus, Savior of souls! Who then will teach them to pray in mind and heart with the Father, if the pastors are not doing so? Or how will they pray, if they do not esteem the practice of prayer? If this heavenly bread of prayer as salutary manna is lacking, how do they do this spiritual office? If they persuade themselves that prayer is not needed, it is an abuse. Prayer helps them do all things well. Far from robbing time needed for their employment, instead they receive more skill and an extraordinary gift of expediting more work with more success.

The pastor therefore needs a double vigilance; first to keep attentive to God and the other to know his flock's state. To sustain this double pastoral vigil, he needs much prayer, so the weakness of the flesh does not distract through unstable senses. As long as the spirit remains united with God and elevated above the flesh, there is nothing to fear, but as soon as the spirit turns away from God, there is everything to fear on the side of the flesh, whose temptations may surprise the mind.

> Again, for the second time, he went away and prayed, "My Father, if this cannot pass unless I drink it, your will be done." (Matt 26:42)

This second prayer of the Savior differs from the first, when he prays to his Father that *if this chalice cannot pass unless I drink it, your will be done*; as if to say, "My *Father*, I enter the pure sacrifice that alone honors you worthily. I enter into this. I agree with all my heart."

What is this pure sacrifice? In this, everything is sacrificed to the most supreme will of God, and consequently nothing is reserved. And what does it mean to have nothing left? Everything has been immolated. No one can understand this except to whom it pleases God to show by a test of last stripping or revelation by a singular illustration. One cannot express this until after having known it. The sacrifice of Jesus Christ is however the true reign and a presentation of faith, because even the annihilation of the whole world would not glorify God in a way worthy of Jesus Christ's annihilation. Only the death of God made to God himself is called the pure sacrifice. The imitation of Jesus Christ has an ineffable excess and abandonment, giving our very selves to the will of God, while setting no limits to abandonment, any more than one should set any limits to the will of God or to the faith that one must have in him.

Therefore, at this moment, Jesus Christ bore the sacrifices of all the saints that were all contained in his own. He drank all the justice of God, so that he might distribute this same justice to humans. He swallowed the chalice of mercy. O who could understand what Jesus Christ suffered in this garden! What was the extent of this sacrifice that his Father demanded of him and to which he consented! O the glory he rendered to his Father, and what he merited for people! All the interior sacrifices of the saints were therefore enclosed in this one, and in this sacrifice, the greatest honor that Jesus Christ could render to God, since by him the victim is entirely destroyed and annihilated, the sovereign being honored only by the destruction of all in the victim who is offered to him. So in the purified being, there remains only the being who emanated from God and all the impure things that have crept into creatures will be destroyed by fire.

The sovereign being wanted to annihilate the sin in human beings in order to substitute beings created in his place, constituting themselves for their own last end. Dying in sin, they will be eternally separated from the sovereign being and united with another being of fire and their torment. For not wanting to leave the creature for the Creator, the continual presence of the creature and the absence of God will be their hell. They will be separated from God and the union of love to which they were called, and also their own being, which cannot subsist without the concurrence of God and dependence on God. Instead, they will be united with creatures to be tormented by them and separated from the support and consolation of the same creatures. So the creatures will serve only to increase their torment.

To the contrary, the blessed, for having separated themselves from all beings in order to give rise to the supreme being of God, will be absorbed in this sovereign being and separated from all beings as much as they can be. Yet united together in God with a height of delight, these created beings united to their all, they will all be together with God by a unity of being, although each of them remains in his true distinction, but a distinction which no longer causes multiplicity, because everything is united in unity. This bond of conformity and love unites them very intimately to God as beings of an infinity united to the Being of beings. Everything is then consumed in unity; as the Son of God asks his Father: *Let them all be one*, says he, *as we are one and be united in one* (John 17:21–23).

> And again he came and found them sleeping, for their eyes were heavy. [44] So, leaving them again, he went away and prayed for the third time, saying the same words again. (Matt 26:43–44)

These apostles had their eyes heavy with sleep, that is to say, their minds were still heavy, so that they could not understand the great mysteries that their Master designated by his repeated prayer and by his comings and goings. Jesus returns to them as many times as he departs to pray, as if to share with them the triple mystery that is happening in him. This triple prayer is extremely mysterious, and it relates to the three sacrifices through which we must pass to arrive at divine unity. Jesus Christ had three sacrifices to make and offers three new abandonments in the garden for himself and for his faithful friends.

The first sacrifice separates us from all creatures, which he accepts with abandon, as if banished from all beings. If he was attached to this sacrifice, he could not go through the remaining two sacrifices to God alone. In the second sacrifice we leave our own self without looking for ourselves in anything. We consent to our destruction for the interests of God. In the third sacrifice we sacrifice God to God. After having renounced all things and leaving himself for love of God, he still must sacrifice God to God.

Jesus Christ made these three sacrifices in the garden of Gethsemane. First, he was abandoned in regard to all beings and creatures. Jesus Christ's disciples left him, and he lived without care from others. All the universe seemed to conspire against him. Whoever is put in this sacrifice of separation from creatures finds all people contrary. Everyone bands together against him. If some people still dare to declare themselves in his favor, they often even contribute to the increase of his evil by surprising providence. Thus, our Lord saw himself abandoned in his holy passion without consolation from others. There remained to him only those who were to torment and afflict him. All the creatures rejected him together, shouting at him, *Crucify him*!

Second, he was separated from himself by a double death, all the more strange as nothing in him was opposed to God. Instead, he was united with God, yet he died a double death, one to God and the other to nature. Jesus enjoyed the beatific vision and sovereign happiness, but his death was not according to nature, all the more so as immortality was due to him by reason of the hypostatic union. So he died because he wanted to, and he gave himself up of his own free will: *Jesus said, No one takes it from me, but I lay it down of my own accord. I have authority to lay it down, and I have authority to take it up again* (John 10:18). It required the power of a God to put to death the author of life, for he had life in himself. The essential life communicates life, but in his reception of death in his bosom, he communicated resurrection and life. Therefore, O Jesus, in order to die you stopped for a few hours the heart of your communicative life for our life. Otherwise, you could not have died, since abundant life flowed in you from its source! And when you gave up your spirit, the tombs opened, because you communicated life to death. Jesus, therefore, by this separation from himself made the greatest and most severe sacrifice that ever was or that is even possible, since his death was against nature and he had within him essential life. The death of Jesus Christ must have caused him infinite and almost incomprehensible torment, since it had to tear his life from him by doing violence to God and nature. O death of the Savior who gave us life! You have indeed been the death of death and the taste of hell.

The third sacrifice was that of abandonment by God. It is the most terrible of all and the one that consumes all the others, because it is the most extreme way of suffering to be put in all the weakness of nature, overwhelmed by the excess of the greatest evils and deprived of all perceived consolation and support, even from the side of God. In truth though, God then sustains with more force, his grace being present. So Jesus Christ cried out on the cross about his abandonment. What! Jesus, hypostatically united to the divinity, could he be abandoned from divinity, he who could not even be separated from it? However, he wanted to suffer this abandonment and how the excess of his love for his Father and people led him to immolate himself. The divine power found the means to make him experience all its rigor, refusing the senses and the lower part the help of the divinity. This abandonment is so appalling that it cannot be understood and presents the most terrible of all trials.

But Jesus Christ experienced this pain in his body, as well as in the lower and upper parts of the soul and spirit. For he said with truth that his soul was *sad unto death*. And the Holy Spirit caused the evangelist to write properly that Jesus was *sad and afflicted* as a pain of the mind and a torment in his soul. Truly this could have been done only by an unheard-of marvel that will forever be unparalleled, since the soul of Jesus Christ, being blessed and enjoying glory, was incapable of pain. But the Son of God dispenses at this point the most inviolable laws of beatitude so that his soul, without leaving its blessedness, can experience our misery and feel for a few moments the agony of sadness and an abandonment harsher than death. And he prevented throughout his immortal life the flow of the glory of the soul upon the body, so he might suffer and die. He also stopped the glorious blessedness of the soul that would prevent him from suffering. The Son of Man's agony of spirit had to be part of his passion.

The three abandonments, or the three sacrifices, of which we have spoken above, are united in the last, which is the pure and sovereign sacrifice. The three times of self-sacrifice have some connection with each other but yet also differ from one another.

Our soul may also experience these three sacrifices. The first occurs when we pass from multiplicity to simplicity and from good activity to passivity. We then immolate our own operations and separate ourselves in some way from ourselves, depriving ourselves of the taste and support that we found in our actions. This is a separation from the creature done with strength and gentleness without experiencing any abandonment of God. On the contrary, we are significantly supported by God's assistance.

The second sacrifice of the soul is made upon leaving the passiveness of light, or the sustained self, to enter into naked faith and the mystical state. In this passage we are still experiencing the three sacrifices, first the separation from creatures, which stimulates crosses. In this second sacrifice, we experience the separation from oneself, not only in what concerns one's own operations but also in what belongs to the natural powers, both acquired and infused. This is indeed a harsher separation than that of one's own operations, as it is much more like losing one's hand than any action of writing or painting with the same hand. They bring about the death of powers, as the first had brought about the death of his own actions. Third, we experience the abandonment of God, who no longer provides any visible help. All are hard to bear, but this last sacrifice is that of total loss and perfect annihilation, where the human loses not only his own actions, not only the use of his powers and all that belongs to them, but also all life, all subsistence, and all being as if it were his. Deprived of the support of all beings, no longer does anyone serve as support for him. For to the measure of his annihilation, he sees them all fall away. In proportion to being lost in God, he becomes lost himself. Far from finding support, everything disappears, and he can have a fixed gaze only on God. This man, thus consumed by the last sacrifice, is consciously separated from all created beings, and they serve him only as a weight. He is moreover deprived of himself, no longer having any correspondence with himself, and feeling himself failing to such an extent that the separation of himself from himself is entirely complete. The superior part disappears from his eyes, and the interior part remains separated and outside of itself, as if it no longer had its part. All good practices and dear virtues are torn from him. Everything that was proper to him is so taken away from him that not he is banished and rejected not only from all beings but also from himself. This beginning of sorrows begins the prelude of the most terrible of sacrifices, abandoned by God, not only with regard to the seen assistance and support but also for hidden support known by its good effects as when a person, although stuck in dryness and bitterness, still produces good actions by the force of a secret grace. But here celestial help appears neither in its principle nor in its fruits. This person is struck by God to his very center, separated and rejected from the Lord, and abandoned to the rage of nature. After having been deprived of sensual satisfactions, he cannot even taste spiritual ones. Losing all support, he suffers, which happens only when the superior part is united to God, but he knows nothing about it. However intimate the union of the upper part may be, it in no way prevents the rigor of the loss, especially as to the inferior part. The superior part of the soul suffers especially when he is still in agony before his total death. The soul finds itself here as the vomit of God. And he recognizes that whichever disaster happened to him in previous states, God supported and consoled him, but now he withdraws his hand so much that nature abandoned to itself falls into rage and despair. By this happy failure of self, the soul is put in the final disposition to pass entirely into God. The second step may be confused with the third stage. Resurrection occurs after death, and the soul can be transformed after it has left itself.

These are the three sacrifices that Jesus Christ made for us in the garden of olives, until he made his sacrifices himself within us, as has been said so many times.

> Then he cometh to his disciples, and saith to them, "Sleep ye now and take your rest; behold the hour is at hand, and the Son of man shall be betrayed into the hands of sinners. 46 Rise, let us go: behold he is at hand that will betray me." (Matt 26:45–46 Douay-Rheims)

First, Jesus commanded his disciples to stay awake, and now he tells them to sleep. He spoke to them that the traitor was approaching to carry out his attack and they should be alert, but now he says to rest. This expression of the Son of God has a great spiritual meaning. When the sacrifice will be performed, the soul must gently acquiesce in the will of God. Yet simultaneously we must get up and come out in faith, to go and consummate this same sacrifice in the manner that providence commands.

Why is this way needed? It is because *the Son of Man shall be betrayed into the hands of sinners.* O to comprehend these things! In the sacrifices of our time, when we are in God and conformed to Jesus Christ, we will be delivered into the hands of sinners, so that it seems that our sinful body is sold to sinners. The word of the Son of Man shows us that in our selfishness that comes from being human, we are sold to sinners, so that we are consummated and receive the divine flowing into God.

The divine Master addresses all this with his disciples, because they will participate in his sacrifice. Exempting them from other sacrifices, he destroys their propriety the moment he dies on the cross, making them die mystically. Remaining in this state of mystical death as in a tomb, they resurrect through the Holy Spirit, giving them a new life in God, an apostolic life. But this anticipated grace will cost them dearly in many works and sacrifices during the ministry of their apostolate and finally martyrdom. The Son of God, who wanted to carry all these states as far as he was capable, could not be sold to sin like other men who pass through this sacrifice because of his divinity and the hypostatic union. Paul himself testifies to having experienced, *For we know that the law is spiritual, but I am of the flesh, sold under sin* like other people (Rom 7:14). Sold to sinners, sinners exercised all their cruelty on Jesus's body, while his soul was plunged into the torrent of bitterness and he drank from the torrent of abjection and agony before raising his head in the height of his glory. Psalm 110:7 reads, *He will drink from the brook by the way; therefore, he will lift up his head.*

> While he was still speaking, Judas came, one of the twelve, and with him a great crowd with swords and clubs, from the chief priests and the elders of the people. [48] Now the betrayer had given them a sign, saying, "The one I will kiss is the man; seize him." (Matt 26:47–48)

The bearable betrayal to be sold by an enemy cannot be compared to the betrayal of a friend, a confidant of the heart, to whom we have given much. To be further betrayed, sold, and delivered by a disciple to whom one had entrusted one's secrets and with whom one acted simply, and by a child prepared for the inheritance, is unbearable. This betrayal of the sensitive heart was needed in the passion of Jesus Christ. Those in whom Jesus Christ expresses himself and are most conformed to him will also know this betrayal. Those to whom they have done much good, their disciples and spiritual children, will accuse, betray, sell, and hand them over.

But why come with a gang of people to take a defenseless Lamb? This Lamb desires to give himself to death. This crowd rushes with force and authority to overwhelm simple people who are not defending themselves. Princes, magistrates, people eminent in the church by their character or by the rumor of their piety use their power to persecute under specious pretexts these souls who have become Jesus Christ. And how do we treat them? As their Master was treated. Judas betrays him with a kiss, trying by this artifice to make him fall into the trap set for him. In the beginning of these relationships, there are only praises and caresses, protests of esteem and friendship, as the artful spirit has learned to express. Then they charge them with blows and mercilessly deliver them either to mockery or to the bad treatment of superiors. The disciples of the Savior walked by his purest ways and now become accused of criminality.

These people thus delivered must be faithful to suffer everything like their divine model, without murmur, complaint, or resistance, but abandoning to God their cause, which is actually God's cause.

We must trust the will of providence, which uses these bad, passionate, and prejudiced dispositions of people to make these children of God similar to his only Son. If they are asked the reason for their conduct and doctrine, or a question of supporting the interior ways of prayer, let them answer according to the talent they have received. But as for themselves, let them suffer in silence with Jesus Christ.

> And he came up to Jesus at once and said, "Greetings, Rabbi!" And he kissed him. (Matt 26:49)

O infamous kiss of the disciple! O incredible charity of the Master in suffering it! A passion as atrocious and a persecution as unjust as that inflicted on Jesus could not begin with an action less black than this betrayal by an apostate apostle who with a sacrilegious kiss betrays his Master and King, his Savior and God. But how many Judases are there still who kiss Jesus Christ to betray him or who commune with his flesh and blood with sin in their hearts? Or who under the color of some piety approach the sacraments full of hatred and venom against their brothers and who would not fail to deliver their Savior to his passion, taking revenge on their brothers and sisters, if they find any opportunity; who notwithstanding vain protests of charity and zeal, tear others apart by extreme slander, a life that they can never restore to them, like the perfidious Judas once he delivered Jesus to them could no longer take his Master out of the hands of the mob?

> Jesus said to him, "Friend, why are you here?" Then they came up and laid hands on Jesus and seized him. (Matt 26:50)

O sweet word! To call a traitor a *friend*, now the most criminal of all men. He was truly your friend, O Lord, since it satisfied your desire to suffer. Would Jesus have treated him as a friend to receive his kiss, invite him to convert, and go and die to earn him eternal salvation, if Jesus had wanted to save himself? This is a big lesson for us. Let us consider those who cause us suffering our best friends. Jesus truly regarded them as such; and he as infallible truth did not speak against his heart. Ah! If we would change our language! We would consider as our best friends those who give us the hardest crosses, and as our true enemies those who are an occasion for us to fall.

> And behold, one of those who were with Jesus stretched out his hand and drew his sword and struck the servant of the high priest and cut off his ear. [52] Then Jesus said to him, "Put your sword back into its place. For all who take the sword will perish by the sword. [53] Do you think that I cannot appeal to my Father, and he will at once send me more than twelve legions of angels?" (Matt 26:51–53)

Jesus Christ allows his disciple in his heated zeal to put his hand to the sword. This shows that we too must sometimes undertake the defense of God's cause with the sword of his word. But immediately Jesus Christ makes him put the sword back, because to defend such a good cause must be through the movement of the Holy Spirit without coming to extreme violence, bitter disputes, or scandals. We should listen peacefully to others so that everyone can understand what is said.

For all who take the sword will perish by the sword. All those who love division and war will certainly perish by the sword. The Son of God also teaches us that he does not need the help of creatures to support his cause and that prayer alone is more effective than all dignitaries. Let us therefore not hurry to convince those who are rebelling against the light by dint of reasoning and disputes. If they do not surrender to simple authority, they must be left to God, and we pray for secret instruction by angels. Colossians 4:3 says, *Pray also for us, that God may open to us a door for the word, to declare the mystery of Christ, on account of which I am in prison.*

> The Son of Man goes as it is written of him, but woe to that man by whom the Son of Man is betrayed! It would have been better for that man if he had not been born. (Matt 26:54)

This passage confirms what has already been said: the Old Testament is the figure of Jesus Christ, and in him and through him all prophecies are accomplished. Jesus Christ points this out to his disciples many times. Luke 24:45 reads, *Then he opened their minds to understand the Scriptures.* Most of us resist entering into the interior states of Jesus Christ because we do not understand the marvelous relationship between the Old and New Testaments or between the life and states of Jesus Christ, and what is interior and exterior in both. If we do not know the interior states of Jesus Christ, we do not know the interior states of the Christian. If we would read the Scripture without preoccupation and humbly listen to the intelligence that God gives us through prayer more than study, we would soon see all error and dispute end. Give, O uncreated Wisdom, your blessing to this work undertaken only to give more light to the Christian interior, showing it in many ways under the clear clouds of your Scriptures!

> At that hour Jesus said to the crowds, "Have you come out as against a robber, with swords and clubs to capture me? Day after day I sat in the temple teaching, and you did not seize me. 56 But all this has taken place that the Scriptures of the prophets might be fulfilled." Then all the disciples left him and fled. (Matt 26:55–56)

Jesus justifies here his quality as a true Shepherd, chosen before all the centuries: *Have you come out as against a robber, with swords and clubs to capture me?* Some had usurped the leadership of the flock. Jesus continues as if he had said, "As if I had come to drink the milk of the sheep, eat their flesh, and clothe myself in their wool, I, who only came to water them with my blood, to feed them with my flesh, and clothe them with myself. *Day after day I sat in the temple teaching*, acting as a good Shepherd and feeding the sheep with my word. I was with you, and for you I carried out this office, yet you have not taken me! Did you believe, when I taught you, that I was the true Pastor? If you believed in it, why do you not still believe in my truth now, or if you thought me a usurper, why would you not be angry with me? *But all this has taken place that the Scriptures of the prophets might be fulfilled.* Which was, that if I was delivered to death by my own sheep, I was there only because I wanted it and when I wanted it." O ravening wolves! It is not by your force that you slaughter the Pastor. Otherwise, you would have done it as soon as he appeared among you; but it is the will of the Father who delivers him to you, according as it had been written in the eternal book of his word. You have not become more powerful than you were when he conversed freely among you. But at this same hour, which for him is the hour to consummate his sacrifice, Luke 22:53 reads, *But this is your hour, and the power of darkness.*

Then all the disciples left him and fled. Peter followed him again later, as will be said below, and John, too, as we will see elsewhere, but at the moment of their master's capture, full of fear, they all fled. Even with this evidence of the fragility of human, we have difficulty being convinced. *Strike the shepherd, and the sheep will be scattered; I will turn my hand against the little ones* (Zech 13:7). Jesus Christ himself applied this prophecy to his passion. His apostles see themselves only as individuals but soon will see themselves filled with the power of the Holy Spirit. God will stretch out his hand on these little ones to gather and join them to their Leader. They will not perish; this weakness will give more entry to the strength of God within them. The Son of Man had to be abandoned by his own children, whom he acquired with a special gift, and by those he had come to save.

Apostolic people will also experience this general neglect at a time of the greatest persecution. Some renounce them openly, others move aside, some conceal, others remain silent and follow them only from afar. But when the time has come, and these gaps that God has permitted for his purposes must end, everything is reunited. Ah! How beautiful it is to see this place of the passion of the Son of God retraced in several places! Ah! How sweet it is to suffer it for the love of him!

> Then those who had seized Jesus led him to Caiaphas the high priest, where the scribes and the elders had gathered. (Matt 26:57)

To be considered guilty by the leaders who have the authority of God in their hands, who would not tremble? This usually happens to the most intimate friends of Jesus Christ, who will be condemned by the prelates, formidable by their divine power. This misunderstanding happens because we believe passionate or poorly informed people. Then we wage war against Jesus Christ without knowing him, under the pretense of supporting the interests of Jesus Christ. How many of these mistakes will come to light; who will see all things according to the truth? However, let those who suffer this suffer it while faithfully carrying a state that the King of justice and the truth itself has deigned to carry. If the Son of God had only been condemned by the populace, it would not have made much of an impression. But having been delivered to death by those who are the greatest, most illustrious, and most holy, this is what is terrible and authorizes the reputation of being guilty. Such persecution aroused on his servants shows their just condemnation and describes them strangely. But how good it is to drink this chalice with the delights of God and in imitation of Jesus his Son!

> And Peter was following him at a distance, as far as the courtyard of the high priest, and going inside he sat with the guards to see the end. (Matt 26:58)

Peter followed Jesus from afar, because fear led him to move away from his Master yet not renounce him. Moving away from Jesus is the first step to falling into sin. Ah! If we knew how disastrous this distance is, we would be careful not to stay there! To stay away from the source of all good pushes us toward the source of all evil. As soon as we begin to move away from Jesus Christ, everything goes wrong, and we tend towards perdition.

> Now the chief priests and the whole council were seeking false testimony against Jesus that they might put him to death, [60] but they found none, though many false witnesses came forward. At last two came forward [61] and said, "This man said, 'I am able to destroy the temple of God, and to rebuild it in three days.'" (Matt 26:59–61)

These wicked and unjust judges wanted to condemn Jesus with some shadow of justice, so that they would not be blamed for having put him to death unjustly. They look for false witnesses to cover their malicious design. But no matter how much care they take, they find nothing convincing. We believe we are well protected from the blame of an unjust persecution when we cover it with some good pretext. A number of people generally accuse servants of God and cry out unanimously against them but cannot convince others of something in particular. All that Jesus Christ is accused of here is having said a truth: namely, that his body, which is the *temple of God*, since *all the fullness of his divinity remains in him bodily*, would be destroyed of his own free will and that he would rebuild it after three days by his resurrection (Col 2:9). A vain and weak accusation comes forth. This weak accusation, even given the false and clever spin, does not judge that the testimony of these two witnesses agrees, so there is no reason to condemn him.

God tests his friends, whom he wants to make like his Son. People of authority use their zeal to look for ways to condemn others. But not finding any positive reason to condemn, certain leaders exaggerate things in a bad sense and say others are monsters.

> And the high priest stood up and said, "Have you no answer to make? What is it that these men testify against you?" [63] But Jesus remained silent. And the high priest said to him, "I adjure you by the living God, tell us if you are the Christ, the Son of God." [64] Jesus said to him, "You have said so. But I tell you, from now on you will see the Son of Man seated at the right hand of Power and coming on the clouds of heaven." (Matt 26:62–64)

Our divine Master gives us an exemplary example of how we are to suffer calumnies without complaining or justifying ourselves and in profound silence. But, O my King! being adjured by the living God, you must respond, and moreover you tell the truth! He is also ready to die for having remained silent in his abasement. O exterior and interior silence in the crosses! You sanctify them all; you give the greatest merit to suffering. But how terrible this silence is, how hard it is to bear! Nothing shows better that nature is tamed in a soul and that pure grace predominates there than this immobility in the midst of slander and persecution by which one does not open the mouth of the body to defend oneself against humans, or that of the heart to complain about it to God, and much less to ask God to be delivered from it! Where do we find people who carry their crosses without complaining about it and without seeking every means to justify themselves? Without accusing those who cause them and without trying to appear innocent? We even make it a principle of conscience to defend ourselves and support our reputation. However,

Jesus Christ is silent and does not respond a single word. Doubtless there is no danger for us in imitating him.

But as soon as the high priest instructs him to speak and adjures him to do so by God himself, Jesus does so to mark the obedience that we owe to the prelates of the church. We must stop looking at the injustice they can commit and consider only their dignity, because although they may be unjust in their judgments, still being our legitimate superiors, they have the right to command us. Jesus Christ therefore declares the truth, neither denying nor disguising it. He, the humblest of all the children of human beings and the model of meekness, declares who he is.

> Then the high priest tore his robes and said, "He has uttered blasphemy. What further witnesses do we need? You have now heard his blasphemy. [66] What is your judgment?" They answered, "He deserves death." (Matt 26:65–66)

To have a poisonous heart is a malignant reality, because it can never be satisfied or escape its malice. The high priest seeks to surprise Jesus in order to condemn him. Jesus is silent; and people complain about it. They ordered him to tell the truth, and he said it. They then accused him of blasphemy, and they judged him worthy of death. If one remains silent, one is considered guilty. If one is questioned about the truth and one simply admits it, one is treated as proud and a blasphemer. Whatever one may do, one is always condemned. *Help us, Lord! in our afflictions because the salvation we hope for from man is only vanity. It is in God alone that we put our trust* (Ps 60:11–13). We must leave ourselves to God and always do our duty. We remain silent in slander when nothing compels us to speak. We break the silence when the glory of God is at stake and there is a need to speak.

> Then they spit in his face and struck him. And some slapped him,
> [68] saying, "Prophesy to us, you Christ! Who is it that struck you?"
> (Matt 26:67–68)

To condemn a man to death and still insult him is against all humanity. However, this is what is done to Jesus Christ, and after him to all those who bear his dominions. The King of heaven and the God of glory is mistreated excessively to please the most unjust of men! The guards received the leader's approval to hit and insult this innocent Lamb. They overwhelmed him like wolves, throwing themselves on him to devour him. However harsh all this was to the man, you were truly peaceful, O

Jesus Son of God! Looking at it in the divine order, you loved this ill treatment no less than the glory with which he was to crown you in heaven! Let us look with the same eye at all our crosses and infinitely prefer them to all crowns. Let us suffer all our ills in this disposition in order to support our faithfulness. We can learn to suffer well only from Jesus Christ, and we never purely carry the cross following him except when he has been revealed in us by the experience of his states.

We *spit in the face* of him whose beauty delights the angels (Job 30:10). This is the latest outrage. The Son of God wanted to experience every kind of contempt, confusion, or bad treatment so that no children of human beings would flee from his share of sufferings for the love of him. Criminals attract compassion, and we try to relieve them in their misery, all the more since we see them ready to be condemned and punished. But for Jesus Christ and his interior friends, *sorrow has been added to my pain* (Jer 45:3). Overwhelmed with reproaches and insults, Jesus Christ is abused, and no one supports or defends him. The beloved Son of the Father suffers such harsh and iniquitous treatment as a grace given to him and to those who resemble him. Let us not complain of any severe treatment or ills. Jesus consecrated them by all his experiences. But let us learn from him through the lively penetration of his holy passion to faithfully carry such great states, so that we will not be unfaithful to them, if one day he deigns to reward us with them.

> Now Peter was sitting outside in the courtyard. And a servant girl came up to him and said, "You also were with Jesus the Galilean."
> 70 But he denied it before them all, saying, "I do not know what
> you mean." 71 And when he went out to the entrance, another servant girl saw him, and she said to the bystanders, "This man was with Jesus of Nazareth." 72 And again he denied it with an oath: "I do not know the man." (Matt 26:69–72)

This circumstance is included in the passion of Jesus Christ to show that he experienced every possible affliction. What! This dear disciple, to whom the divine Master always gave preference, the one in whom he entrusted himself entirely as witness to his greatest mysteries and revealed his most secret actions. The one whom he made the first of his apostles, and who must lead and govern the church; Peter himself firmly renounces Jesus publicly several times. Tremble, little saplings, seeing one of the tallest cedars in Lebanon fall! Ah! When we are ashamed of following Jesus Christ, we are soon ashamed of confessing him, and we then renounce him.

O Peter! This is what happened to you because you moved away from Jesus Christ. From a fault that seems slight to you, you have fallen into a crime of perjury and carried it to the last excess. Through your presumptuous love you protested that when all others abandoned your Master, you would never abandon! However, you immediately abandoned and renounced him! Such a disastrous fall is clear proof that you relied on your own natural courage and resolution. For if you had relied only on the Almighty, you would never have been lacking. These people who promise many beautiful things are the ones who do them the least.

Peter needed this fall as a test for his weakness to make him compassionate for others and be in this the model for all the pastors of the church.

A pastor and an apostle needs to have experienced everything. From his perjury, Peter learned to rely on God alone. We must never rely on the creature or on the strength and fervor of sensitive love, because being still mixed with a lot of self-love, it cannot stand the test of contradiction. He who believed himself to be an apostle succumbs to the reproaches of a servant and a weak sinner. Let one rely only on abandonment and surrender to God.

How many friends and loved ones are there who say in times of persecution, "I do not know that man!" Some claim a spiritual fortune based on this friendship. Yet seeing their friend fall into disarray before humans, they withdraw from this union, as it was wrong. Very few have the courage to bear abjection with the other friends of Jesus Christ or dare *to go to him outside the camp and bear the reproach he endured* (Heb 13:13).

When we trust others and they fail us, this causes great pain, especially with the first unexpected blow of the betrayal. Even if we had warnings, nothing equals experience, and the creature always feels its blows.

> After a little while the bystanders came up and said to Peter, "Certainly you too are one of them, for your accent betrays you."
> 74 Then he began to invoke a curse on himself and to swear, "I do not know the man." And immediately the rooster crowed. 75 And Peter remembered the saying of Jesus, "Before the rooster crows, you will deny me three times." And he went out and wept bitterly. (Matt 26:73–75)

Peter falls three times, and his last fall is the worst. O the great weakness of humans! How does he not learn through the experience of his fragile and desperate faith to abandon himself totally to God? Only relying on God himself brings great strength, but relying on ourselves brings only weakness.

As soon as we rely on our own faith, we find ourselves in disorder more or less to the extent of the support given to us. Support on something outside of God, however great and lofty it may be, causes all falls. Seeking strength outside of God is the root of all evil. He who delights in the creature to the detriment of God's presence makes the creature his last end and destination, becoming full of complacency. We owe everything to the Creator, who causes within us the strength of God. If the person makes himself the first principle, this breaks under him and pierces him. Many fatal falls come even from souls who had noble beginnings and made very great progress. This is why only a few who having started well complete with good fortune. The secret presumption that they nourish, the vain confidence in their efforts and practices, the excessive esteem of their actions, the support they have from their mortifications and austerities, the assurance with which they flatter themselves of not falling, and the search for themselves almost in all things make ruinous foundations. Then with the first temptation, everything is lacking. God not being the only principle and the only end of this edifice, they unfortunately fall into ruin.

But when God allows these falls in people, God says, *I have loved you with an everlasting love; therefore, I have continued my faithfulness to you* (Jer 31:3). God makes admirable use of these people. He uses this conviction of their weakness to bring them into the renunciation of their self-support within themselves, so that nothing prevents them from returning and being united to God without an intervening middle ground. Otherwise, their return would be impossible.

Thus, Peter remembers the words of his Master, and this memory alone, accompanied by a look from his same Master, brings about his conversion. And in what way is he converted? Peter leaves, remembering the place and occasion of sin; he weeps bitterly. O! What pain for a heart that tasted God to have offended by renouncing God! The greater the love, the more extreme the pain. We cannot understand unless we have experienced this painful love after the fall, having tasted the goodness and the infinite kindnesses of God. This strange pain makes the heart feel it is going to burst through excess of contrition. When the fall is real, the soul experiences this mortal pain in its return to God, but when God takes and possess the soul, she cannot have pain. She finds herself protected and insensitive like iron. By this fall, or by God's merciful actions following it, Peter was taken entirely out of himself and away from all support in creation; Peter passed into God. This good disciple was after that so full of self-distrust that he no longer dared to risk undertaking anything, not even daring to attend the crucifixion of his Master, for fear that his weakness would carry him to do again on Calvary what he had done in the house of the high priest. Broken and destroyed by his fall, Peter was now more disposed to be clothed with strength from above and filled with the Holy Spirit. Peter preached Jesus Christ, founded the church, and governed it for many years with zeal and united apostolic intrepidity to the point of consummating his ministry with his strong and glorious martyrdom on the cross. To feel our weakness and misery caused by our faults is a great good, so that, no longer expecting anything from our strength, which is in itself a weakness, we hope for everything from the strength of God alone, by whom we can do all things.

> When morning came, all the chief priests and the elders of the people took counsel against Jesus to put him to death. [2] And they bound him and led him away and delivered him over to Pilate the governor. (Matt 27:1–2)

The priests and people in authority over this innocent man delivered Jesus into the secular arm. For we know that the law is spiritual, but I am of the flesh, sold under sin to the secular arm. It is deplorable that priests, whose dignity is so great, know Jesus Christ so little. Many declared themselves against him and opposed his reign in souls. That they do this is inexcusable, since being the persons who have knowledge and authority, they should be the ones to know the most about the interior Kingdom of Jesus Christ and work fervently to extend this.

Spiritual directors and confessors are also jealous against God, unable to tolerate him leading souls in his own way. They are more jealous of their own authority than of that of their Master and do not understand what is most pleasant and glorious to Jesus Christ. If a believer wants to abandon himself fully to God in trust, searching in the simplicity of his heart, responsive to God's attractions, the confessor calls this deception, opposing him and frightening him with terrors. There is no one who needs the interior life as much as a priest so to be able to lead souls in the way of the Spirit. The church groans to see so few devoted to the way of the Spirit. However, we have some faithful sheep and true pastors bringing us consolation in this corrupt century. Divine Jesus! When will we see according to your prediction in John 6:45, *all* the faithful *will be taught by God?* This will happen when the priests who lead them draw God into their interior life and teach others what they learn.

> Then when Judas, his betrayer, saw that Jesus was condemned, he changed his mind and brought back the thirty pieces of silver to the chief priests and the elders, [4] saying, "I have sinned by betraying innocent blood." They said, "What is that to us? See to it yourself." [5] And throwing down the pieces of silver into the temple, he departed, and he went and hanged himself. (Matt 27:3–5)

If Judas's penitence had been honest and humble confidence, however great and horrible his crime was, God would have forgiven him. The character of true penitence is peaceful sorrow, although strong and sovereign. Two disciples offend their Master; one betrays him, and the other renounces him. The two repent: Peter's true repentance with trust and sincerity, but Judas's repentance was willed with pride and despair. In human despair, we mistrust God's goodness, which is for us whichever crimes we may have committed. We bring great honor to God after a fall to have sorrow filled with hope. Those who see themselves fallen may inflict disorder on themselves, become troubled and worried, while distrusting the mercy of God because of their own self-love. They pity the harm they have done to themselves rather than the offense they have committed against God. True penitence comes from God and leads effectively to God, since God gives us this to make happy return. Yet those who occupy themselves with self-love know discouragement and turn away from God out of self-preoccupation. To the contrary, those who are peacefully afflicted, without being frightened by the terrors of the fall, hope in the infinite goodness of God, abandon themselves to God with resignation, and have a healthy sorrow, which is accompanied by love.

People who are troubled after their fall consider only their regret for their sins. They mourn the loss of their virtue to which they were attached naturally or the danger of eternal loss. In their torment, they do not think only of God's interests. We see the same in people who have advanced quickly into spiritual consummation. Their own self-interest, hidden in their sorrows, is built on the strong foundation of self-love, which animates their devotion. They need to discover this monster of self-preoccupation and destroy it. God allows this in his mercy, yet looking only at the interests of God, we remain in peace. Hating sin as much as it deserves, we are content in humiliation. We want God to take glory from everything. We are delighted that he rescues us from the ignominy of his creature. Happy are the falls that give a place to a prompt resurrection, great sacrifices, and a disinterested love! People who are troubled after their fall barely correct themselves, and they return to fall heavily like Judas, who consummated his iniquity with despair. But those who remain in peaceful sorrow rise again, as we see in St. Peter.

God touched Judas to bring him to repentance to show us that he does not fail to warn us and give us graces needed for salvation if we put them to good use. If this betrayer had not despaired, his repentance would have been good. But who will not be surprised at the hardness of these priests, who seeing this repentance of Judas and the declaration he made to them of having handed over an innocent man to them, far from correcting themselves, become even harsher? Whether you have delivered up a just man or an innocent one, they tell him, that is none of our business. What then is your business, O blind men! If the obvious danger of committing such injustice does not affect you, if a just man has been handed over to you, will you be able to condemn him justly? Or did he become a criminal just because he was handed over to you? The hardness of heart in people whose lives are not visibly disordered is worse than that of the greatest sinners, because when covered with self-esteem and supported by obstinacy, it is no longer curable.

> But the chief priests, taking the pieces of silver, said, "It is not lawful to put them into the treasury, since it is blood money." [7] So they took counsel and bought with them the potter's field as a burial place for strangers. [8] Therefore that field has been called the Field of Blood to this day. (Matt 27:6–8)

The judges show an impertinent scruple not to dare put into the *treasury of the temple* the money that the traitor returned to them, because, they said, these pieces of silver are the price of a man's life. They persisted, though, in taking the life of the most innocent of men as an effect of the envy they had conceived against him. In this action, the chief priests want to appear charitable in their act of injustice. Sons of the patriarchy, they want to seem compassionate for the corpses of foreign strangers while they cruelly overwhelm the benefactor of the patriarchy. Their hypocritical nature seeks to hide their iniquities from the eyes of people. But will they be able to hide them from the eyes of God? Jesus Christ wants everything that concerns him to serve the benefit of men: *the price of his blood* is used to buy a place suitable for the burial of strangers, and this place is a *potter's field*. This signifies that all who were strangers to Jesus Christ and did not know him will receive union with him at the price of his blood. After they have been called to his church and united with his body, they are hidden and buried with him in the bosom of his Father. The *potter's field* marks that Jesus Christ came by his blood to restore these earthen vessels that the divine worker had made, but which were spoiled by their fragility. The incarnate Word by whom everything was made came to break these first-infected vessels in Adam and to make them cemented together again with his blood. As St. Paul says, *If anyone is in Christ, he is a new creation* (2 Cor 5:17). This happens when the old has passed away and the new has come.

> Then was fulfilled what had been spoken by the prophet Jeremiah, saying, "And they took the thirty pieces of silver, the price of him on whom a price had been set by some of the sons of Israel, [10] and they gave them for the potter's field, as the Lord directed me." (Matt 27:9–10)

Nothing happens to Jesus Christ that is not prophesied; the evangelists clarify this in this place and in others. What! God has poured out graces to show us that this is the Son of God, yet the leaders place a price on him. Without recognizing him, they make a business deal on him who is infinitely worth more than all possible worlds and who comes to redeem those who had sold themselves to the demon and sin. In our unfaithfulness, something similar happens to our interior. We hesitate to declare ourselves for God. We bargain over him. As soon as we falter over the sovereignty of the divine presence, we soon fall like Lucifer, who hesitated on this point and fell heavily. Falls of this kind are the most profound ones. One of the premier angels, Lucifer became the most evil of devils, because his malice went as far as the graces he had received.

> Now Jesus stood before the governor, and the governor asked him, "Are you the King of the Jews?" Jesus said, "You have said so." (Matt 27:11)

O Love! How do they betray you who are the *King of the Jews*? Far from treating Jesus as the one who should reign in them and on them, they treat him as a slave. The governor talks about the Jews as who they should be under Jesus's reign, yet they had become corrupted and rejected Jesus's right to rule over them. Through them he was to reign in them, yet instead of being delighted in his legitimate reign, they opposed his Kingdom because he reigns perfectly only in abandoned souls. The Jews were to be his people, as seen both in the character of the patriarchs and in Genesis.

> But when he was accused by the chief priests and elders, he gave no answer. [13] Then Pilate said to him, "Do you not hear how many things they testify against you?" [14] But he gave him no answer, not even to a single charge, so that the governor was greatly amazed. (Matt 27:12–14)

In an occasion of such consequence, Jesus remains quiet. He keeps his silence and does not respond to the accusations that are made against him. This surprises and astonishes the governor. Where have we seen an innocent man charged with crimes who does nothing to justify himself?

The Savior gives us an example that we are to follow on certain occasions. O such an efficacious silence! This does more for the conversion of sinners than many words. The silence of Jesus is not affected but shows his abandon to the will of his Father. An abandoned soul does not open his mouth to defend himself. He sees God in all that happens, and he loves God's order. No longer able to think about oneself or take any care of it, he leaves all things to God with an indifference whether to be justified or to be left without justification.

> Now at the feast the governor was accustomed to release for the crowd any one prisoner whom they wanted. [16] And they had then a notorious prisoner called Barabbas. [17] So when they had gathered, Pilate said to them, "Whom do you want me to release for you: Barabbas, or Jesus who is called Christ?" [18] For he knew that it was out of envy that they had delivered him up. (Matt 27:15–18)

Pilate knew Jesus Christ was delivered to him out of envy. Out of a vain fear of the Caesar's indignation, Pilate will soon condemn an innocent man to death. Nothing is more dangerous than the consideration of human beings to the detriment of the presence of God. It restrains and holds back almost all that is good. A thousand people would embrace the way of God if they did not allow themselves to be dominated by human respect. Could our Lord inspire us with more horror than by allowing it to result in his death? There are many kinds of unjust judges of Jesus; some condemn him out of malice, others out of weakness and cowardly complacency. They also overwhelm his loyal followers. As soon as through the progress of the spirit they have the happiness of resembling him, they are favored by the same treatments that he suffered in his holy passion.

> Besides, while he was sitting on the judgment seat, his wife sent word to him, "Have nothing to do with that righteous man, for I have suffered much because of him today in a dream." [20] Now the chief priests and the elders persuaded the crowd to ask for Barabbas and destroy Jesus. (Matt 27:19–20)

Through God's Spirit, Pilate's wife knows about Jesus's innocence, and she informs her husband. But Pilate's respect for humans blinds him, and he does not profit from this warning. He despises this wisdom and refuses to follow it. She says, *Have nothing to do with that righteous man.* The Spirit of God causes a pagan woman to prophesy, so that she bears witness to the innocence of Jesus Christ, calling him only the righteous. By this name, we should also call the Lord our righteous, who by his justice must judge all men and punish all injustice. But an unjust judge has no eyes to see this justice by which he himself must be judged, no matter how much anyone shows it to him or tries to make him fear it. Useless opinions captivate and pressure blinds unjust judges. Only rarely are their judgments not corrupted either by one or by the nature of these bad impressions.

The priests and the elders use the credit and the authority that they have over people to persuade them to ask for Barabbas and to kill Jesus. They compare the Son of God to a murderer. Deliberating which of the two deserves death, they conclude that the author of life must die and the murderer must live. Do we not often commit the same injustice, preferring a vile creature, perhaps even infamous, to our Creator? What is worse is that the people who should dissuade us are those who persuade us to do so through bad advice. They tempt us, persuading us to prefer Barabbas to Jesus Christ. We accept their pretexts and do an injustice to give precedence to the criminal over the innocent. Simple people and people of good will go to consult Jesuit confessors and receive bad advice from them, either because the confessors surprise them or deceive them in what they explain to them; or because the confessors' ignorance, passion, or interest makes them too indulgent. They decide in our favor things that we cannot approve in our interior, because we know that this is repugnant to our conscience and that God has put in us a light of truth, which makes us discover the just within our being.

> The governor again said to them, "Which of the two do you want me to release for you?" And they said, "Barabbas." [22] Pilate said to them, "Then what shall I do with Jesus who is called Christ?" They all said, "Let him be crucified!" [23] And he said, "Why? What evil has he done?" But they shouted all the more, "Let him be crucified!" (Matt 27:21–23)

All the people ask for Barabbas and abandon Jesus Christ. The governor regards Jesus Christ as a useless man fit for nothing. The people, on the contrary, consider him a seducer to be rid of and cry with all their might, *Let him be crucified!* O Love! God had nothing better to give you than the cross! And there was nothing you cared about so much and wanted to share with your friends in this life. Pilate asks, *What evil has he done?* O cowardly judge, and more than unworthy of being so! Why do you not take away from oppression the one in whom you cannot find any crime?

What! This people, Lord, to whom you have done so much good, who followed you day and night to listen to your word, whom you fed miraculously in the desert, whose *sorrows you bore and healed their illnesses*, are those who cry, *Let him be crucified!* These people who received you with so much honor only six days ago, recognizing you as the true Messiah and the messenger of the Lord, are today mutinying against you with such excess that they want to take your life! Who will dare to believe the promises of such people, since they repay the benefits of God with such black ingratitude? But this is the fate of apostolic people when they live in imitation of their Master. Those to whom they have done the most good and have delivered from thousands of sorrows, those they have served with bonding and warmth, are the ones who then cry, *Let him be crucified.* At the right time, O Savior! The creature prepares crosses with such injustice, yet God regards these crosses with grace and love. Clearly God entrusted his own Son with the cross. However, nothing is so strange as the inconstancy of creatures; they persecute those whom previously they esteemed and applauded. Today we revere them as apostles, yet in a few days they will be placed among the despised. The best friends of Jesus Christ must experience this state as well as the others, and all kinds of people agree when it comes to condemning them.

> So when Pilate saw that he was gaining nothing, but rather that a riot was beginning, he took water and washed his hands before the crowd, saying, "I am innocent of this man's blood; see to it

> yourselves." [25] And all the people answered, "His blood be on us and on our children!" (Matt 27:24–25)

By washing his hands, Pilate wants to cast this injustice on the people. On the contrary, he is more guilty out of his knowledge that Jesus's blood is innocent, yet Pilate spreads it. How many people still do the same thing, believing that as long as we wash or polish the exterior of things, everything is permitted? They believe that as long as one says a word in favor of a person, one is permitted to dip one's tongue in his blood with the blackest slander. For pretexts of honor and decorum, or out of imaginary necessity, beneficiaries rob the poor and the churches of what Jesus Christ acquired for them at the price of his blood. Sadly, pastors give their time to trifles and abandon souls for whom the Son of God died. It is assumed that a contract adroitly palliated arises to require usury. We imagine that injustice is permitted when it is covered by some formality. Pleasing the world, we create an unjust conscience, while releasing a murderer free. This is how the world uses Jesus. What is all this, Pilate believing himself innocent of the blood of Jesus Christ when he is even more guilty of it because he sinned with full knowledge of the malicious crime, yet seeks to justify the crime at the same time as he was resolved to commit it? Neither the authors nor the accomplices of such excesses can be excused: and although they try to force the responsibility on another person, neither can be exonerated from it.

> Then he released for them Barabbas, and having scourged Jesus, delivered him to be crucified. (Matt 27:26)

Pilate's strange process makes us afraid. Because finally, if Pilate knows Jesus to be innocent, why does he condemn him to torture? Or if it is out of weakness that Pilate hands Jesus over, why scourge him before crucifying him? The final torture is rigorous enough without adding this cruel torment. Yet, *he who did not spare his own Son* (Rom 8:32), having destined him for the pain and ignominy of scourging to heal all our wounds, allowed the cruelty of an unjust judge to make him suffer. Who will not admire the conduct of God towards his Son and his servants? He allows those who cannot deny their innocence be persecuted and insulted. All agree the morals of such people are beyond reproach, and yet we cannot prevent them from suffering. Scandalous sinners, obliged by duty, are allowed to live in peace while we mercilessly pursue innocent people who suffer attacks from the whole world. Also, some inadvertently cause them suffering. We must see that the sufferers' transcendence is higher than in the creatures who persecute them. God has countless means of crucifying his friends; the love he has for them is measured by the crosses he sends them.

> Then the soldiers of the governor took Jesus into the governor's headquarters, and they gathered the whole battalion before him. [28] And they stripped him and put a scarlet robe on him, [29] and twisting together a crown of thorns, they put it on his head and put a reed in his right hand. And kneeling before him, they mocked him, saying, "Hail, King of the Jews!" (Matt 27:27–29)

Nothing is harder to bear than confusion, mockery, and consequences. Any other torment would be more bearable than this martyrdom. But because of this, Jesus wanted to bear this torment and have his friends also participate in this. He reserves this grace for his privileged friends. Happy are those who drink long drinks from the chalice of abjection and who, at the end of a life soaked in deep humiliation, can say with truth, *For it is for your sake that I have borne reproach, that dishonor has covered my face* (Ps 69:7). Rarely do people suffer for the love of God. Frequently we suffer because the miseries of nature or the malice of others creates the torments of hell. Yet Jesus Christ taught us to love and suffer a martyrdom of charity in these torments.

That all this happened to Jesus Christ is extremely mysterious and a great consolation for us. First, he is stripped of his clothing, so we understand that to be consummated in the final sacrifice, we must be entirely stripped of ourselves. In Jesus's stripping, he was then dressed in a *scarlet robe*. This shows us that when we are stripped of ourselves, we must be clothed in pure love. All of this was done to Jesus in mockery to reveal that the most profound abjection completes the stripping of ourselves and disposes us to pure love, as it is through this that the sacrifice is consummated.

Second, they place a *crown of thorns* on the head of our Lord to show the mark of his Kingdom and his sovereignty over souls. This costs him dearly, although he is already the legitimate king. When the soul reigns, this also causes the soul to suffer. She must be pierced with thorns, just as her Spouse suffered the stings to acquire this Kingdom. Having the Master crowned with thorns means that his most dear souls must also be pierced.

Third, the *reed* they put in his right hand takes the place of a scepter and shows his sovereign power by which he leads human beings, for even the wicked while acting with malice know the truth of God, which accomplishes great mysteries. But this scepter is a reed that men put in his hand, and which they take away at the same time to strike him on the head. Nothing could better mark the inconstancy of men in letting themselves be led to God yet after giving themselves to God become unfaithful. Having taken him for their King and God, they reclaim themselves, withdraw, and offend him by rising against him. They aim blows to his head trying to escape his sovereignty. They strike him with a reed to abandon him with cowardice after having devoted themselves to him. Or they become upset and agitated with fears and sorrows after having placed themselves in the hands of an entirely good, all-wise, and all-powerful God. But those who insult him most shamefully, who mock his reign in souls, and who ridicule the treasure of eternity are like a chimera, missing what is most divine under heaven.

> And they spit on him and took the reed and struck him on the head. (Matt 27:30)

Jesus Christ wanted to suffer these last outrages and the most extreme contempt to teach us that we must not put limits to our patience in insults, however extreme they may be. We use a thousand excuses not to suffer. We say that others must respect our character, state, and person. Yet who has had a more eminent and elevated state than Jesus Christ? What person was ever more worthy of respect than him? These people who want to avoid all suffering are in love with self and also want to give themselves and others a reason not to suffer. Instead, let us suffer all kinds of pain until death. All martyrdoms are good, even those accomplished by confusion, contempt, censure, and opprobrium, as well as those accomplished through pain and sorrow. Our dignified self-love and all that glorifies us must instead be used to humiliate and make us suffer. Jesus Christ's quality of being a King and the marks of his royalty made him suffer.

> And when they had mocked him, they stripped him of the robe and put his own clothes on him and led him away to crucify him. (Matt 27:31)

Jesus Christ shows us in all these strippings that he wanted to suffer what also happens in the interior person and what must be consummated by the last sacrifice. After having made him go through the strangest losses and abjections, he was again stripped of this outer *robe*, which as a priestly vestment portrayed a sign of charity and God's love in these terrible states. They tear away the appearance of pure love from him, but they cannot tear away the reality. The exterior garment is only a perception, and in truth he never loved more with purity. This very deep love, withdrawn in the most supreme part of the soul, was not perceived with external powers.

Jesus is given his clothes before being taken to Calvary to consummate his sacrifice. All of these circumstances have mystery, not only for the public edification of the church but also to confirm the truth from within. The soul who must bear its last sacrifice seems to be placed in its pure nature in order to consummate it by a martyrdom. In this extreme torment, she is stripped of the strength of love that sustained her, although it was already well hidden. Moreover, she is clothed with all the weaknesses of nature and must go under this dejection to her last torture.

This martyrdom of the spirit differs by being much harsher than that of the body, both by the excess and the duration of its punishments. Jesus Christ carries it to its full extent, a martyrdom that also makes interior people suffer. Invisible tyrants and executioners torment them beyond anything we can imagine. The martyrdom of the soul goes through a long series of inconceivable pains, making her die to herself. These interior martyrs are weakened to the point that I have just said, but for the exterior martyrs, it was quite the contrary, since to suffer their tortures, they were stripped of their weakness and clothed with strength; their spirit was supported by love and enjoyment while their body was torn apart. They also had assurance of making a sacrifice to God.

Being thus stripped, there is nothing left but to be taken to the place of torture, where we must go in the manner that God has ordered, according to what is manifested to us by the divine moment of the infallible oracle of God's plans for us. These moments, which follow one another in the eternal order, surely lead us to God, but they lead us there through the cross. This having been the means of consummation for Jesus Christ is also the plan for the consummation for his elect (Heb 2:10).

> As they went out, they found a man of Cyrene, Simon by name. They compelled this man to carry his cross. (Matt 27:32)

Many people who carry the *cross* of Jesus are forced to do so against their inclination, yet this becomes their happiness since its mere touch has a sanctifying virtue. Although this violent injustice burdens them in spite of themselves, making it for a time forced and unbearable, yet subsequently this becomes a pleasant and voluntary cross. Blessed are the people who carry the cross for Jesus! They truly carry it externally, but Jesus himself supports them with a secret force. He even teaches us by this that the unexpected and forced crosses that come through human violence are as much Jesus's cross as all the others. For Simon Cyrene did not stop carrying the cross of Jesus, though they had to force him to do so. O inestimable happiness to encounter the cross of Jesus when you least expect it! It is the same with all the afflictions that surprise us. These unexpected crosses destroy an abusive value that creeps into the world, even among spiritual people, to value crosses only of one's own choice, or those that one expected or that one first accepts with approval. These self-chosen crosses have their value, I admit, but the unexpected crosses that come only from pure providence and for which one initially feels a strange repugnance are the best. These are the crosses of Jesus Christ because we do not choose them, and they are freer from self-love.

> And when they came to a place called Golgotha (which means Place of a Skull), [34] they offered him wine to drink, mixed with gall, but when he tasted it, he would not drink it. (Matt 27:33–34)

Jesus Christ is finally led to the place of his final sacrifice at the Mount of Calvary, the place of torture and death, infamous for the uses for which the justice of judges destined it but now the most celebrated and holy of all the places in the world by the use that God's will made of this, the choice for the theater of crucifixion of his Son. Through his torture, humanity is freed from eternal death. This is very mysterious. There is not a circumstance of this extremity of the passion of our Lord that his interior friends do not experience in their last sacrifice. The cross then rises to the summit of the spirit, which is equivalent to ascending Calvary. Then, we must taste the beverage mixed with wine and gall, which is presented by the best friends who have become the cruelest enemies. But as the Savior having tasted it did not want to drink it, we must not drink it either. This wine that was presented to Jesus Christ was, according to St. Mark, mixed with myrrh, which gives rise to St. Matthew calling it bitter like gall. Customarily, they gave it to those tortured so that they would feel less their torments. But the King of martyrs teaches us by his refusal to drink that we too refuse it in such a parallel extremity. The wine mixed with *myrrh or gall* is a strength and a secret support that we want to give to the interior martyrs to relieve them at the end of their sacrifice, but this slows the consummation and very much diminishes the cost. We want to force them to mix bitterness with wine, that is to say, to rely on some penance or mortification of their own choice to secure themselves in some way in a state where everything seems lost. I admit that this experience is filled with bitterness, yet let them take care of taking this wine with gall, for it mixes in a wine that prevents them from dying. Let them remain engulfed in the gall and bitterness where God holds them and neither add nor diminish anything of their own accord.

The wine mixed with gall shows again that in the state of affliction, cruel in both external and interior life, people frequently suggest that they carry their bitterness in the shell of comfort or pleasures of the world. This way they will dissipate their sorrows. But this is a wine mixed with gall that we should not drink, because only bitterness and torment would remain. Jesus Christ instructs us that weak souls who try this will find only bitterness, and they would have to leave. The comforts and pleasures themselves would be bitter.

> And after they had crucified him, they divided his garments, casting lots; that it might be fulfilled which was spoken by the prophet, saying: They divided my garments among them; and upon my vesture they cast lots. (Matt 27:35)

O how divine Scripture is succinct and profound! *After they had crucified him* meaning this unequaled prodigy of the ignominious torture of the King of glory and of the death of a God. It says in a few words the infinite torments that the Savior suffered to deliver us from the pain of eternal death. It relates only in passing what the world had wished for and prepared for for more than forty centuries and which will be the delight and adoration of all blessed spirits in eternity. But it says a lot, since it declares what the Holy Spirit wanted us to be. The measure of all things is the will of God. Divine movement is the reign of the most just expression.

Jesus is *crucified*, but he does not crucify himself. He is crucified *by the hands of men, as he predicted, and by the hand of his Father, who did not spare his own Son but gave him up for us all.* Let us learn from this that active crosses and mortifications, that is to say, those taken up by ourselves, must cease and give way to passive ones when it is time to be consummated by them. People who remain all their lives in external penances of their own choice never enter the true crosses sent from God himself or provided by humans. O exterior crosses, you are only shadows of crosses compared to the interior ones! O crosses procured by ourselves, you are only straws compared to those that are sent to us from elsewhere and which surprise us by unforeseen providence!

Those who crucified Jesus Christ *divide his garments*. He also died for the salvation of those who put him to death, and his blood shed by their sacrilegious hands was shed for their redemption. At the same time that he was made to suffer strange torments, those who were the perpetrators received the advantage. It is the same with the crosses that we make most interior people suffer when they are in this last sacrifice: those who torment them the most and who cause them the most crosses receive their first, great fruits, either by their conversion from sin to grace or by their entry into the interior Kingdom.

These interior martyrs, all the more famous before God because they are more unknown to the world, suffer in two ways. First, by persecution, and second, by spiritual generation. Now those who incite persecution or foment it are often won and sanctified by the same people they persecute and even when they crucify them, they share their spoils. God gives extraordinary graces to sinners in consideration of the loyalty of their friends who suffer these last trials. As for spiritual generation, Christ suffered this eagerness to give birth to his children, when he said to his disciples, *I have earnestly desired to eat this Passover with you before I suffer* (Luke 22:15). That is to say, Jesus says, "I communicate my life and Spirit to you. May this Passover, or this passing of my life into you, happen continually." Here, in the same way, the mothers of grace chosen by God have the same pain to communicate his Spirit to many hearts, having been filled with superabundance for this purpose.

The true apostles are mothers of grace, who feel the violence that this Spirit of Jesus Christ does in them so they can flow into others. Paul had experienced this well when he cried, *My little children, for whom I am again in the anguish of childbirth until Christ is formed in you!* (Gal 4:19). The reproach that God makes to the children of Israel for having been unfaithful to him is grounded in the affection and tenderness of the Father God's love and the pain he has at the little correspondence that he finds in his creatures who have abandoned him and forgotten the Lord who created them. Yet nothing compares with the love and tenderness of parents of grace toward their spiritual children.

Therefore, one of the principal pains of Jesus Christ on the cross was to generate all his elect. This incomprehensible pain in his heart from which all the children of God were to be born could have opened and burst his heart in a thousand places if he had not had divine strength. So, he wanted his side to be opened with a spear as if to give birth through this opening to his church and all his children. The strength of the blood of his heart marked the true generation taking place; the blood of God produced children of God. He also fortified this with water to designate the purity of this same generation. His children were begotten by the blood of his love and washed in the water of his grace. O little-known and little-tested mystery! O Christians! If you knew what you cost Jesus on the cross, what love would you not want to know? Children of grace, how dearly do your spiritual parents beget you in Jesus Christ through their prayers, sufferings, and love and obtain you for Jesus Christ! The divine Master communicates this divine fertility to the apostles and the subsequent apostleship that enters into this spiritual generation, which takes place singularly through the cross. *For I became your father in Christ Jesus through the gospel* (1 Cor 4:15). St. Paul had the best part there. Ah! That he was a great apostle and a very fruitful father of Christians! We know the number of our children only in eternity. We must not even persuade ourselves that his generation is finished: the outpouring of his Spirit and the preaching of his word will last for centuries, or rather the Spirit of Jesus Christ and the word of God communicate to infinite people through the mouth of Paul and are perpetuated in the church through his epistles and through his intercessions.

> Then they sat down and kept watch over him there. (Matt 27:36)

Every place in Scripture has admirable meanings. These soldiers sharing the clothing of Jesus Christ represent the Christians who were to share in his graces, because certainly we have all crucified the same Savior by our hands. Although these particular people are evil, they are the figure of what happens among Christians who cause his death and take the spoils, yet his death gives us all life. A soul adopted by grace in the filiation of Jesus Christ must sit and repose in the grace communicated to them. Grace requires great repose, either to let it act in its full extent or to not lose it by spreading itself quickly outside. In this repose, we must keep Jesus Christ by watching over him with loving attention. Children of grace newly born from the side of Jesus Christ must do this. This carefully preserves our spiritual firstfruits.

> And over his head they put the charge against him, which read, "This is Jesus, the King of the Jews." (Matt 27:37)

Jesus Christ died to be the King. O Love! The cause of your death! If Scripture did not expressly say so, it would be difficult to believe it. Yes, this is the cause of Jesus's death. It is not only to bring about our salvation that the Son of God wants to die. That was not necessary in the strict sense, because his incarnation, circumcision, the slightest of his actions, a single sigh was more than enough to save everyone. But he wants to die in order to be the King of the spiritual Jews and to reign absolutely over the interior people. This can be done only through the mystical death of these souls, so he dies to merit it for them. This is why he takes the cross, for the mark of *his government shall be upon his shoulders* (Isa 9:6). The church sings that he reigned by the wood, interior torture being the means that God uses to bring about the mystical death of his friends. It cost his Son his life to reign over us, and we do not want to let him reign. Those who oppose this interior empire oppose the fruit of his death. O crucified Love! You died only to be King but singularly the King of pure hearts, hidden in God with you. So be truly King. No one disputes your royalty anymore.

> Then two robbers were crucified with him, one on the right and one on the left. (Matt 27:38)

The passion of the Savior was needed *to be numbered with the transgressors* in order to consummate in him in a very eminent way. Jesus Christ needed to experience the same tortures to which criminals are condemned. To have the reputation of have committed criminal excess is an excellent thing! This also shows the contempt of men in their judgments when they mix innocence with crime and treat the saints as guilty and give criminals the praise and rewards that the righteous deserve. The fate of the dearest friends of Jesus Christ for a time must be confounded among the malefactors. Those placed in this infamous rank would not suffer much as long as they had a clear testimony of good conscience, which still gives glory and assurance before God and in one's own eyes. Yet to die under the weight of the ultimate abjection, even we must be convinced of faults in appearance and have the eye of conscience so obscured by whichever means God makes that we can see ourselves only as criminals among transgressors. This happens with such a conviction that we are not separated from abandonment, peace, or the love of Jesus crucified. We have given ourselves to him without reservation, but this is so hidden so we are not prevented from drinking in all the ignominy of the torture.

> And those who passed by derided him, wagging their heads [40] and saying, "You who would destroy the temple and rebuild it in three days, save yourself! If you are the Son of God, come down from the cross." (Matt 27:39–40)

We further increase the persecution that we inflict on the righteous in that we offer them insults that we will not do to evildoers. They insult Jesus and say nothing to the thieves. What! They say, is this the one who made the interior and the spiritual! He helps others to save themselves, and he cannot save himself! Ah! A hard blow for a soul who is truly God's! Yet it is a greater grace to her to have such a good share in the ignominy of the cross that she was lifted up to heaven and tasted its sweetness. If they are the children of God, they say again, and abandoned to his guidance, let them come down from this cross to which they are attached. Their accusers justify themselves in this slander and believe it. In this universal outcry and being condemned by all these people of authority, they question, could they have the Spirit of God? They say, "If we see them emerge from this oppression, we will enter the interior path that they strive so hard for, but it is clear enough from the desperate state to which they are reduced that God is not with them." They even use what they say to insult them more cruelly.

But O souls too fortunate to be treated in this way after your dear Master! You, like him, are a spectacle of mockery to those who have never entered either his rest or his sanctuary. If seeing you they shake their heads, having only contempt for your affliction, be faithful to imitate him in this point, and do not come down from the cross, if you are offered, even to save the world. Do not justify yourself; do not seek to prove your innocence, but be happy to be considered guilty with Jesus Christ and to die as such. If he had come down from the cross, this people would not have believed in him, since he would have deprived his Father of infinite glory. Jesus Christ had performed other miracles that could have engaged their belief. Let each one therefore remain on his cross and remain there without leaving it until God removes him. We will help souls infinitely more by this fidelity to remain in ignominy than by all great and prodigious things we can do to save others. From God alone as the only source flow all graces. As his Son merited them all by his crucifixion, he also communicates them most abundantly through the merit of the crucified souls.

> Also the chief priests, with the scribes and elders, mocked him, saying, [42] "He saved others; he cannot save himself. He is the King of Israel; let him come down now from the cross, and we will believe in him. [43] He trusts in God; let God deliver him now, if he desires him. For he said, 'I am the Son of God.'" (Matt 27:41–43)

Doctors of the law do not understand the interior kingdom well and will always oppose the reign of Jesus in souls. They rejoice to see the interior kingdom treated in this way, believing that they have ruined this interior kingdom of which truly spiritual people say such great things. They triumph in their opinion that they must have overwhelmed him. They add malice to error when they persecute Jesus Christ in the hearts of those most dear to him. And the doctors of the law raise trophies to their false zeal, imagining that those in the interior Kingdom were a pernicious sect, although in reality the chief priests have crucified their God and *mocked* his truth.

To so many outrages, we add the bloodiest reproaches. Behold, it is said, these people of sublime prayer who wanted to rise rashly to contemplation have thrown themselves into the abyss of error and vice! Wanting to work for the perfection of others, they cannot save themselves. Having strayed from the high road, they have visibly lost their way in their paths. If they have found this interior Kingdom that they so praise, if Jesus reigns in them, *let them come down from this cross*! These ill-intentioned people applaud themselves for having prevented souls from going this way that they supposed to be deceptive. In derision, they carry the excess of their derision to the point of ridiculing the confidence that these interior and simple souls have in God. They trust in God in their abandonment, they say, "What use has all this been to them? Would it not have been better for them to rely on their own strength and lead themselves along the common path than to wander along unknown paths? For wanting to blindly follow faith and abandonment, here they are lost without resources!" Since *they trusted in God, if he loves them, let him deliver them now*, because they boasted of being *the children of God*, abandoned to the care of their heavenly Father, called to freedom, and delivered from the fear of slavery. If this were true, could they be treated as they are? But since *they glory in having God for Father; let us see if their words are true: let us test what will happen to them, and we will see what their end will be* (Wis 2:16–17). This is how those who ignore the secrets of God speak.

> The rebels who were crucified with him also taunted him in the same way. (Matt 27:44)

Criminal persons, seeing themselves punished with the punishments they deserve, also attack interior people and find relief in their ills by charging them with outrages, as if they could justify themselves by blaming those who are closest to God or find consolation in seeing interior persons also pass for criminals. It is strange, but it is only too true that good people, who moreover are opposed to sinners, agree with them in decrying and persecuting the interior souls.

> From noon on, darkness came over the whole land until three in the afternoon. (Matt 27:45)

This darkness not only shows the violence that nature suffered, seeing the agony of the one by whom nature was made and without whom nothing was made. The darkness is also the sign of the terrible state to which the lower part was abandoned so that a general darkness covered the whole lower soul of the Savior without allowing any light of divinity to shine there. Jesus Christ also resembles in his last sacrifice the state of souls. When this sacrifice is about to be consummated, these souls are for some time in complete darkness, so that they find themselves plunged into universal darkness, and so horrible that they know dread and terror in all the lower powers. All that is left for them is the feeling of extreme pain in incomprehensible darkness.

> And about three o'clock Jesus cried with a loud voice, "Eli, Eli, lema sabachthani?" that is, "My God, my God, why have you forsaken me?" (Matt 27:46)

This horrible darkness happens because God withdraws into the most supreme part of the spirit and seems to abandon the soul. The stronger this abandonment becomes, the more the darkness increases, since it is an effect of the eclipse of the interior sun. Ah! If one only knew what it is to be thus abandoned by God, or if one could understand the rigor of this test! But this is inconceivable. A soul having been united to God and no longer able to find anything in creation, whatever it may be, even in the most holy things, finds itself in a terrible solitude.

And the more the soul is deserted into solitude, the more violent its pain. So some souls find this abandonment more cruel than hell. However distressing this abandonment of God may be in souls who are in this last sacrifice, it is only the shadow of Jesus Christ's sufferings of abandonment and pain, although to human beings this appears to be extreme, and indeed it is. It seems that without a miracle one could not bear it.

To understand in part this excessive abandonment of God with regard to his Son, we know the pain caused by this same abandonment lies in proportion to the loneliness of the soul. That Jesus Christ carries this loneliness to infinity, because his only support is divinity, he even wanted to be deprived of divinity as much as possible. The abandonment of his Father to which Jesus Christ was reduced was the most crushing thing, for it can never be so in any creature. So Jesus Christ by the rigor of this abandonment found himself in his lower part, and even in his soul by an extraordinary effect of divine power deprived of the support of the divinity, which was needed, because without the Father he could not survive. He would also have ceased to exist, for he lacks the full flow of divinity that he ordinarily had. He suffered this agony and mortal abandonment. His excessive pain, then, in this extremity was like immense solitude, since he was deprived of the divine force and of infinite support.

The feeling that our Lord had in his abandonment was so penetrating that nothing more could be done. This is why, God though he is, he cries out about this and forgets all the rest. The other pains are nothing to him in comparison with this one. So he bore and sanctified this state of abandonment by his own, teaching others by his example that we should not refrain from crying out in the extremity of abandonment or be surprised when we cry out. There are people who bear great crosses and harsh privations without opening their mouths to complain; and they are well. But at this point, they are far from the last abandonment, however they feel. If they had tasted even a little of it, they would utter loud cries of pain because of it then being unbearable to be able to contain. A hidden pain is very light. Some souls are so weak that they cry out for the slightest privations, but it is not of these that I want to speak. They are far from carrying such a strange pain.

> When some of the bystanders heard it, they said, "This man is calling for Elijah." 48 At once one of them ran and got a sponge, filled it with sour wine, put it on a stick, and gave it to him to drink. (Matt 27:47–28)

In such a desolate state, humans can hardly console. With whichever feelings of compassion they allow themselves to be touched, they still have nothing but vinegar to offer to the interior martyrdom of Jesus Christ, who is in this agony. Besides taking everything in the wrong direction, all they could do to soften such great evils would be only bitterness. These consolations are even unbearable to a heart that is reduced to this extremity. Ah! If one only knew what it is to even have the thought of looking for it! Alas! How far one is from being able to find any! Everything that comes then from the side of the creature is like vinegar, which serves only to sour the pain of a cheek, far from relieving it. There is not a place of this state that Jesus Christ did not want to bear in order to sanctify it and strengthen by the experience he had of it for other souls who were to pass through it. He knew others would also conform with him into these circumstances of his passion either in an interior or exterior way.

> But the others said, "Wait, let us see whether Elijah will come
> to save him." 50 And Jesus cried out again with a loud voice and
> yielded up his spirit. (Matt 27:49–50)

Abandonment has reached its last extremity. No one comes to help this poor, dying man. There is nothing left but to die. God sends no help from his sanctuary, and no help comes from Zion. There is nothing left but to consummate all the sacrifices by this last sacrifice and to make the pleasing and perfect holocaust. The measure of torments and tortures is filled. The interior martyr must die. A single breath remains in this crucified soul, which will soon pass away, and all that was of this person will die. The soul happy enough to have been faithful up to this point, released from his own life, will be received into the bosom of God to participate excellently in his life. By this lack of all that was his own and sensual, God alone has become the God of his heart and his only share forever. O souls who experience this strange abandonment of God, one thing should console you: the more extreme it is, the nearer it approaches its end. This abandonment consummates the sacrifice and causes the soul to fail in sustaining itself, either on the side of God or on the side of the creature, to lose all life. O God! You seem to abandon such a soul, but it is on purpose to receive her forever in your arms!

You leave her, so that, dying entirely to herself, she no longer lives except in you! And the moment at which she comes out of herself by this terrible abandonment is the consummation of her sacrifice and the ruin of her life of propriety and self-centeredness.

> And behold, the curtain of the temple was torn in two, from top
> to bottom; and the earth shook, and the rocks were split; 52 the
> tombs also were opened, and many bodies of the saints who had
> fallen asleep were raised. (Matt 27:51–52)

O God! How admirable you are in expressing to us what happened at the death of your dear Son, giving us ideas of what happens in the mystical death of your most chosen souls! O Love crucified! You made a real and true sacrifice of yourself! It cost you your natural life to sanctify all our sacrifices! By your very real death, you gave value to our mystical death, teaching at the same time to all Christians that it was necessary to die like you on Calvary, if not really, at least mystically!

The curtain of the temple was torn in two, from top to bottom, not only to show the real death of Jesus Christ and the *division of his soul from his body*, which is like the curtain in the temple that covers the divinity, but to confirm what has been said before: the moment of mystical death is when the superior part entirely divides from the inferior part. This separation happens gradually to stop us from resting in propriety. This itself is figured in the corruption of the body after death. The soul leaves, the body corrupts gradually and becomes dust. This did not happen to the body of Jesus Christ, because he had no propriety. Divinity was his support. His flesh was incorruptible because of justice, but other bodies do not have this grace.

When these two parts divide, the inferior part designated by the *earth trembles.* It suffers more from this than the separation of the soul from the body. Here the spirit separates from the soul, although it is but one and the same substance with it, is more united to the soul than the soul is to the body. This is what strikes such a strange terror in the lower powers.

This makes the earth tremble at the death of Jesus Christ by the horror it had of such a terrible deicide, because the earth felt deprived of the most noble life that ever was. Also, because the earth's sovereign Lord had to abandon it soon to return to heaven, the earth also wanted to give this testimony to the divinity of our adorable, crucified God and contribute to the grief of all nature for the death of its God. But the trembling also is singularly ordained by God to be the figure of what happens in the mystical death.

The stones were split. A soul who seemed hard as a rock, splits, breaks, and reduces to powder. Propriety is no other thing than a hard and inflexible quality that resists the perfect penetration of the Spirit of God, giving the soul a restraint and consistency in itself that prevents it from being dilated, enlarged, and losing its form. Instead, it becomes restricted and cannot pass into another being. These qualities are common both to the stone and to the proprietary soul. Mystical death splits this stone, puts it into powder, and causing it to lose its first form, yet puts it in a condition to receive another. Who would believe that glass was made from the stone, and that the sand could be changed into a fine crystal, if experience did not teach us? A soul is infinitely more surprised when, after having experienced the resistances and restrictions of its propriety, it finds itself finally freed from them and sees itself penetrated by light. The soul become as it were immense, raised to a high participation in the divine attributes.

After these things have taken place, this hidden soul, as if hidden and buried by its state of death, experiences that this state of death is gradually lost and that its monument opens. But this miracle can be done only by Jesus Christ, as the tombs of the saints opened when his soul, penetrating the earth, descended into hell. Coming therefore himself into this tomb from the state of death, he opens the tombs, and then the bodies of the saints rise. What are these bodies of saints interpreted for interior life? These are all the usages and practices of holiness that the soul had as it were lost, no longer being able to use them, as has been seen in a number of places. All this is returned to them by the descent of Jesus into her. All these bodies of outward godliness are resurrected. We no longer have pain or difficulty for anything. We have a facility in all things. What if we have a difficulty or repugnance for some things? I say we are again in a state of death and not in resurrection. Truly we spend some time in the beginning of new life without knowing it, but gradually the full and free use of this life is given.

> After his resurrection they came out of the tombs and entered the holy city and appeared to many. (Matt 27:53)

This passage confirms admirably what has been said. For the tombs were opened at the time that Jesus died, although the Jews did not immediately notice it because of the Sabbath, during which they rested, and the tombs were outside the city. The dead did not come out until after the resurrection of our Lord to show that he put the soul in the state of resurrection. When this is done, all reunite in *the holy city*, the soul no longer using things for herself but only in God and for God. Not everybody is capable of seeing this resurrection, but God destines the witnesses of *many people*, who judge this either by the characters and the fruits of so great a state or by the advantages they receive. And the soul discovers also by the effects it feels the happiness of its resurrection.

> Now when the centurion and those with him, who were keeping watch over Jesus, saw the earthquake and what took place, they were terrified and said, "Truly this man was God's Son!" (Matt 27:54)

Those who do not know Jesus Christ in life know him at death and recognize this in the prodigious signs that appear. Seeing that all nature groans and trembles with fear at the moment he dies, one cannot but exclaim, *Truly this man was God's Son!* These wonders happen as long as the state of death lasts, yet even spiritual directors do not distinguish this mystical state of death unless in an extraordinary light. But soon at the sight of all these signs, one can no longer doubt the death of the soul or that Jesus Christ came to operate his resurrection. And then we exclaim with truth: This soul belongs to God; she has become a child of God, since Jesus lives and operates in her.

> Many women were also there, looking on from a distance; they had followed Jesus from Galilee, ministering to him. [56] Among them were Mary Magdalene, and Mary the mother of James and Joseph, and the mother of the sons of Zebedee. (Matt 27:55–57)

Jesus Christ did not refuse to be assisted by women, and some women followed him everywhere. This shows that God gives to the female sex the ministry of the apostolate. This is also seen in the apostles, the parents of the Lord, and particularly Peter, having also allowed women to follow them in their missions and to render them continual assistance.

Clearly God can unite persons of different sexes to work together in very great purity for his glory, salvation, and perfection of many souls. For example, the patriarchs of religions associated themselves with holy women in order to extend their patriarchal institute to the female sex. In the marvelous order of God, the church authorized a public justification of their conduct. Thereby St. Paula united with St. Jerome, St. Scholastica with St. Benedict, St. Claire with St. Francis, St. Teresa with St. John of the Cross, St. Jane Chantal with St. Francis de Sales. All were illustrious missionaries, of both sexes, whom God used to draw to himself an infinity of souls.

As we see in the circumstance of his life, our Lord confounded the slander of those who, seeing these liaisons of grace, could condemn them as inappropriate or criminal unions, although they were even purer than many between people of the same sex. Jesus Christ reassured us about such unions, seeing that there was nothing to fear. He wanted his apostles to do the same to teach us that once the soul participates in Jesus Christ and is placed in the apostolic state, these unions are always very helpful, since these unions subsist in God. The more the human is drawn out of himself and from Adam's corruption, the less he participates in the malignity and fury of Adam's flesh. But until this transformation happens, we need to be cautious. For one legitimate and truly bound in God, there are a hundred counter-saints either by the demon or by nature. Some may also be easily mistaken by what is naturally pleasing and masked by the colors of grace. We know this is of God if we are not acting quickly or too occupied. The communications should purify and vivify and have a *je ne sais quoi* of tranquility, simplicity, and purity, which already has the aroma of paradise. One washes one's stains with such souls, instead of soiling oneself there; and what would be death in others gives life through them.

> When it was evening, there came a rich man from Arimathea named Joseph, who also was himself a disciple of Jesus. 58 He went to Pilate and asked for the body of Jesus; then Pilate ordered it to be given to him. 59 So Joseph took the body and wrapped it in a clean linen cloth 60 and laid it in his new tomb, which he had hewn in the rock. He then rolled a great stone to the door of the tomb and went away. (Matt 23:57–60)

Jesus Christ wanted not only to die but also to be buried in order to rise gloriously from the bosom of death and the tomb. The soul must pass through burial before resurrection. This is something more than death: the soul is there in the oblivion of all things, and all creatures forget this soul too. But Jesus Christ could not carry this state either as long or in the same way or for the same ends as we carry him. He enters the sepulcher only to sanctify it and to teach all those who have this happiness to keep him company in his tomb of the mystical truth of these great words: that all those who *have been buried with Jesus Christ will rise with him* and come out of the tomb glorious like him (Rom 6:4). The sepulcher is like the seal and the confirmation of the death. In each state, there is both a state and a confirmation of the state. The same happens in the state of mystical death: the sepulcher is the confirmation of the death and a result of submission to God's Kingdom. Just as Jesus entered the sepulcher only to emerge alive in the life of glory, so all who enter the mystical sepulcher are assured of having a part in the glorious resurrection of the Son of God. Finally, moreover, his state was strengthened by the stone that was placed at the entrance of the sepulcher, which shows that one acquires perfect immobility of the spirit.

> The next day, that is, after the day of Preparation, the chief priests and the Pharisees gathered before Pilate [63] and said, "Sir, we remember what that impostor said while he was still alive, 'After three days I will rise again.' [64] Therefore command the tomb to be made secure until the third day; otherwise, his disciples may go and steal him away and tell the people, 'He has been raised from the dead,' and the last deception would be worse than the first." [65] Pilate said to them, "You have a guard of soldiers; go, make it as secure as you can." [66] So they went with the guard and made the tomb secure by sealing the stone. (Matt 27:61–66)

Mary Magdalene and the other Mary were there sitting opposite the tomb. Mary Magdalene, who had more part than any other in all the mystical states and who is given to us as an outstanding example of the interior life, could not depart from the sepulcher of her Master. She died mystically in the moment of Jesus Christ's natural death and was thus separated by a double death from the author of her life. But when she was deprived of the natural presence of her Savior and the consolation she received from him, she was never deprived for a moment of his real and intimate presence. She was hidden with him in his sepulcher. She not only took part in his entombment, she remained all her life hidden with him, no longer in the tomb of his life or in the sepulcher of his death, but in God. She wanted to enclose herself alive in a cave that served as a tomb for her.

The state of a tomb is a mystical state. To take it properly, all mystical life is a state of sepulcher but in very different tombs. First, when a human being enters into the interior life, he feels an attraction to sink into himself as into a sepulcher. There he separates himself from all created things by a generous renunciation in order to give himself entirely to God and to think only of him. He no longer has a taste for anything but interior recollection. In this first sepulcher all the operations of the soul are gradually buried, hidden, and lost in those of God. Like a dead person bound in shrouds, one is deprived of all means of using one's limbs. Second, one enters the sepulcher of pure faith where all lights, reflections, and reasonings are in captivity, and where one must remain until it pleases God to draw one out into a deeper sepulcher. The third is that of death, in which not only the operations, powers, and lights are buried, but also one's own life, and all that in which one subsists is lost in the bosom of death so that there is nothing left. Finally, we lose ourselves in God where we remain hidden and buried forever with Jesus Christ; and the last sepulcher of the sepulcher of death becomes the sepulcher of life. The soul rises to hide itself in God with Jesus Christ, or rather, Jesus Christ raises the soul to hide with him in the bosom of his Father.

Those souls opposed to the interior life fight the life of Jesus Christ hidden in the souls. They cannot suffer that one speaks of mystical death and still less of resurrection. They treat everything that is said about it as an illusion and call us seducers who uphold these great truths and speak or write soberly for the interests of the Spirit of God, who is the author of these secret marvels for the edification of souls who have the happiness to experience it. We speak of the state of freedom and the new life in God, yet they are scandalized because we dare (they say) not only to aspire to these things but also to encourage others to them. They write that this last error is worse than the first or that these last extremities of the mystics are more extravagant than all the others. But peacefully suffering these cruel reproaches, after so many others who have already suffered them for the confession of the gospel of the interior Kingdom, let us say only to them that they should beware of pronouncing curses on what they *do not understand* (Jude 10). Let us pray to God that he will let them enter the interior temple, so that they may one day admire what they now disprove, when they will recognize that what they considered to be monsters of error were prodigies from the finger of God.

However, we go further in Matthew. Guards are placed around the sepulcher of these souls hidden in God. Authorities want to convince, surprise, or overwhelm others by authority, argument, and violence. What can they do to those *blessed* who have *died in the Lord* (Rev 14:13)? Just as Jesus Christ rose glorious from the tomb, notwithstanding all the guards that had been placed there, he also rose victorious in all souls who are happy to have a share in his death. Jesus Christ resurrects himself in them as soon as their death is perfectly consummated. Nothing can prevent their resurrection. To be dead with Jesus Christ is a sure pledge of rising with him. O good, blind people who deprive yourselves of such great states by your own fault and who, not wanting to pay to enter them, try to exclude others from them! You cannot suffer the state of resurrection. God does not bring a soul into death with the intention of leaving it there forever but to bring it to a new life. Death is not a state of consistency; it is a passage from a life subject to a thousand changes to an entirely new and entirely admirable life in God, an entirely immutable, firm, and constant life.

> After the Sabbath, as the first day of the week was dawning, Mary Magdalene and the other Mary went to see the tomb. [2] And suddenly there was a great earthquake, for an angel of the Lord, descending from heaven, came and rolled back the stone and sat on it. [3] His appearance was like lightning and his clothing white as snow. (Matt 28:1–3)

The resurrection takes place *at the end of the Sabbath night*, that is to say, in the deepest darkness when the soul buried in a long death thinks only of resting in its sepulcher without hope to ever leave. Psalm 88:5 says in the following passage:

> Like those forsaken among the dead,
> like the slain that lie in the grave,
> like those whom you remember no more,
> for they are cut off from your hand.

But while the soul waits in the night of the repose, she does not realize that the more the night advances, the more the day approaches. As the sun rises from the bosom of the night, so Jesus Christ rises in her from his darkest obscurity and resurrects her little by little by his coming. *Mary Magdalene* was this impatient lover who ahead of the day searches for her Beloved. She still looks for him in death, and when she does not think she can find him anywhere, she suddenly sees him in life. Having learned to be content with death, she still wants to seek him in death itself. A soul in the same state of death and persuaded to abide in death is deprived of the perceived presence of Jesus Christ. However, he is not there: we find him only in the new life, which is the soul's life, when Jesus Christ deigns to allow us to discover him and hence to manifest himself.

The sacred Virgin who loves her son infinitely more than any other did not seek him in the tomb. She knew too well that this was neither the place where he should be nor the way to look for him in this state, but instead this would stir up again some eagerness to see him again. We must suffer our privation in grand repose, which has become a perfect abandonment, waiting for him to manifest himself. This is the difference between those who have not yet arrived at its consummation and those who are in a consummated death. Let the former still seek with some desire what they love, seeing themselves deprived of it; but the others, equally content with privation, die peacefully in the will of God, seeking nothing for themselves but letting God be all things as he wills to be. The divine Mary was in a consummated degree so that the exterior privation of her soul was not a privation to her, because the union within and intimate communication were not hindered by distance. And although outward conversation is useful, it must nevertheless cease in order to enter into a spiritually more intimate communication.

This angel affixed on the stone was the figure of the resurrected soul and of what happens at its resurrection. When the mystical resurrection takes place, the lower part enters into a certain trembling with the abundance of graces that are communicated, overflowing on the body, which is moved deeply by this newness of life. She enters into a kind of weakness but very different from the ecstasy that occurs in the first fervor and even from any other. This operation is not so sensitive nor violent as that of ecstasy. In this deep and intimate union, the body also feels something in its own way. This essential union manifests itself, and the soul feels enclosed in intimacy somewhat felt in the senses. She notices a trembling of the whole body, represented by the earthquake that makes itself felt at the resurrection of the Lord, as if from a weakness more like pleasure than pain, although it is no longer a pleasure that takes away the senses or to which the body succumbs as before; but it is a *je ne sais quoi* as delicate as it is profound, which can be perceived only by a subtle feeling. The soul then enters into an absorption so graded that it cannot discern it. This is no longer done as it used to be by recollection or drawn within but by enlargement and expanse into the immense. She feels herself lifted out of herself and passed into another, where she remains submerged. Therefore at this moment, the angel of the Lord or, rather, a powerful and sudden grace like the forerunner of Jesus Christ, because Jesus Christ immediately follows this, knocks down the stone that held the soul as locked up and sealed in herself to give it the freedom to act outside. At the same time this, grace, which is a grace of confirmation, sits on the stone. The death is perfected in the consummation of this resurrection; the soul remains confirmed in grace forever; this grace, being a final grace, rests on and affirms the soul. This grace can never be merited by the soul on its own. Jesus Christ alone deserved it and gives it freely without any care whether the creature is worthy of obtaining it. Our Lord by his pure goodness gives his merit at the time of this resurrection, but by no means does the soul have the certainty of it by herself; God removes from the soul the knowledge of such a great good, so she remains abandoned for the rest of her life to all purposes of God, perfectly subject to all that he might will or do, whether in time or in eternity. After the total destruction of propriety as the root of all evil that took place by death, and after the renewal of life in God, which takes place through the mystical resurrection, there is every reason to believe that a soul so happy to have reached this degree enters into the eternally reciprocal love between God and herself (Jer 31:3). And being born of God by an excellent participation of his life, she will never again be separated from God, and nothing will be able to remove her from the love of Jesus Christ (1 John 3:1). But these wonders of grace are hidden in God the Father with Jesus Christ.

After such a prodigious change, the supreme part of the soul becomes all luminous and brilliant, being filled with sublime knowledge and participating in the advantages of glory, since she entered into a share in the divine life. And the lower inferior part like the garment becomes white and entirely pure by the communication making purity within the soul. She appears from then on with a candor and innocence that are not natural and which all admire without knowing her, without penetrating the cause of her purity. In her external bearing she appears like the milk of the most innocent and lovable childhood. All that comes only from the outpouring of the Spirit, which makes extreme purity in the soul's foundation.

> For fear of him the guards shook and became like dead men. (Matt 28:40)

We have two spiritual interpretations of these terrified guards. First, they can be interpreted as the reaction of our senses during these grace-filled changes. We become almost disoriented in this operation, since the senses absorbed by grace receive only slight sensory impressions, almost like we do not feel them. Second, spiritual directors may become frightened by such rapid and unhoped-for changes in their proteges.

> But the angel said to the women, "Do not be afraid, for I know that you are looking for Jesus who was crucified. [6] He is not here, for he has been raised, as he said. Come, see the place where he lay. [7] Then go quickly and tell his disciples, 'He has been raised from the dead, and indeed he is going ahead of you to Galilee; there you will see him.' This is my message for you." (Matt 28:5–7)

This grace, or this angel, who assists the coming of Jesus Christ in the soul, says to the women, "Do not be afraid!," because they seek only Jesus Christ. And why should they not fear? Because they seek only Jesus

Christ and Jesus Christ crucified. Ah! There is nothing to fear for such souls: neither the illusion of nature, nor the temptation of the demon, nor the malignity of sin can harm them. As soon as they are in a state of wanting only what St. Paul wants of *knowing nothing except Jesus Christ and him crucified* (1 Cor 2:2), they find him glorious and triumphant. Jesus is no longer in death or in the tomb. You will no longer find him there, devoted and passionate souls for him! He is risen. He himself will come to you, full of life, to give you your life and give you a share in his resurrection.

Then the mission is given to these women to exercise the office of apostles. And to whom? Towards the apostles themselves. What? The pillars of the church will learn from women the resurrection of their Savior, which is the fundamental truth of religion? Is it, O Lord! to keep the apostles in humility or to reward with this sublime employment the love that these women have for you, that you honor them with such a celebrated embassy? It is at least to show your sovereign authority; your absolute will cannot be hampered or limited by any sex or condition. Who will not admire that God uses ordinary women to teach the greatest mysteries to learned men? But the women must be annihilated to be prepared for the great things for which God destines them. By this marvelous conduct, the majesty of God shines forth in his works. Not only does God cause great men to be instructed by women, but moreover, even those who are called to the apostolate in a more eminent way are sometimes instructed by women and learn from their mouths the most profound truths. Having sought God in the simplicity of their heart, these pure souls not only find God for themselves but moreover discover him for others. O how efficacious is this conduct of God in destroying self-sufficiency! Women cannot appropriate these great gifts of God, seeing that they come neither from their study nor from their talent but that they are given to them very gratuitously. And men have less reason to get caught up in pride when, in order to penetrate the divine mysteries, they must become the disciples of women.

But women should serve only to announce what has been committed to them without entering into a dispute or usurping more power than they have been given. They simply carry out the order they have received. Also, the state is no sooner announced by women to these apostles than the apostles first enter and receive the experience of the resurrection. Jesus Christ even precedes the coming of these women to dispose hearts to listen and believe them. The angel adds to these women that in the very place where they will announce to the apostles that Jesus is risen, they *will see him*. O how mysterious is this circumstance! The soul who possesses this state of resurrection discovers it in faith only in proportion to the manifestation that she makes of it to others. She possesses this treasure for a long time without knowing it, and it is shown to her only when she points it out to others. A soul of this degree has no inclination to manifest itself: and she thinks only of remaining hidden and unknown when suddenly she is given a mission to speak. Remaining faithful and hidden as long as God willed it, now out of this same faithfulness, she discovers and appears when God commands it. A virtue at one time will be a fault at another. All fruits, old and new, must be preserved for God alone, and his will alone sets the price for all things. Virtue must therefore be practiced for love of God, according to the ancient custom while there is time, and at another time we keep them hidden. But when God wants new fruits and directs us to change our methods, we must also be prompt and firm in obeying him. This true and entirely divine discretion is unknown to those who give the same rules and practices for all and who do not want a soul to change its conduct. Certainly, they deviate from the soul's perfection, because they persist in wanting its interior to always march in the same train of thought along with conformity in exterior behavior also.

> So they left the tomb quickly with fear and great joy and ran to tell his disciples. (Matt 28:8)

These holy women have no sooner received their apostolic mission than without delay they emerge from the sepulcher, that is to say, from the hidden and completely interior state by which they were enclosed within themselves to obey the command of heaven. We must have great faithfulness to do without delay and hesitation all that God wants of us without looking to our own interest, or whether there is more security for us in retreat or in an exposed life for the service of souls or for external occupations. Anyone who still makes use of these observations is not released from self-love or abandoned to God to the point where he should be. But those who have lost all will in that of God's and drown all reasoning in faith no longer know how to hesitate or discern. On the contrary, letting themselves go at the whim of providence, they are convinced that they will enter more infallibly into the order of God, the less they examine it and the more simply they deal with it.

We no longer think of ourselves, because we have abandoned ourselves to divine guidance. After an irrevocable gift of ourselves to God, it is an infidelity to still want to seek our ways. When the mission is given, it must be carried out in the will of God, but we must never help others in our own way. However, in the beginning, when a soul is placed in the apostolic state, she enters *with fear* because God's ways are quite contrary to what she did formerly. She might even consider this as a fault within her. Yet this must be done: the time has come.

God wants all new things from her, and yet she feels a superficial fear. Deep down within herself, she finds herself filled with joy in the sight and experience of her new freedom. And this is how she fulfills her mission.

> And behold, Jesus met them and said, "Hail!" And they came up and took hold of his feet and worshiped him. [10] Then Jesus said to them, "Do not be afraid; go and tell my brethren to go to Galilee, and there they will see me." (Matt 28:9–10)

As soon as the soul leaves the captivity of its sepulcher and of herself to enter into the new freedom given to her, Jesus Christ appears and manifests himself to her. All she had known of him before was only a sketch and a shadow compared to what she discovers of him here. For she sees Jesus in himself, whereas hitherto she had seen him only as in a shadow. She then receives from him a permanent and lasting peace that will not be altered or interrupted. God brings peace and salvation together.

These faithful women therefore approached and became united and connected to their Savior. They kissed his feet and adored him, paying him sovereign homage, worthy of his grandeur, so they were united to the Word-God to carry him into their interior and exterior states. That is why they kissed his feet externally and worshiped him internally. He expressly told them *not to fear* this new state, although it seemed to them so different from the first. Jesus Christ reassured them by declaring that this state is glorious and that they would perform the office of apostles with which he charged them. He confirmed at the same time the mission given to them by the angel and ordered them to go to his apostles. But why, O Son of God, do you call them your brothers? Because you associate them with your mission for the salvation of the world, and you inform them of your divine filiation.

The resurrected Jesus also tells these Marys to go and wait for him in Galilee where they will see him. As long as the soul is still within herself, she seeks Jesus Christ in Jerusalem, or around the same city that is her background and her center, but as soon as she is resurrected and called to the apostolate, she must go further. And leaving herself, go to Galilee, the place of the apostolic missions. This is where Jesus Christ leads her. We note that he does not say that he will be found. But he says, That is where they will *see* me, that is to say, I will be manifested to them. There they will not only possess and taste me, but even what they taste and possess will be revealed to them. To understand this, one must know that throughout faith, death, and even the beginning of life with God, the soul has no distinct knowledge of Jesus Christ. What she had known of him by the illumination of the powers was taken away from her so that she no longer saw it. She has not yet received what is to be given to her by the *revelation of Jesus Christ* in her (Gal 1:16). During this time of darkness and loss, she possesses and unites to him in an excellent degree, but without thinking about it or noticing it. So absorbed in a certain general cloud, she cannot distinguish anything. If she could distinguish something, that very thing would harm her and prevent her from flowing back into her essential unity. But when her flowing back is perfect, the manifestation now no longer withdraws her from its unity: on the contrary, the manifestation reaffirms it there and articulates it more because, being established in God, she sees and does things in a divine way, without unity preventing distinction or that distinction removing it from unity.

> While they were going, behold, some of the guard went into the city and told the chief priests all that had taken place. [12] And when they had assembled with the elders and taken counsel, they gave a sum of money to the soldiers [13] and said, "Tell people, 'His disciples came by night and stole him away while we were asleep.' [14] And if this comes to the governor's ears, we will satisfy him and keep you out of trouble." [15] So they took the money and did as they were directed; and this story has been spread among the Jews to this day. (Matt 28:11–15)

Some spiritual directors, although very few, seeing the truth of this state of mystical resurrection in the experience of souls, have enough faithfulness to declare it. But the devil makes every effort to quell the belief in the mystical resurrection; he succeeds by making it seem incomprehensible, although it is the most divine state. Now the demon does this because he knows that if Jesus Christ is not resurrected and we do not live mystically with him, then the resurrection itself becomes vain and useless, because as Matt 22:32 says, *He is not God of the dead, but of the living.* He reigns absolutely in souls in the state of life and not of death.

Death is advantageous only because it introduces us into the divine life. Death is a means and not an end, and it would be difficult to let oneself go into a complete death if one did not hope for the resurrection. This hope always remains in the bosom of these blessed dead, although they do not always perceive it. The germ of the life that they take up one day accompanies them in the tomb and cannot be consummated no matter how long they are in the tomb. As Paul declares, *Jesus Christ delivers the kingdom to God the Father after destroying every rule and every authority and power. After this, all the dead shall be resurrected, and the end shall have come* (1 Cor 15:24). Likewise, the reign of God over the interior person cannot be perfected until after his resurrection, for God does not reign in all the extent of his Kingdom, except over hearts in which he lives without resistance and which live in him without restriction.

Some say that these states are invented by the partisans of the interior and allege as much to prevent souls from letting themselves be led fully to God. They assert that we use artifices and bad reasoning to persuade others; that we add lies and calumny to temerity; that witnesses are corrupted with money; that we try to engage others by interest or by favor. Yet the truth will exist in the eyes of God and his angels and to all those to whom he chooses to reveal it. They stir up tumults in the sensible world against the interior world. Yet the unalterable interior life will be the same during all the centuries. Those who died there in the Lord will rise there through Jesus Christ. Could there by anything more ridiculous than what the Pharisees and elders said and did when they should have had more common sense and skill? Isn't that a good testimony of a person sleeping? If those guards were sleeping, how could they know what happened? If they were not sleeping, why did they not prevent this kidnapping? It is so, O Jesus! King of the interior, when unjust witnesses rise up against you, may iniquity lie against itself. Blind passion takes them out of their minds, and full of extravagance, they do not know what they are. The testimony of these soldiers won by money was more proof of the resurrection of Jesus Christ than all they would have published without it. For if they had first declared the truth, it might have been said that they had been corrupted. But not ignoring that they had been won over by means of money to make them say the opposite, their testimony was no longer believable. There are people who, by wanting to decry the interior, establish it because of their artifices being discovered and the ridiculous things that they invent being recognized; the credence they lose is returned with justice to the defenders of the interior ways.

> Now the eleven disciples went to Galilee, to the mountain to which Jesus had directed them. [17] When they saw him, they worshiped him, but they doubted. (Matt 28:16–17)

As soon as the apostles find themselves at the place that Jesus Christ has marked out for them, they do not fail to see him, according to the word given to them. When, therefore, they saw him, they truly adored him with interior adoration. However, some did not fail to doubt. One must have great faith or be well advanced to be without fear and doubt, particularly in extraordinary things, when all that one has understood passes away. When reason runs short, rest in faith.

> And Jesus came and said to them, "All authority in heaven and on earth has been given to me. [19] Go therefore and make disciples of all nations, baptizing them in the name of the Father and of the Son and of the Holy Spirit [20] and teaching them to obey everything that I have commanded you. And remember, I am with you always, to the end of the age." (Matt 28:18–20)

Jesus Christ approaches and unites even more, or rather, incarnates himself in the soul in the way we have said so many times. Then he teaches her this great truth, the full discovery of which makes all the happiness of life, that all power has been given to him in heaven and on earth. Ruler of the universe! Why then do we dispute this supreme power? Why are we afraid of losing and abandoning ourselves for all things, since all power is in your hands? How dare we think this will lead us to a precipice? This is nevertheless what the partisans of property and propriety assert. But Jesus must reign as sovereign both in heaven and on earth. He reigns on earth as in heaven. He alone must govern and lead everything, without anything resisting him any longer.

God has given his power to his Son, full of the Spirit, which is superior and like *heaven*. The *soul* is inferior and like the *earth*. All the secret of the spiritual life consists in remaining in his power and not disputing his rights over us, without limiting or hindering either the power or the rights, because we submit all to him in the divine order. Whoever no longer resists him in anything is perfect. There are some who give all power to Jesus Christ in heaven, never doubting that he reigns there absolutely, but they do not give him power on earth, since they always want to lead themselves, and they never abandon themselves fully to the Spirit of his grace. O Jesus, Son of God! This is your right that you have acquired through your death, O Jesus, Son of God! Although you already had it by your origin, you now have absolute power over the soul and the body, on the interior and on the exterior, on the superior part and on the inferior! Why then are we so unjust as to dispute it with you and try to retain a part for ourselves?

We cannot interfere with ourselves for any reason or concern whatsoever. We cannot act, fight, defend, foresee, or desire by ourselves without trespassing the rights of Jesus Christ. All movement out of an effect of nature that we begin for ourselves is impure. Without seeking ourselves, we must therefore abandon ourselves to Jesus without reserve, so that he may act, fight, defend, foresee, and desire for us. We leave to Jesus Christ the full use and all the glory of the power his Father gave him. Not that he does all this in us without us, for we sit very truly with him, but Jesus Christ moves us by the movement of his divine Spirit.

Also, Jesus Christ wants his apostles to preach and teach to all nations about this absolute power he has over us, which is the foundation of their mission. He teaches them the principle of the great things they must do in the saving of souls. Certainly nothing should be preached so much as this reign of the Savior and the manner of establishing it internally. The kings on earth reign over material good and bodies. Their authority, though, is limited to the exterior and in time. The King of kings has power to reign in spirits and hearts, and his reign is eternal. As the Canticle of Moses says, *The Lord will be King forever* (Exod 15:18). Because this gives Christian perfection, this most important point of morality must be preached. We pray to heaven that the gospel be announced in an interior way, teaching us to surrender to Jesus Christ and stand united to him. We must remain subject to his power and abandon ourselves to his will. Nothing brings more glory to God than when we remain attached to the source of God so that we may see all good and find the remedy to all our evils. Penetrate an infinity of hearts with your grand word, O Jesus, with all *power that has been given on heaven and earth.* Bring us back from our wanderings with sweet assurance of your law. Above all, do not allow, my God and my King, that I take any power away from you that the Father has given you, and do not let me retain anything in myself that is yours.

After having taught the peoples this sovereign power of Jesus Christ, we must *baptize in the name of the Father, and of the Son, and of the Holy Spirit.* This properly explains the spiritual regeneration that comes with baptism, but this must also be explained mystically. After a soul knows the power of Jesus Christ and Jesus Christ begins to exercise his power fully over the soul, he places the soul in the sublime participation of the operations of the Trinity. This new grace comes like a baptism and purifies her more and more. This new presence of God, which is given by a union of powers, has been explained in many places. Now one can accept this saving grace by entering into the prayer of simple exposition before God, feeling invited to do so. Souls need to stay there after their introduction, because Jesus Christ operates within us a second baptism, giving us a close union with the Holy Trinity.

Finally, the divine Master tells his disciples to *teach people to obey everything he has commanded us.* We must preach this and not amuse ourselves with futile discourse and human inventions, which do no good to the people and infinitely harm the preachers. Ministers of Jesus Christ, entrusted with his word, *do not preach yourself* but only Jesus Christ our Lord (2 Cor 4:5). Remain faithful to his orders. Teach the whole world to obey and follow all that he has commanded. But do not forget the most important of the precepts about the interior. Teach all the people to worship God in spirit and in truth: to pray without ceasing and without interruption, to live in faith and abandon, in prayer and love. To practice intimately the theological virtues, to walk in the presence of God, to talk familiarly with him. To have only God in view, to act and suffer with the only intention of pleasing him. In a word, to establish a secret communion with him in his interior Kingdom, because this is what he most desires and is what is called the gospel of the gospel. How many times did our Lord preach the interior to his disciples? How much more did he give them his Holy Spirit? The Spirit of the church works principally in the interior, since it brings us to unite with God through spirit to Spirit, which is without doubt very intimate. Clearly we may not teach Christians to obey all that Jesus Christ commands without preaching and strongly inculcating *the interior life.*

Jesus Christ assures his apostles, *Remember, I am with you always, to the end of the age.* O happiness of no longer being able to lose God! This assurance, which apostolic persons have, is not in them but in Jesus Christ, who gives it to them, which makes them very free and very happy. *For I am convinced,* says Paul, *that no creature will be able to separate us from the love of God in Christ Jesus our Lord* (Rom 8:38–39). Paul did not look at this assurance in himself, but it was founded and supported in God, since it is declared elsewhere, *No one can tell whether he is worthy of love or hate* (Eccl 9:1). The apostles do not regard this assurance on the side of the merit or demerit of the creature, but on the side of the infallible word of God. This assurance is known by apostolic people by their annihilation; they expect nothing more from others, as they are sure of having everything in God, unto whom they gave all things. But if they are never more separated from Jesus Christ, then they will never again lose his grace. This apostolic state is not an inclination to produce things, even in favor of souls, which is ordinarily quite natural. Instead, the apostolic state is a pure and efficacious disposition, doing everything that God wants, nothing more nor less, according as one is committed to it by his order. But to get there, you have to pass all the other states.

This same passage is still a certainty of the firmness and immobility of the church founded by Jesus Christ on the apostles. The church must last without interruption until the end of the centuries, and since Jesus Christ assures that he will always be with her until the end of the world, it is certain that she will never be separated, not even for a moment, from Jesus her Bridegroom.

THE END OF THE GOSPEL ACCORDING TO MATTHEW.

Bibliography

Angela of Foligno. *Complete Works*. Translated by Paul Lachance. Mahwah, NJ: Paulist, 1993.

Aquinas, Thomas. *Summa Theologica*. Translated by Fathers of the English Dominican Province. London: Burns, Oates & Washbourne, 1927.

Aumann, Jordan. *Spiritual Theology*. London: Bloomsbury, 1980.

Benedict XIV. "*Deus Caritas Est*: On Christian Love." Vatican, Dec. 25, 2005. https://www.vatican.va/content/benedict-xvi/en/encyclicals/documents/hf_ben-xvi_enc_20051225_deus-caritas-est.html.

Bossuet, Jacques Bénigne. *Quakerism à-la-mode, or, A history of quietism: Particularly that of the Lord Arch-bishop of Cambray and Madam Guyone*. London: Harris and Bell, 1698.

Bremond, Henri. *Apologie pour Fénelon*. Paris: Perrin, 1910.

Catherine of Genoa. *Purgation and Purgatory. The Spiritual Dialogue*. Translated by Serge Hughes. Classics of Western Spirituality. Mahwah, NJ: Paulist, 1979.

Catholic Church. *Catechism of the Catholic Church*. 2nd ed. Vatican City: Vatican, 1997.

Caussade, Jean Pierre de. *Abandonment to Divine Providence*. New York: Image, 1975.

———. *On Prayer: Spiritual Instructions on the Various States of Prayer According to the Doctrine of Bossuet, Bishop of Meaux*. Translated by Algar Thorold. London: Burns, Oates & Washbourne, 1931.

Conzemius, Viktor. "Quietism." In *Sacramentum Mundi*, edited by Karl Rahner, 5:169–72. New York: Herder & Herder, 1970.

De la Bedoyère, Michael. *The Archbishop and the Lady: The Story of Fénelon and Madame Guyon*. New York: Pantheon, 1956.

Eire, Carlos. *The Christian Mysticism Podcast*. Season 3, episode 5, "Madame Guyon: A Mystic for Catholics and Protestants." Aired May 15, 2025, on Acast. https://shows.acast.com/the-christian-mysticism-podcast/episodes/madame-guyon-a-mystic-for-catholics-and-protestants.

Fénelon, Francois de Salignac de La Mothe. *The Archbishop of Cambray's Dissertation on Pure Love, with an Account of the Life and Writings of the Lady, for Whose Sake the Archbishop Was Banished from Court*. London: Thomson, 1750.

———. *The Complete Fénelon*. Edited and translated by Robert J. Edmonson and Hal M. Helms. Paraclete Giants. Brewster, MA: Paraclete, 2008.

———. *The Maxims of the Saints Explained, Concerning the Interior Life*. Bordeaux: N.p., 1913.

Gondal, Marie-Louise. *Madame Guyon: Un nouveau visage*. Paris: Beauchesne, 1989.

Gough, J. [James]. "Comparative View of the Lives of St. Teresa and M. Guion." In *The Life of Lady Guion*, 2:237–39. Bristol: Farley, 1772.

———. "Life of Michael de Molinos and Progress of Quietism." In *The Life of Lady Guion*, 2:308–24. Bristol: Farley, 1772.

Griffin, John Howard. *Follow the Ecstasy: The Hermitage Years of Thomas Merton*. Maryknoll, NY: Orbis, 1993.

Guyon, Jeanne de la Mothe. *Autobiography of Madame Guyon*. Translated by Thomas Taylor Allen. 2 vols. London: Kegan Paul, Trench, Trübner, 1897.

———. *Divine Love: The Emblems of Madame Jeanne Guyon and Otto van Veen, Volume 1*. Illustrations by Otto van Veen. Translated by Nancy Carol James. Eugene, OR: Pickwick, 2019.

———. *Jeanne Guyon's Apocalyptic Universe: Her Biblical Commentary on Revelation with Reflections on the Interior Life*. Translated by Nancy Carol James. Eugene, OR: Pickwick, 2019.

———. *Jeanne Guyon's Christian Worldview: Her Biblical Commentaries on Galatians, Ephesians, and Colossians with Explanations and Reflections on the Interior Life*. Translated by Nancy Carol James. Eugene, OR: Pickwick, 2018.

———. *Jeanne Guyon's Interior Faith: Her Biblical Commentary on the Gospel of Luke with Reflections on the Interior Life*. Translated by Nancy Carol James. Eugene, OR: Pickwick, 2019.

———. *Jeanne Guyon's Mystical Perfection Through Eucharistic Suffering: Her Biblical Commentary on the Gospel of John with Reflections on the Interior Life*. Translated by Nancy Carol James. Eugene, OR: Pickwick, 2020.

———. *Les justifications de Mme J.-M.B. de La Mothe-Guyon, écrites par elle-meme, avec un examen de la IXe et Xe conferences de Cassien touchant l'état fixe d'oraison continuelle, par M. De Fénelon*. 3 vols. Cologne: N.p., 1720.

———. *Les livres de l'Ancien Testament de Notre-Seigneur Jésus-Christ avec des explications et réflexions qui regardent la vie intérieure*. 12 vols. Cologne: N.p., 1714–15.

———. *Les livres du Nouveau Testament avec des explications et réflexions qui regardent la vie intérieure*. N.p.: Poiret, 1713.

———. *Le Nouveau Testament de Notre-Seigneur Jésus-Christ avec des explications et réflexions qui regardent la vie intérieure*. 12 vols. Cologne: Poiret, 1714–15.

———. *The Way of the Child Jesus: Our Model of Perfection*. Translated by Nancy Carol James. Arlington, VA: European Emblems, 2015.

Guyon, Jeanne de la Mothe. *See also* Guyon, Madame.

Guyon, Madame, and Herman Hugo. *The Soul, Lover of God*. Translated by Nancy Carol James. New York: University Press of America, 2014.

Holcombe, William H. *Aphorisms of the New Life: With Illustrations and Confirmations from the New Testament, Fénelon, Madame Guyon, and Swedenborg*. Philadelphia: Claxton, 1883.

James, Nancy. *I, Jeanne Guyon*. Jacksonville, FL: Christian, 2014.

James, Nancy. *See also* James, Nancy C., *and* James, Nancy Carol.

James, Nancy C., ed. *The Complete Madame Guyon*. Paraclete Giants. Brewster, MA: Paraclete, 2011.

———. *The Pure Love of Madame Guyon: The Great Conflict in King Louis XIV's Court*. New York: University Press of America, 2007.

———. *Standing in the Whirlwind: The Riveting Story of a Priest and the Congregations That Tormented Her.* Cleveland: Pilgrim, 2005.

———, trans. "Supplement to the Life of Madame Guyon." In *The Pure Love of Madame Guyon: The Great Conflict in King Louis XIV's Court*, by Nancy C. James, 85–104. New York: University Press of America, 2014.

James, Nancy C. *See also* James, Nancy, *and* James, Nancy Carol.

James, Nancy C., and Sharon D. Voros. *Bastille Witness: The Prison Autobiography of Madame Guyon.* New York: University Press of America, 2012.

James, Nancy Carol. *The Apophatic Mysticism of Madame Guyon.* Ann Arbor: UMI Dissertation, 1998.

———. "Jeanne Marie Bouvier de la Mothe Guyon." World Religions and Spirituality Project, Mar. 15, 2023. https://wrldrels.org/2023/03/14/jeanne-marie-bouvier-de-la-mothe-guyon/.

James, Nancy Carol. *See also* James, Nancy, *and* James, Nancy C.

James, William. *Varieties of Religious Experience.* New York: Collier, 1961.

Kuffel, Thomas P. "St. Thomas' Method of Biblical Exegesis." *Living Tradition* 38 (1991). https://rtforum.org/lt/lt38.html.

Kuffel, Thomas P., and Nancy Carol James. *The Ascent to God: Divine Theosis Revealed and Realized in the Teaching of John Paul II.* Eugene, OR: Pickwick, 2022.

La Combe, François. *A Short Letter of Instruction, Shewing the Surest Way to Christian Perfection.* Translated by J. [James] Gough. In *The Life of Lady Guion*, 2:295–307. Bristol: Farley, 1772.

Macarius the Great, St. *Spiritual Homilies.* Elpenor in Print, n.d. https://www.elpenor.org/macarius/homilies.asp.

Millare, Roland. *A Living Sacrifice: Liturgy and Eschatology in Joseph Ratzinger.* Steubenville, OH: Emmaus Academic, 2022.

Mudge, James. *Fénelon the Mystic.* Cincinnati: Jennings and Graham, 1906.

Poiret, Pierre. "The Theology of Emblems: Preface to the Emblems of Father Hugo and Madame Guyon." In *The Soul, Lover of God*, by Madame Guyon and Herman Hugo, translated by Nancy Carol James, xxxiii–xl. New York: University Press of America, 2014.

Ramsay, Chevalier. "Life of Francis de Salignac de la Mothe Fénelon, Archbishop and Duke of Cambray." In *The Life of Lady Guion*, 2:325–72. Bristol: Farley, 1772.

Saint-Simon, Duc de. *Historical Memoirs of the Duc de Saint-Simon.* Edited and translated by Lucy Norton. 2 vols. New York: McGraw-Hill, 1967.

Teresa of Avila. *The Interior Castle.* Translated by Kernan Cavanaugh and Orthlio Rodriguez. 2nd ed. Classics of Western Spirituality. Mahwah, NJ: Paulist, 1979.

Underhill, Evelyn. *Mysticism: A Study in the Nature and Development of Man's Spiritual Consciousness.* 12th ed. Cleveland: World, 1965.

Upham, Thomas C. *Life and Religions Opinions and Experience of Madame de la Mothe Guyon.* 2 vols. New York: Harper & Brothers, 1847.

Wesley, John. *An Extract of the Life of Madame Guion.* London: Hawes, 1776.

Index

www.ingramcontent.com/pod-product-compliance
Lightning Source LLC
LaVergne TN
LVHW050631100826
845148LV00011B/1824

* 9 7 9 8 3 8 5 2 4 5 1 8 5 *